DENTAL ASSISTING EXAM

LearningExpress ®

NEW YORK

Library of Congress Control Number: 20099 22727

Printed in the United States of America

9 8 7 6 5 4 3 2 1

ISBN: 1-57685-679-8
ISBN: 978-1-57685-679-6

Developed and Produced by Focus Strategic Communications Inc.
Project Managers: Ron Edwards, Adrianna Edwards
Developmental Editor: Ron Edwards
Copy Editor: Ann Firth
Proofreaders: Layla Moola, Linda Szostak
Compositor: Carol Magee
Illustrators: Carolyn Tripp, Sarah Waterfield

For more information or to place an order, contact LearningExpress at:
    2 Rector Street
    26th Floor
    New York, NY 10006

Or visit us at:
    www.learnatest.com

Contents

Contributors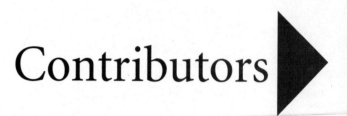

Colleen Kirby-Banas, CDA, RDAEF, BS, MS, is a graduate of the College of San Mateo (CSM) Dental Assisting Program in San Mateo, California. She has worked in the dental field for over 15 years. She has been teaching at CSM for a decade, and is currently the Director of the Dental Assisting Program. She also teaches at Foothill College.

Renee Ostini-Herold, CDA, RDA, CDPMA, is a graduate of the College of San Mateo (CSM) Dental Assisting Program in San Mateo, California. She has worked in the dental field for nearly three decades, and has been teaching Dental Assisting at CSM (Foothill College and College of Alameda) for over a decade.

▶ Additional Contributors

Denise Murphy, BA, CDA, CDPMA, FADAA, EFDA, graduated from the dental assisting program at Orlando Vocational-Technical Center and holds a BA in Psychology from Columbia College, also in Orlando, Florida. In addition to 20 years of industry experience, she has been a teacher for two decades.

Marie Eubanks, CDA, EFDA, graduated from the Dental Assisting Program at Palm Beach Community College (PBCC) in Lake Worth, Florida. After some years in the industry, she returned to PBCC as an adjunct instructor, Dental Health Services Department, a position she has held for five years. She is currently working on a degree in psychology at Florida Atlantic University. She is the president of the Palm Beach County Dental Assistants Society (PBCDAS).

Renee Filippo, CDA, is a Dental Assistant/Treatment Coordinator in Mississauga, Ontario, Canada. She attended George Brown College in Toronto, Ontario, Canada, for programs in Dental Office Administration and Dental Assisting. She has been working in the dental field for 15 years.

Corey B. Lietzke, CDA, EFDA, graduated from Palm Beach Community College's (PBCC) dental assisting program. She also holds an associate of arts degree from Florida Atlantic University. After working in the dental industry for five years, she began teaching at PBCC, where she is now an adjunct instructor in the Dental Health Services Department.

Roberta Wirth, CDA, is Dental Assistant Program Co-Director at Clover Park Technical College (CPTC) in Lakewood, Washington, where she has taught dental assisting for two decades. She also has seven years of industry experience. She graduated from the Dental Assistant program at CPTC and is currently working on her bachelor degree through University of Washington.

How to Use This Book ▶

CHAPTER OVERVIEW

Passing the RDA or the CDA exams is essential to your career as a dental assistant, and this book can help you achieve that goal. This is not a substitute for your textbook. This book is a supplement to the text and your classroom lessons. It will help you review the material you have already covered in the text and classroom.

DENTAL ASSISTING OFFERS you unlimited potential for a career in healthcare, and there are many possibilities for advancement and growth. Salary rewards and professional development go hand in hand.

Chapter 1 provides general information on how to use this preparation guide. Chapter 2 offers some information on the dental assistant profession. Chapter 3 discusses the two major exams for dental assistants.

Chapter 4 explains the "secrets" of test taking and how to improve your scores on multiple-choice exams through strategic planning. LearningExpress has developed a system to help you prepare for your exam by giving the following recommendations:

- becoming familiar with the format of the exam(s)
- planning to have sufficient time to practice taking the exam(s)
- learning how to overcome test anxiety and exam fear
- learning critical test-taking skills, such as pacing yourself through the exam, using the process of elimination, and knowing when to guess
- planning to get enough rest and exercise before the test (and while preparing as well)
- preparing your test supplies and having last-minute details ready

The "core" of the book is found in Chapters 4 through 10, which cover the essential topics of dental assisting: Dental Science (4), Infection Control (5), Chairside Assisting (6), Dental Materials (7), Dental Radiology (8), Dental Office Procedures (9), and Dental Law and Ethics (10).

The final chapters (11 and 12) are the "heart" of the book, as they contain the two practice exams. This is the place to start. Prepare yourself as if for the actual exam with pencils, erasers, and other supplies. Wear an accurate wristwatch, or use a stopwatch to allow yourself time to answer questions and skip those that hold you up. Before you read Chapters 4–10, take the first 100-question exam, allowing yourself 75 minutes to complete it. Generally, the CDA exam will have 300 multiple-choice questions to be answered over the course of three hours. The RDA exam, if it exists in your state, generally will have 150 multiple-choice questions, to be answered over the course of three hours. Both examinations are given at computer testing centers at a location near you. Each applicant must provide current picture identification prior to being admitted to the exams. Of course, cheating is prohibited on the actual exam, and there really is no point in cheating on the practice test in this book since you will only be cheating yourself out of a chance to improve your knowledge and pass the actual exam.

Once you are finished, turn to the section called Practice Answers and Explanations. Score your exam carefully. Now, take note of the sections in which you did particularly poorly. You will want to review these with extreme care. We suggest that your exam preparation include all of the core chapters (4–10), but you may want to concentrate on those sections in which you are weakest. Review each topic chapter here and in your textbook as well. At the end of the topic chapter, you will find a set of 30–50 questions. Remember to time yourself. Score these questions as you did the Practice Exam to see how solid your knowledge of this topic is.

At the end of the seven reviews, take the second exam in Chapter 12. Remember to time yourself. Score the exam, and identify which topics still need improvement.

Take the exams repeatedly. Remember, practice makes perfect.

TIME BEFORE EXAM	WHAT YOU CAN DO
Three Months	Read through this entire book, making notes about what you need to know and where you need improvement.
Two Months	Become familiar with the format and wording of the questions in the Practice Exams.
One Month	Set aside 75 minutes, and take the first Practice Exam in Chapter 11. Time yourself, and avoid all distractions such as TV, radio, or cell phones. Score yourself, and note in which topics/sections you are the weakest. Concentrate your review on those topics.
Two Weeks	Review Chapters 4 to 10. You can cover one chapter per day. Take the short test at the end of each chapter, timing yourself. Note which topics need more work.
One Week	Review the Practice Exam you took three weeks ago, as well as the mini-tests in each chapter. Reread the explanations (rationale) of each answer, taking particular care over those you still do not understand. Sometimes, it may help to read them aloud to yourself.
Three Days	Gather together all of the materials that you will need to take the exam (watch, pens, pencils, erasers, etc.) and put them somewhere secure but within easy reach. Note that the DANB does not allow you to take anything other than your ID into the exam room. Check the exam location, and make sure that you know how to get there. It can help to actually visit the site to locate the entrance and the exam room.
One Day	Relax. Take it easy. Get some exercise, and get a good night's rest.
Exam Day	Arrive early, with all your exam materials and ID ready.

CHAPTER

1 ▶ Dental Assisting as a Profession

CHAPTER OVERVIEW

Dental assisting is a challenging and rewarding career offering job satisfaction, financial rewards, and the opportunity to help others. Dental assistants are professionals who understand the difference between a job and a career. They are very important members and essential components of a cohesive dental healthcare team.

THE DENTAL ASSISTANT works closely with a supervising dentist. Dentists depend on dental assistants for a great many things. Assistants are responsible for sterilizing and preparing instruments and equipment, keeping patient records, and preparing materials and instruments in the treatment rooms. Many dentists would not know where to locate their instruments and supplies, how to sterilize them, and how to set up and break down the treatment room without the dental assistant present in the office.

▶ The Dental Healthcare Team

The dental healthcare team consists of the following:

- Dentist/Operator
- Dental Assistant (in various roles throughout the office)
- Dental Hygienist
- Dental Laboratory Technician

One of the most important roles dental assistants play is to reassure patients and make them comfortable while they are prepared for treatment. Compassion is an essential quality in dental assistants. When a professional dental assistant treats a patient with compassion and concern, along with respect, the dental assistant is respected in return. A chairside dental assistant will escort the dentist throughout the entire day, moving from one treatment room to the next. The assistant will pass instruments and materials to the dentist as needed, often anticipating the dentist's needs. The dental assistant also ensures that patient records are accurate and educates patients about oral healthcare.

A professional dental assistant adds to the overall efficiency of the dental practice. Treatment procedures run more smoothly and effectively with a professional dental assistant in place. The members of the dental healthcare team and their roles are discussed on the following pages.

Dentist/Operator

The dentist is often the owner/operator of the dental practice. Although dentists treat patients and are healthcare providers, they are also running a business. A dentist can be either a generalist or a specialist. A general dentist treats patients of all ages and can perform a wide variety of dental procedures. The general dentist must take approximately seven to eight years of post-secondary schooling (four years of undergraduate work to obtain a bachelor degree, and then another three to four years of dental school) to become eligible to take his or her national and state board examinations. The national exams are written, whereas individual states give clinical board examinations.

One may notice that dentists have initials after their names: DDS or DMD. These letters represent the degree they earned from their dental school. Dental schools on the east coast of the United States generally offer Doctor of Medical Dentistry degrees, or DMD. Dental schools on the west coast of the United States generally offer Doctor of Dental Surgery degrees, or DDS. There is no difference between the two degrees.

A specialty dentist must complete the same education as the general dentist and receives a DDS or DMD. After that, the individual applies to be admitted to a specialized area of dentistry that is of interest to her or him. Depending upon the specialty chosen, the dentist may attend school for another three to six years. A specialty dentist treats patients depending on their needs. For example, an endodontist will treat patients who need a root canal performed, a pediatric dentist treats children, and so on. These are two of the nine specialties recognized by the American Dental Association, which are discussed in more detail on page 95.

Dental Assistant

A dental assistant takes on many roles in a dental practice. This individual is very versatile, adaptable, and knowledgeable. The following four positions are fulfilled by dental assistants in the office:

- clinical dental assistant
- sterilization assistant
- expanded-function dental assistant (EFDA)
- business assistant

Clinical Dental Assistant

The clinical assistant is the individual most closely involved in patient care. This function is further broken down into chairside assistant and circulating/roving assistant.

Chairside Assistant

This person is responsible for running the clinical end of the dental practice and is involved with direct patient care. This assistant has many duties and performs various functions for the dentist. Chief among them is four-handed dentistry. This term refers to the teamwork between the dentist and assistant when treating patients. Some examples of a chairside assistant's duties are:

- greeting and seating patients
- preparation of the treatment/clinical areas
- proper disinfection and sterilization procedures (infection control)
- clinical charting on both paper and/or computerized dental chart
- assisting the dentist during 'procedure'
  - manipulating and passing materials
  - instrument transfer
  - patient safety and comfort
- patient management
- radiograph exposure and processing
- dental lab procedures
- patient education and post-op instructions
- ordering supplies and inventory control
- adhering to national and state Occupational Safety and Health Administration (OSHA) regulations

Circulating/Roving Assistant

This assistant performs all of the same duties and functions as the chairside assistant, but also serves as an extra set of hands where needed. This assistant is most effective in offices that practice six-handed dentistry, which refers to the efficient teamwork between the dentist and two assistants. Not all offices have a circulating/roving assistant or practice six-handed dentistry.

Sterilization Assistant

This assistant is responsible for the preparation, pre-cleaning, disinfection, and sterilization of all instruments, and for properly disposing of biohazard waste. This assistant enforces infection control protocol along with universal and standard precautions. In addition to overseeing the management of biohazard waste, this assistant often monitors sterilizers and compiles regular reports. Not all dental offices have a separate sterilization assistant, so the duties would fall back on the chairside assistant.

Expanded-Function Dental Assistant (EFDA)

An EFDA is a dental assistant who has additional training in patient procedures beyond the traditional duties of a dental assistant. These expanded functions vary from state to state, depending on local laws.

Business Assistant

Business assistants are responsible for the management of the front office area in the practice. They are sometimes known as front-desk assistants, administrative assistants, secretarial assistants, or receptionists. Patients are greeted by these assistants, which means that these assistants create the first impressions of the dental practice. They perform various support services for the clinical team. Some examples are:

- welcoming patients
- answering the phone
- returning phone calls
- scheduling of patients
- managing clinical records
- handling insurance services
- managing accounts receivables
- managing accounts payable
- maintaining the recall/continuing care systems
- adhering to national Health Insurance Portability and Accountability Act (HIPAA) standards
- managing internal and external marketing

Dental Hygienist

The dental hygienist is responsible for oral prophylaxis and soft-tissue management. He or she usually works independently in a treatment room, maintaining a separate schedule from the dentist. A hygienist attends school for two years full-time after completing an extensive list of prerequisites, primarily in the field of science. Dental hygienists are required to pass both national and state board examinations successfully to become registered and to practice as a hygienist. Registered dental hygienists (RDH) are eligible to join the American Dental Hygienists Association (ADHA).

Dental Laboratory Technician

The dental laboratory technician is primarily responsible for the fabrication of crowns, bridges, dentures, and any other complex laboratory devices. Sometimes, the lab technician works onsite in a dental office, but often she or he will work offsite in a private laboratory. The lab technician follows the dentist's instructions in fabricating the dental appliances. These are delivered in lab cases to the dental office by the lab. A dental laboratory technician can become certified as a dental technician (CDT), by successfully completing a written examination. Once they pass this exam and are certified, dental laboratory technicians may join the American Dental Laboratory Technician Association (ADLTA).

▶ Becoming a Dental Assistant

Do you have what it takes to become a professional dental assistant?

To work as a professional dental assistant and be part of the dental team requires a number of personal characteristics. You should ask yourself the following questions:

- Do I possess a compassionate nature?
- Am I friendly to everyone I meet?
- Am I respectful?
- Am I honest and trustworthy?
- Do I want to help people?

- Can I manage time wisely?
- Am I efficient and organized?
- Can I abide by rules?
- Can I speak professionally to patients?
- Can I communicate well with all age ranges?
- Am I flexible?

If your answer to these questions is yes, a dental assisting career will be a wise choice for you.

Professional Appearance of a Dental Assistant

The manner in which an assistant presents himself or herself reflects upon not only the individual but also upon the dental practice as a whole. It is important for dental assistants to be aware of how they are presenting themselves as they work in such close proximity to patients and dentists.

Professional dental assistants present themselves in the following way:

- clean and neat appearance
- freshly showered and washed hair
- simple jewelry
- no artificial nails
- limited use of perfume
- appropriate make-up
- hair off the face and eyes
- fresh breath and good oral hygiene (smoking is not recommended)
- freshly laundered uniform
- clean uniform shoes

Dental Assisting as a Career

As of 2006, there were 280,000 dental assistants in the United States, almost all working for individual dentists or small partnerships. A small percentage worked in large clinics and hospitals, and some worked for the government or the military. About 35% of dental assistants worked part-time.

Employment in the field is expected to grow by almost 30% by 2016 to 362,000, making dental assisting one of the fastest-growing professions. In 2006, the average hourly wage of a dental assistant was $14.53. The lowest 10% earned $9.87, and the highest 10% earned $20.69 per hour. The middle 50% earned between $11.94 and $17.44 an hour.

American Dental Assistants Association (ADAA)

The American Dental Assistants Association (ADAA) is a component of the American Dental Association (ADA). It was formed in 1924 by Juliette Southard and is headquartered in Chicago, Illinois. There are chapters in almost every state of the union. This is a professional organization exclusively designed for dental assistants that encourages education, professional development, and licensure. The ADAA is involved with lobbying for legislative changes, and updates members about such issues. Members receive a subscription to *The Dental Assistant*, the journal of the ADAA. This journal outlines the latest trends and techniques in the field of dental assisting. The ADAA also provides free continuing education courses that are outlined in the journal.

2 ▶ Dental Assistant Credentials

CHAPTER OVERVIEW

While it is possible to work as a dental assistant without being certified —this is known as on-the-job trained (OJT)—being a certified dental assistant demonstrates your dedication to the field of dentistry. The two leading credentials for dental assistants are the Certified Dental Assistant (CDA) offered by the Dental Assisting National Board (DANB), and the Registered Dental Assistant (RDA), offered in many states.

Most dental assistants seek certification to demonstrate their professionalism. The national certifying board is the Dental Assisting National Board (DANB), which oversees examinations for regular dental assistants, as well as specialized assistants. The CDA Exam has three components: general chairside (GC), radiation health and safety (RHS), and infection control (ICE). There are three pathways to eligibility for the CDA Exam. Many states offer a license of Registered Dental Assistant (RDA). Both certifications are widely recognized and accepted.

▶ Dental Assisting National Board (DANB)

The DANB administers the following national certification examinations:

- Certified Dental Assistant (CDA)
- Certified Orthodontic Assistant (COA)
- Certified Dental Practice Management Administrator (CDPMA)

The DANB is headquartered in Chicago, Illinois. This agency oversees the national certificants who hold the above certifications, as well as administers the exam to new applicants. Every state in the union recognizes the CDA credential.

The *DANB Review* is the DANB's official study guide. Candidates for the CDA Exam need to submit a written application to the DANB along with an application fee. Applications are available to download on the DANB Web site: *www.danb.org*

The CDA Exam has three components:

1. General Chairside (GC)
2. Radiation Health and Safety (RHS)
3. Infection Control (ICE)

To receive CDA certification, a candidate must pass all three parts of the exam within a five-year period, although many candidates choose to do all three parts in a single sitting.

Pathways

There are three pathways to eligibility for the CDA Exam.

- **Pathway I**
  Graduation from an ADA-accredited dental assisting school
  and
  DANB-approved cardiopulmonary resuscitation (CPR) certification

- **Pathway II**
  High-school graduation or GED
  and
  Two years (minimum 3,500 hours over 24 months) practical experience as a dental assistant, or at least 3,500 hours combination full- and part-time work experience over a 24-month period, and a maximum 48 months as a dental assistant
  and
  DANB-approved cardiopulmonary resuscitation (CPR) certification

- **Pathway III**
  CDA certification or graduation from a DDS or DMD program, or a foreign-degree program
  and
  DANB-approved cardiopulmonary resuscitation (CPR) certification

Additionally, the DANB offers two other certifications (mentioned previously). These are the Certified Orthodontic Assistant (COA) and the Certified Dental Practice Management Assistant (CDPMA) credentials. Both are excellent certifications to have if these are the areas in which you are specializing. However, this book is recommended for applicants interested in the Certified Dental Assistant Examination.

Registered Dental Assistant (RDA)

Each state decides individually if it will offer the license of Registered Dental Assistant (RDA). If you have a question regarding whether or not your home state offers an RDA examination, please consult your state's Dental Practice Act. It will outline the duties a dental assistant can perform and the licenses available in that state.

For example, the state of California offers an RDA examination and license, while Florida does not. The RDA in California is administered by the Committee on Dental Auxiliaries (COMDA) and the State Board of Dental Examiners. One must apply if interested in taking the RDA examination. The examination consists of two portions: a written portion and a practical portion. The written portion is given in a computer–testing center in various locations throughout the state. The practical exam is given at most dental schools. Information and details will follow from your state regarding these locations.

The duties of a dental assistant vary greatly from state to state, so this book cannot cover what is tested in each portion of the RDA examinations for each and every state. It is best to look for a review course in your general location that will tell you exactly what will be tested on your particular RDA examination.

State associations are listed in Appendix IV at the back of this book.

Why Be Certified?

As a certified dental assistant—either the certified dental assistant (CDA) or the registered dental assistant (RDA)—you will become a more desirable candidate in job interviews. With a certification, you will be offered better pay, and be able to perform additional duties at the chair. Having this certification tells the dentist that you have a certain level of knowledge of dentistry, which you proved by passing the rigorous examination process. Patients also appreciate your knowledge, and often ask the dental assistant for clarification.

The CDA certification is the nationally recognized credential, and even in states that offer an RDA license, the CDA is often the pathway to obtaining an RDA. It is always a good idea to have the fullest credentials possible. In states that do not offer an RDA license, the CDA is the only option for licensure. You will be allowed to perform additional duties holding this license as well. If you ever need to move from one state to another, the CDA license is honored and recognized in every state in the union. Dental educators everywhere recommend that you apply for, take, and successfully pass both exams.

CHAPTER

3 ▶ The LearningExpress Test Preparation System

CHAPTER OVERVIEW

Taking any written exam can be tough. It demands a lot of preparation if you want to achieve a top score, and your rank on the eligibility list is often determined largely by this score. The LearningExpress Test Preparation System, developed exclusively for LearningExpress by leading test experts, gives you the discipline and attitude you need to be a winner.

TAKING THIS WRITTEN exam is no picnic, and neither is getting ready for it. Your future career in dental assisting depends on you getting a high score on the various parts of the test, but there are all sorts of pitfalls that can keep you from doing your best on this all-important exam. Here are some of the obstacles that can stand in the way of your success:

- being unfamiliar with the format of the exam
- being paralyzed by test anxiety
- leaving your preparation to the last minute or not preparing at all
- not knowing vital test-taking skills: how to pace yourself through the exam, how to use the process of elimination, and when to guess
- not being in tip-top mental and physical shape
- messing up on exam day by having to work on an empty stomach or shivering through the exam because the room is cold

11

What's the common denominator in all these test-taking pitfalls? One word: *control*. Who's in control, you or the exam?

The LearningExpress Test Preparation System puts you in control. In just nine easy-to-follow steps, you will learn everything you need to know to make sure that you are in charge of your preparation and your performance on the exam. Other test takers may let the exam get the better of them; other test takers may be unprepared or out of shape, but not you. After completing this chapter, you will have taken all the steps you need to get a high score on the dental assisting exam.

Here's how the LearningExpress Test Preparation System works: nine easy steps lead you through everything you need to know and do to get ready for this exam. Each of the steps listed below and on the following pages includes both reading about the step and one or more activities. It's important that you do the activities along with the reading, or you won't be getting the full benefit of the system. Each step tells you approximately how much time that step will take you to complete.

Step 1. Get Information (30 minutes)
Step 2. Conquer Test Anxiety (20 minutes)
Step 3. Make a Plan (50 minutes)
Step 4. Learn to Manage Your Time (10 minutes)
Step 5. Learn to Use the Process of Elimination (20 minutes)
Step 6. Know When to Guess (20 minutes)
Step 7. Reach Your Peak Performance Zone (10 minutes)
Step 8. Get Your Act Together (10 minutes)
Step 9. Do It! (10 minutes)

Total time for complete system (180 minutes—3 hours)

We estimate that working through the entire system will take you approximately three hours. It's perfectly okay if you work at a faster or slower pace. If you can take a whole afternoon or evening, you can work through the whole LearningExpress Test Preparation System in one sitting. Otherwise, you can break it up, and do just one or two steps a day for the next several days. It's up to you—remember, you are in control.

▶ Step 1: Get Information

Time to complete: 30 minutes
Activities: Read Chapter 2, "Dental Assistant Credentials"

Knowledge is power. The first step in the LearningExpress Test Preparation System is finding out everything you can about the types of dental assisting exams offered. For example, the Dental Assisting National Board (DANB)'s *Review* (Third Edition) outlines all the details about taking the CDA exam. Your local state dental assisting boards will have information for you on the RDA exam requirements, which vary from state to state (see Appendix IV).

What You Should Find Out

The more details you can find out about the exam, either from the national or state boards' publications, the more efficiently you will be able to study. Here's a list of some things you might want to find out about your exam:

- What skills are tested?
- How many sections are on the exam?
- How many questions are in each section?
- Are the questions ordered from easy to hard, or is the sequence random?
- How much time is allotted for each section?
- Are there breaks between sections?
- What is the passing score, and how many questions do you have to answer right in order to get that score?
- Does a higher score give you any advantages, like a better rank on the eligibility list?
- How is the exam scored, and is there a penalty for wrong answers?
- Are you permitted to go back to a prior section or move on to the next section if you finish early?
- Can you write in the exam booklet, or will you be given scratch paper?
- What should you bring with you on exam day?

What's on Most Dental Assistant Exams (CDA and RDA)

The skills that are tested in the dental assisting written exam vary from state to state. That's why it's important to contact the DANB as well as your local state association to find out what skills are covered. If you haven't already done so, stop here and read Chapter 1 of this book, which gives you an overview of the entire process of becoming a dental assistant. Then, move on to the next step to get rid of that test anxiety.

▶ Step 2: Conquer Test Anxiety

Time to complete: 20 minutes
Activity: Take the Test Anxiety Quiz (page 16)

Having complete information about the exam is the first step in getting control of it. Next, you have to overcome one of the biggest obstacles to test success: test anxiety. Test anxiety can not only impair your performance on the exam itself, but it can even keep you from preparing properly. In Step 2, you will learn stress management techniques that will help you succeed on your exam. Learn these strategies now, and practice them as you work through the questions in this book, so they'll be second nature to you by exam day.

Combating Test Anxiety

The first thing you need to know is that a little test anxiety is a good thing. Everyone gets nervous before a big exam—and if that nervousness motivates you to prepare thoroughly, so much the better. It's said that Sir Laurence

Olivier, one of the foremost British actors of the twentieth century, threw up before every performance. His stage fright didn't impair his performance; in fact, it probably gave him a little extra edge—just the kind of edge you need to do well, whether on a stage or in an examination room.

On page 16 is the Test Anxiety Quiz. Stop here and answer the questions on that page to find out whether your level of test anxiety is something you should worry about.

Stress Management before the Exam

If you feel your level of anxiety is getting the best of you in the weeks before the exam, here is what you need to do to bring the level down again:

- **Get prepared.** There's nothing like knowing what to expect and being prepared for it to put you in control of test anxiety. That's why you're reading this book. Use it faithfully, and remind yourself that you're better prepared than most of the people taking the exam.
- **Practice self-confidence.** A positive attitude is a great way to combat test anxiety. This is no time to be humble or shy. Stand in front of the mirror and say to your reflection, "I'm prepared. I'm full of self-confidence. I'm going to ace this exam. I know I can do it." Say it into a recorder, and play it back once a day. If you hear it often enough, you will believe it.
- **Fight negative messages.** Every time someone starts telling you how hard the exam is or how it's almost impossible to get a high score, start telling them your self-confidence messages above. If the someone with the negative messages is you—telling yourself you don't do well on exams, that you just can't do this—don't listen. Turn on your recorder and listen to your self-confidence messages.
- **Visualize.** Imagine yourself reporting for duty on your first day of dental assisting. Think of yourself wearing your uniform with pride and learning skills you will use for the rest of your life. Visualizing success can help make it happen—and it reminds you of why you're doing all this work in preparing for the exam.
- **Exercise.** Physical activity helps calm down your body and focus your mind. Besides, being in good physical shape can actually help you do well on the exam. Go for a run, lift weights, go swimming—and do it regularly.

Stress Management on Exam Day

There are several ways you can bring down your level of test stress and anxiety on exam day. They'll work best if you practice them in the weeks before the exam, so you know which ones work best for you.

- **Deep breathing.** Take a deep breath while you count to five. Hold it for a count of one, and then let it out on a count of five. Repeat several times.
- **Move your body.** Try rolling your head in a circle. Rotate your shoulders. Shake your hands from the wrist. Many people find these movements very relaxing.
- **Visualize again.** Think of the place where you are most relaxed: lying on the beach in the sun, walking through the park, or whatever relaxes you. Now, close your eyes and imagine you're actually there. If you practice in advance, you will find that you need only a few seconds of this exercise to experience a significant increase in your sense of well-being.

When anxiety threatens to overwhelm you during the exam, there are still things you can do to manage your stress level:

- **Repeat your self-confidence messages.** You should have them memorized by now. Say them quietly to yourself, and believe them!
- **Visualize one more time.** This time, visualize yourself moving smoothly and quickly through the exam, answering every question correctly and finishing just before time is up. Like most visualization techniques, this one works best if you've practiced it ahead of time.
- **Find an easy question.** Skim over the test until you find an easy question, and answer it. Getting even one circle filled in gets you into the test-taking groove.
- **Take a mental break.** Everyone loses concentration once in a while during a long exam. It's normal, so you shouldn't worry about it. Instead, accept what has happened. Say to yourself, "Hey, I lost it there for a minute. My brain is taking a break." Put down your pencil, close your eyes, and do some deep breathing for a few seconds. Then, you're ready to go back to work.

Try these techniques ahead of time, and see if they work for you!

You need to worry about test anxiety only if it is extreme enough to impair your performance. The following questionnaire will provide a diagnosis of your level of test anxiety. In the blank before each statement, write the number that most accurately describes your experience.

0 = Never

1 = Once or twice

2 = Sometimes

3 = Often

_____ I have gotten so nervous before an exam that I simply put down the books and didn't study for it.

_____ I have experienced disabling physical symptoms such as vomiting and severe headaches because I was nervous about an exam.

_____ I have simply not showed up for an exam because I was scared to take it.

_____ I have experienced dizziness and disorientation while taking an exam.

_____ I have had trouble filling in the little circles because my hands were shaking too hard.

_____ I have failed an exam because I was too nervous to complete it.

_____ **Total: add up the numbers in the blanks above.**

Understanding Your Test Stress Scores

Here are the steps you should take, depending on your score.

- **Below 3:** Your level of test anxiety is nothing to worry about. It's probably just enough to give you that little extra edge.

- **Between 3 and 6:** Your test anxiety may be enough to impair your performance, and you should practice the stress-management techniques listed in this section to try to bring your test anxiety down to manageable levels.

- **Above 6:** Your level of test anxiety is a serious concern. In addition to practicing the stress-management techniques listed in this section, you may want to seek additional, personal help. Call your local high school or community college and ask for the academic counselor. Tell the counselor that you have a level of test anxiety that sometimes keeps you from being able to take the exam. The counselor may be willing to help you or may suggest someone else you should talk to.

▶ Step 3: Make a Plan

Time to complete: 50 minutes
Activity: Construct a study plan, using Schedules A–D (pages 18–20)

Many people do poorly on exams because they forget to make a study schedule. The most important thing you can do to better prepare yourself for your exam is to create a study plan or schedule. Spending hours the day before the exam poring over sample test questions not only raises your level of anxiety, but it is also not a substitute for careful preparation and practice over time.

Don't cram. Take control of your time by mapping out a study schedule. There are four examples of study schedules on the following pages, based on the amount of time you have before the exam. If you're the kind of person who needs deadlines and assignments to motivate you for a project, here they are. If you're the kind of person who doesn't like to follow other people's plans, you can use the suggested schedules to construct your own.

In constructing your plan, you should take into account how much work you need to do. If your score on the sample test wasn't what you had hoped, consider taking some of the steps from Schedule A and fitting them into Schedule D, even if you do have only three weeks before the exam. (See Schedules A–D on the next few pages.)

You can also customize your plan according to the information you gathered in Step 1. If the exam you have to take doesn't include dental office procedures, for instance, you can skip Chapter 4 and concentrate on other areas that are covered.

Even more important than making a plan is making a commitment. You can't review everything you learned in your dental assisting course in one night. You have to set aside some time every day for studying and practice. Try to set aside at least 20 minutes a day. Twenty minutes daily will do you more good than two hours crammed into a Saturday.

If you have months before the exam, you're lucky. Don't put off your study until the week before the exam. Start now. Even ten minutes a day, with half an hour or more on weekends, can make a big difference in your score—and in your chances of becoming a dental assistant.

Schedule A: The Leisure Plan

This schedule gives you at least six months to sharpen your skills and prepare for your exam. The more prep time you give yourself, the more relaxed you'll feel.

TIME	PREPARATION
Exam minus 6 months:	Read the Introduction and Chapters 1 and 2. Start going to the library once every two weeks to read books or magazines about dental assisting. Start gathering information about working as a dental assistant. Find other people who are preparing for the exam, and form a study group.
Exam minus 5 months:	Read Chapter 4 and work through the exercises. Use at least one of the additional resources for each chapter.
Exam minus 4 months:	Read Chapters 5 and 6 and work through the exercises. You're still continuing with your reading, aren't you?
Exam minus 3 months:	Read Chapters 7 and 8 and work through the exercises.
Exam minus 2 months:	Read Chapters 9 and 10 and work through the exercises.
Exam minus 1 month:	Use your scores from the chapter execises to help you decide where to concentrate your efforts this month. Go back to the relevant chapters and use the additional resources listed there. Continue working with your study group.
Exam minus 1 week:	Take and review the sample exams in Chapters 11 and 12. See how much you've learned in the past months. Concentrate on what you've done well, and decide not to let any areas where you still feel uncertain bother you.
Exam minus 1 day:	Relax. Do something unrelated to the dental assisting exam. Eat a good meal and go to bed at your usual time.

Schedule B: The Just-Enough-Time Plan

If you have three to six months before the exam, that should be enough time to prepare. This schedule assumes four months; stretch it out or compress it if you have more or less time.

TIME	PREPARATION
Exam minus 4 months:	Read the Introduction and Chapters 1 and 2. Start going to the library once every two weeks to read books or magazines about dental assisting. Start gathering information about working as a dental assistant.
Exam minus 3 months:	Read Chapters 4–7 and work through the exercises.
Exam minus 2 months:	Read Chapters 8–10 and work through the exercises. You're still continuing with your reading, aren't you?

TIME	PREPARATION
Exam minus 1 month:	Take one of the sample exams in Chapter 11 or Chapter 12. Use your score to help you decide where to concentrate your efforts this month. Go back to the relevant chapters and use the extra resources listed there, or get the help of a friend or teacher.
Exam minus 1 week:	Review the sample exams in Chapters 11 and 12. See how much you've learned in the past months. Concentrate on what you've done well, and decide not to let any areas where you still feel uncertain bother you.
Exam minus 1 day:	Relax. Do something unrelated to the dental assisting exam. Eat a good meal and go to bed at your usual time.

Schedule C: More Study in Less Time

If you have one to three months before the exam, you still have enough time for some concentrated study that will help you improve your score. This schedule is built around a two-month time frame. If you have only one month, spend an extra couple of hours a week to get all these steps in. If you have three months, take some of the steps from Schedule B and fit them in.

TIME	PREPARATION
Exam minus 8 weeks:	Read the Introduction and Chapters 1–5. Work through the exercises in Chapters 4 and 5. Review areas you're weakest in.
Exam minus 6 weeks:	Read Chapters 6–8 and work through the exercises.
Exam minus 4 weeks:	Read Chapters 9 and 10 and work through the exercises.
Exam minus 2 weeks:	Take one of the sample exams in Chapter 11 or Chapter 12. Then, score it and read the answer explanations until you're sure you understand them. Review the areas where your score is lowest.
Exam minus 1 week:	Review the sample exams, concentrating on the areas where a little work can help the most.
Exam minus 1 day:	Relax. Do something unrelated to the dental assisting exam. Eat a good meal and go to bed at your usual time.

Schedule D: The Cram Plan

If you have three weeks or less before the exam, you really have your work cut out for you. Carve half an hour out of your day, every day, for studying. This schedule assumes you have the whole three weeks to prepare; if you have less time, you will have to compress the schedule accordingly.

TIME	PREPARATION
Exam minus 3 weeks:	Read the Introduction and Chapters 1–6. Work through the exercises in Chapters 4–6. Review areas you're weakest in.
Exam minus 2 weeks:	Read the material in Chapters 7–10 and work through the exercises.
Exam minus 1 week:	Evaluate your performance on the chapter exercises. Review the parts of Chapters 4–10 that you had the most trouble with. Get a friend or teacher to help you with the section you had the most difficulty with.
Exam minus 2 days:	Take the sample exams in Chapters 11 and 12. Review your results. Make sure you understand the answer explanations.
Exam minus 1 day:	Relax. Do something unrelated to the dental assisting exam. Eat a good meal and go to bed at your usual time.

▶ Step 4: Learn to Manage Your Time

Time to complete: 10 minutes to read, many hours of practice
Activities: Practice these strategies as you take the sample exams

Steps 4, 5, and 6 of the LearningExpress Test Preparation System put you in charge of your exam by showing you test-taking strategies that work. Practice these strategies as you take the sample exams in Chapters 11 and 12. Then, you will be ready to use them on exam day.

First, you will take control of your time on the exam. The first step in achieving this control is to find out the format of the exam you're going to take. Dental assisting exams have different sections that are each timed separately. If this is true of the exam you will be taking, you will want to practice using your time wisely on the practice exams and trying to avoid mistakes while working quickly. Other types of exams don't have separately timed sections. If this is the case, just practice pacing yourself on the practice exams so you don't spend too much time on difficult questions.

- **Listen carefully to directions.** By the time you get to the exam, you should know how the test works, but listen just in case something has changed.
- **Pace yourself.** Glance at your watch every few minutes, and compare the time to how far you've gotten in the section. Leave some extra time for review, so that when one-quarter of the time has elapsed, you should be more than a quarter of the way through the section, and so on. If you're falling behind, pick up the pace.
- **Keep moving.** Don't spend too much time on one question. If you don't know the answer, skip the question and move on. Circle the number of the question in your test booklet in case you have time to come back to it later.
- **Keep track of your place on the answer sheet.** If you skip a question, make sure you skip on the answer sheet, too. Check yourself every five to ten questions to make sure the question number and the answer sheet number match.
- **Don't rush.** You should keep moving, rushing won't help. Try to keep calm and work methodically and quickly.

▶ Step 5: Learn to Use the Process of Elimination

Time to complete: 20 minutes
Activity: Complete worksheet on Using the Process of Elimination (pages 24–25)

After time management, the next most important tool for taking control of your exam is using the process of elimination wisely. It's standard test-taking wisdom that you should always read all the answer choices before choosing your answer. This helps you find the right answer by eliminating wrong answer choices. And, sure enough, that standard wisdom applies to this exam, too.

Let's say you're facing a question that goes like this:

13. "Biology uses a *binomial* system of classification." In this sentence, the word *binomial* most nearly means

    a. understanding the law.

    b. having two names.

    c. scientifically sound.

    d. having a double meaning.

If you happen to know what *binomial* means, you don't need to use the process of elimination, but let's assume that, like most people, you don't. So, you look at the answer choices. "Understanding the law" sure doesn't sound very likely for something having to do with biology. So, you eliminate choice **a**—and now you only have three answer choices to deal with. Mark an **X** next to choice **a** so you never have to read it again.

Move on to the other answer choices. If you know that the prefix *bi-* means *two*, as in *bicycle*, you will flag answer **b** as a possible answer. Make a check mark beside it, meaning "good answer, I might use this one."

Choice **c**, "scientifically sound," is a possibility. At least it's about science, not law. It could work here, though, when you think about it, having a "scientifically sound" classification system in a scientific field is kind of redundant. You remember the *bi-* in *binomial*, and probably continue to like answer **b** better. But you're not sure, so you put a question mark next to **c**, meaning "well, maybe."

Now, look at choice **d**, "having a double meaning." You're still keeping in mind that *bi-* means *two*, so this one looks possible at first. But then you look again at the sentence the word belongs in, and you think, "Why would biology want a system of classification that has two meanings? That wouldn't work very well!" If you're really taken with the idea that *bi-* means *two*, you might put a question mark here. But if you're feeling a little more confident, you will put an **X**. You've already got a better answer picked out.

Now, your question looks like this:

13. "Biology uses a *binomial* system of classification." In this sentence, the word *binomial* most nearly means

  X **a.** understanding the law.

  ✓ **b.** having two names.

  ? **c.** scientifically sound.

  ? **d.** having a double meaning.

You've got just one check mark, for a good answer. If you're pressed for time, you should simply mark answer **b** on your answer sheet. If you've got the time to be extra careful, you could compare your check mark answer to your question mark answers to make sure that it's better. (It is: The *binomial* system in biology is the one that gives a two-part genus and species name like homo sapiens.)

It's good to have a system for marking good, bad, and maybe answers. We recommend using this one:

  X = bad

  ✓ = good

  ? = maybe

If you don't like these marks, devise your own system. Just make sure you do it long before exam day—while you're working through the practice exams in this book—so you won't have to worry about it during the exam.

Even when you think you're absolutely clueless about a question, you can often use the process of elimination to get rid of one answer choice. If so, you're better prepared to make an educated guess, as you will see in Step 6.

More often, the process of elimination allows you to get down to only two possibly right answers. Then you're in a strong position to guess. And sometimes, even though you don't know the right answer, you find it simply by getting rid of the wrong ones, as you did in the example above.

Try using your powers of elimination on the questions in the worksheet Using the Process of Elimination beginning on the next page. The answer explanations there show one possible way you might use the process to arrive at the right answer.

The process of elimination is your tool for the next step, which is knowing when to guess.

Use the process of elimination to answer the following questions.

1. Ilsa is as old as Meghan will be in five years. The difference between Ed's age and Meghan's age is twice the difference between Ilsa's age and Meghan's age. Ed is 29. How old is Ilsa?
   a. 4
   b. 10
   c. 19
   d. 24

2. "All drivers of commercial vehicles must carry a valid commercial driver's license whenever operating a commercial vehicle." According to this sentence, which of the following people need **NOT** carry a commercial driver's license?
   a. a truck driver idling his engine while waiting to be directed to a loading dock
   b. a bus operator backing her bus out of the way of another bus in the bus lot
   c. a taxi driver driving his personal car to the grocery store
   d. a limousine driver taking the limousine to her home after dropping off her last passenger of the evening

3. What has smoking been linked to?
   a. increased risk of stroke and heart attack
   b. all forms of respiratory disease
   c. increasing mortality rates over the past ten years
   d. juvenile delinquency

4. Which of the following words is spelled correctly?
   a. incorrigible
   b. outragous
   c. domestickated
   d. understandible

Answers

Here are the answers, as well as some suggestions as to how you might have used the process of elimination to find them.

1. **d.** You should have eliminated answer **a** off the bat. Ilsa can't be four years old if Meghan is going to be Ilsa's age in five years. The best way to eliminate other answer choices is to try plugging them in to the information given in the problem. For instance, for answer **b**, if Ilsa is 10, then Meghan must be 5. The difference in their ages is 5. The difference between Ed's age, 29, and Meghan's age, 5, is 24. Is 24 two times 5? No. Then answer **b** is wrong. You could eliminate answer **c** in the same way and be left with answer **d**.

2. c. Note the word *not* in the question, and go through the answers one by one. Is the truck driver in choice **a** "operating a commercial vehicle"? Yes, idling counts as "operating," so he needs to have a commercial driver's license. Likewise, the bus operator in answer **b** is operating a commercial vehicle; the question doesn't say the operator has to be on the street. The limo driver in **d** is operating a commercial vehicle, even if it doesn't have a passenger in it. However, the cabbie in answer **c** is not operating a commercial vehicle, but his own private car.

3. a. You could eliminate answer **b** simply because of the presence of the word *all*. Such absolutes hardly ever appear in correct answer choices. Choice **c** looks attractive until you think a little about what you know—aren't fewer people smoking these days, rather than more? So how could smoking be responsible for a higher mortality rate? (If you didn't know that *mortality rate* means the rate at which people die, you might keep this choice as a possibility, but you'd still be able to eliminate two answers and have only two to choose from.) And choice **d** is plain silly, so you could eliminate that one, too. And you're left with the correct choice, **a**.

4. a. How you used the process of elimination here depends on which words you recognized as being spelled incorrectly. If you knew that the correct spellings were *outrageous*, *domesticated*, and *understandable*, then you were home free. Surely you knew that at least one of those words was wrong!

▶ Step 6: Know When to Guess

Time to complete: 20 minutes
Activity: Complete Worksheet on Your Guessing Ability (pages 28–29)

Armed with the process of elimination, you're ready to take control of one of the big questions in test-taking: Should I guess? The first and main answer is yes. Unless the exam has a so-called "guessing penalty," you have nothing to lose and everything to gain from guessing. The more complicated answer depends both on the exam and on you—your personality and your "guessing intuition."

Most dental assisting exams don't use a guessing penalty. The number of questions you answer correctly yields your score, and there's no penalty for wrong answers. So most of the time, you don't have to worry— simply go ahead and guess. But if you find that your exam does have a guessing penalty, you should read the section below to find out what that means to you.

How the Guessing Penalty Works

A guessing penalty really only works against random guessing—filling in the little circles to make a nice pattern on your answer sheet. If you can eliminate one or more answer choices, as outlined above, you're better off taking a guess than leaving the answer blank, even on the sections that have a penalty.

Here's how a guessing penalty works: Depending on the number of answer choices in a given exam, some proportion of the number of questions you get wrong is subtracted from the total number of questions you got right. For instance, if there are four answer choices, typically the guessing penalty is one-third of your wrong answers. Suppose you took an exam of 100 questions. You answered 88 of them right and 12 wrong.

If there's no guessing penalty, your score is simply 88. But if there's a one-third point guessing penalty, the scorers take your 12 wrong answers and divide by three to come up with four. Then they subtract that four from your correct answer score of 88 to leave you with a score of 84. Thus, you would have been better off if you had simply not answered those 12 questions. Then your total score would still be 88 because there wouldn't be anything to subtract.

What You Should Do About the Guessing Penalty

You now know how a guessing penalty works. The first thing this means for you is that marking your answer sheet at random doesn't pay. If you're running out of time on an exam that has a guessing penalty, you should not use your remaining seconds to mark a pretty pattern on your answer sheet. Take those few seconds to try to answer one more question right.

But as soon as you get out of the realm of random guessing, the guessing penalty no longer works against you. If you can use the process of elimination to get rid of even one wrong answer choice, the odds stop being against you and start working in your favor.

Sticking with our example of an exam that has four answer choices, eliminating just one wrong answer makes your odds of choosing the correct answer one in three. That's the same as the one-out-of-three guessing penalty—even odds. If you eliminate two answer choices, your odds are one in two—better than the guessing penalty. In either case, you should go ahead and choose one of the remaining answer choices.

When There Is No Guessing Penalty

As noted above, most dental assisting exams don't have a guessing penalty. That means that, all other things being equal, you should always go ahead and guess, even if you have no idea what the question means. Nothing can happen to you if you're wrong. But all other things aren't necessarily equal. The other factor in deciding whether or not to guess, besides the guessing penalty, is you. There are two things you need to know about yourself before you go into the exam:

- Are you a risk-taker?
- Are you a good guesser?

Your risk-taking temperament matters most on exams with a guessing penalty. Without a guessing penalty, even if you're a play-it-safe person, guessing is perfectly safe. Overcome your anxieties, and go ahead and mark an answer.

But what if you're not much of a risk-taker, and you think of yourself as the world's worst guesser? Complete the worksheet Your Guessing Ability on the next two pages to get an idea of how good your intuition is.

The following are ten really hard questions. You're not supposed to know the answers. Rather, this is an assessment of your ability to guess when you don't have a clue. Read each question carefully, as if you were expected to answer it. If you have any knowledge at all of the subject of the question, use that knowledge to help you eliminate wrong answer choices. Use this answer grid to fill in your answers to the questions.

1. September 7 is Independence Day in:
   a. India.
   b. Costa Rica.
   c. Brazil.
   d. Australia.

2. Which of the following is the formula for determining the momentum of an object?
   a. $p = mv$
   b. $F = ma$
   c. $P = IV$
   d. $E = mc^2$

3. Because of the expansion of the universe, the stars and other celestial bodies are all moving away from each other. This phenomenon is known as:
   a. Newton's first law.
   b. the big bang.
   c. gravitational collapse.
   d. Hubble flow.

4. American author Gertrude Stein was born in:
   a. 1713.
   b. 1830.
   c. 1874.
   d. 1901.

5. Which of the following is NOT one of the Five Classics attributed to Confucius?
   a. the *I Ching*
   b. the *Book of Holiness*
   c. the *Spring and Autumn Annals*
   d. the *Book of History*

6. The religious and philosophical doctrine that holds that the universe is constantly in a struggle between good and evil is known as:
   a. Pelagianism.
   b. Manichaeanism.
   c. neo-Hegelianism.
   d. Epicureanism.

7. The third Chief Justice of the U.S. Supreme Court was:
   a. John Blair.
   b. William Cushing.
   c. James Wilson.
   d. John Jay.

8. Which of the following is the poisonous portion of a daffodil?
   a. the bulb
   b. the leaves
   c. the stem
   d. the flowers

9. The winner of the Masters golf tournament in 1953 was:
   a. Sam Snead.
   b. Cary Middlecoff.
   c. Arnold Palmer.
   d. Ben Hogan.

10. The state with the highest per capita personal income in 1980 was:
   a. Alaska.
   b. Connecticut.
   c. New York.
   d. Texas.

Answers

Check your answers against the correct answers below.

1. c.
2. a.
3. d.
4. c.
5. b.
6. b.
7. b.
8. a.
9. d.
10. a.

How Did You Do?

You may have simply gotten lucky and actually known the answer to one or two questions. In addition, your guessing was more successful if you were able to use the process of elimination on any of the questions. Maybe you didn't know who the third Chief Justice was (question 7), but you knew that John Jay was the first. In that case, you would have eliminated answer **d** and, therefore, improved your odds of guessing right from one in four to one in three.

According to probability, you should get two and a half answers correct, so getting either two or three right would be average. If you got four or more right, you may be a really terrific guesser. If you got one or none right, you may be a really bad guesser.

Keep in mind, though, that this is only a small sample. You should continue to keep track of your guessing ability as you work through the sample questions in this book. Circle the number of questions you guessed on as you make your guess; or, if you don't have time while you take the practice tests, go back afterward and try to remember which questions you guessed at. Remember, on a test with four answer choices, your chances of getting a right answer is one in four. So keep a separate "guessing" score for each exam. How many questions did you guess on? How many did you get right? If the number you got right is at least one-fourth of the number of questions you guessed on, you are at least an average guesser, maybe better—and you should always go ahead and guess on the real exam. If the number you got right is significantly lower than one-fourth of the number you guessed on, you need to improve your guessing skills.

▶ Step 7: Reach Your Peak Performance Zone

Time to complete: 10 minutes to read; weeks to complete!
Activity: Complete the Physical Preparation Checklist (page 31)

To get ready for a challenge like a big exam, you also have to take control of your physical, as well as your mental, state. Exercise, proper diet, and rest will ensure that your body works with, rather than against, your mind on test day, as well as during your preparation.

Exercise

If you don't already have a regular exercise program going, the time during which you're preparing for an exam is actually an excellent time to start one. And if you're already keeping fit—or trying to get that way—don't let the pressure of preparing for an exam fool you into quitting now. Exercise helps reduce stress by pumping wonderful good-feeling hormones called endorphins into your system. It also increases the oxygen supply throughout your body, including your brain, so you will be at peak performance on exam day.

A half hour of vigorous activity—enough to raise a sweat—every day should be your aim. If you're really pressed for time, every other day is OK. Choose an activity you like and get out there and do it. Jogging with a friend always makes the time go faster, as does running with a radio.

But don't overdo it. You don't want to exhaust yourself. Moderation is the key.

Diet

First of all, cut out the junk. Go easy on caffeine, and try to eliminate alcohol and nicotine from your system at least two weeks before the exam.

What your body needs for peak performance is simply a balanced diet. Eat plenty of fruits and vegetables, along with protein and carbohydrates. Foods that are high in lecithin (an amino acid), such as fish and beans, are especially good "brain foods."

The night before the exam, you might "carbo-load" the way athletes do before a contest. Eat a big plate of spaghetti, rice and beans, or whatever your favorite carbohydrate is.

Rest

You probably know how much sleep you need every night to be at your best, even if you don't always get it. Make sure you do get that much sleep, though, for at least a week before the exam. Moderation is important here, too. Too much sleep will just make you groggy.

If you're not a morning person and your exam will be given in the morning, you should reset your internal clock so that your body doesn't think you're taking an exam at 3 A.M. You have to start this process well before the exam. The way it works is to get up half an hour earlier each morning, and then go to bed half an hour earlier that night. Don't try it the other way around; you will just toss and turn if you go to bed early without having gotten up early. The next morning, get up another half an hour earlier, and so on. How long you will have to do this depends on how late you're used to getting up. Use the Physical Preparation Checklist on the next page to make sure you're in tip-top form.

Physical Preparation Checklist

For the week before the exam, write down 1) what physical exercise you engaged in and for how long and 2) what you ate for each meal. Remember, you're trying for at least half an hour of exercise every other day (preferably every day) and a balanced diet that's light on junk food.

Exam minus 7 days

Exercise: _____ for _____ minutes

Breakfast: _____

Lunch: _____

Dinner: _____

Snacks:_____

Exam minus 6 days

Exercise: _____ for _____ minutes

Breakfast: _____

Lunch: _____

Dinner: _____

Snacks:_____

Exam minus 5 days

Exercise: _____ for _____ minutes

Breakfast: _____

Lunch: _____

Dinner: _____

Snacks:_____

Exam minus 4 days

Exercise: _____ for _____ minutes

Breakfast: _____

Lunch: _____

Dinner: _____

Snacks:_____

Exam minus 3 days

Exercise: _____ for _____ minutes

Breakfast: _____

Lunch: _____

Dinner: _____

Snacks:_____

Exam minus 2 days

Exercise: _____ for _____ minutes

Breakfast: _____

Lunch: _____

Dinner: _____

Snacks:_____

Exam minus 1 day

Exercise: _____ for _____ minutes

Breakfast: _____

Lunch: _____

Dinner: _____

Snacks:_____

▶ Step 8: Get Your Act Together

Time to complete: 10 minutes to read; time to complete will vary
Activity: Complete Final Preparations worksheet (page 33)

You're in control of your mind and body; you're in charge of test anxiety, your preparation, and your test-taking strategies. Now, it's time to take charge of external factors, like the exam site and the materials you need to take the exam.

Find Out Where the Exam Is and Make a Trial Run

The testing agency or your dental assisting instructor will notify you when and where your exam is being held. Do you know how to get to the exam site? Do you know how long it will take to get there? If not, make a trial run, preferably on the same day of the week at the same time of day. Make note, on the worksheet Final Preparations on the next page, of the amount of time it will take you to get to the exam site. Plan on arriving 10–15 minutes early so you can get the lay of the land, use the bathroom, and calm down. Then, figure out how early you will have to get up that morning, and make sure you get up that early every day for a week before the exam.

Gather Your Materials

The night before the exam, lay out the clothes you will wear and the materials you have to bring with you to the exam. Plan on dressing in layers; you won't have any control over the temperature of the examination room. Have a sweater or jacket you can take off if it's warm. Use the checklist on the worksheet Final Preparations on the next page to help you pull together what you will need.

Don't Skip Breakfast

Even if you don't usually eat breakfast, do so on exam morning. A cup of coffee doesn't count. Don't do doughnuts or other sweet foods, either. A sugar high will leave you with a sugar low in the middle of the exam. A mix of protein and carbohydrates is best. Cereal with milk and just a little sugar or eggs with toast will do your body a world of good.

Final Preparations

Getting to the Exam Site

Location of exam site: _____

Date: _____

Departure time: _____

Do I know how to get to the exam site?   Yes _____   No _____   If no, make a trial run.

Time it will take to get to exam site: _____

Things to Lay Out the Night Before

Clothes I will wear   _____

Sweater/jacket _____

Watch _____

Photo ID   _____

No. 2. pencils   _____

Other Things to Bring/Remember

_____   _____

_____   _____

_____   _____

_____   _____

▶ Step 9: Do It!

Time to complete: 10 minutes, plus test-taking time
Activity: Ace the dental assisting exam!

Fast forward to exam day. You're ready. You made a study plan and followed through. You practiced your test-taking strategies while working through this book. You're in control of your physical, mental, and emotional state. You know when and where to show up and what to bring with you. In other words, you're better prepared than most of the other people taking the dental assisting exam with you. You're psyched.

Just one more thing. When you're done with the exam, you will have earned a reward. Plan a celebration. Call up your friends and plan a party, or have a nice dinner for two, or pick out a movie to see—whatever your heart desires. Give yourself something to look forward to.

And then do it. Go into the exam, full of confidence, armed with test-taking strategies you've practiced until they're second nature. You're in control of yourself, your environment, and your performance on the exam. You're ready to succeed. So do it. Go in there and ace the exam. And look forward to your future career as a dental assistant.

Dental Science

CHAPTER OVERVIEW

Knowledge of the dental sciences is the foundation for a dental assistant's career. The dental assistant will utilize this knowledge in many aspects of his or her career including radiology, infection control, and chairside assisting with four-handed dentistry.

TOOTH NUMBERING SYSTEMS, tooth surfaces, cavity classifications, anatomic features of the teeth, and angles and divisions of the teeth are the framework for understanding most dental procedures. Oral embryology and histology, along with head and neck anatomy, are also important subjects of interest for the dental assistant.

KEY TERMS

abscess	anatomy	calculus
alveolar process	apex	carcinoma
ameloblasts	apical foramen	caries
ameloclasts	biopsy	cementoblasts
anatomic crown	buccal	cementoclasts

KEY TERMS (continued)

cementum
central nervous system
cingulum
clinical crown
cranium
cusp
deciduous teeth
demineralization
dental sealant
dentin
dentition
distal
embrasure
enamel
eruption
exfoliation
fluoride
gingiva
gingivitis
glossitis
hematoma
histology
hydroxyapatite
incipient caries
incisal
inflammation
integumentary system

interproximal
labial frenum
labial/facial
lactobacilli (LB)
lamina dura
lingual
lingual frenum
mamelon
marginal ridge
masseter
mesial
midline
mixed dentition
morphology
mutans streptococci (MS)
nutrients
occlusal
occlusion
odontoblasts
odontoclasts
osteoblasts
osteoclasts
parotid salivary gland
periodontitis
periodontium
peripheral nervous system
physiology

planes
plaque
pre-natal
preventive dentistry
prism
pulp
quadrant
rampant caries
remineralization
resorption
sarcoma
secondary dentin
Sharpey's fibers
stomodeum
subgingival
sublingual salivary gland
submandibular salivary gland
succedaneous teeth
supragingival
temporomandibular joint
 (TMJ)
uvula
vermilion border
vestibule
xerostomia

▶ Concepts and Skills

Dental Science is broken down into 11 main areas:

- Dentition Overview
- Tooth Morphology
- Oral Embryology and Histology

- Head and Neck Anatomy
- Dental Caries Process
- Periodontal Disease Process
- Preventive Dentistry
- Nutrition
- Oral Pathology
- General Anatomy
- General Physiology

In this chapter, we will present questions relating to each of these 11 areas of Dental Science. The outline below chronicles the most current information available regarding each area of Dental Science, but remember to study your textbook as well.

Dentition Overview

A dentition is a complete set of teeth. Humans have two dentitions, or sets of teeth, in their lifetimes. These are the primary and the permanent dentitions.

The Dentitions

Primary Dentition – 20 teeth

The primary dentition, commonly referred to as "baby teeth," occurs between six months and six years of age. Other names for this dentition include the deciduous dentition and the succedaneous dentition. These teeth are exfoliated, or "lost," beginning at approximately age six.

Mixed Dentition – varied numbers

This dentition occurs on a child between the ages of approximately seven to 12 years of age. In a mixed dentition, there are both primary and permanent teeth present in the mouth at the same time.

Permanent Dentition – 32 teeth

The permanent dentition, also known as "adult teeth," begins erupting at about age six. The teeth will continuously erupt until approximately age 12. There will be a pause in eruption until ages 17 to 21, when the wisdom teeth, or third molars, begin the eruption process. These are the last teeth to erupt.

Dental Arches

Maxillary

The upper arch in the mouth is referred to as the maxillary arch. This is named for the bone of the upper arch, which is called the maxilla. The maxillary arch holds 16 of the 32 permanent teeth and 10 of the 20 primary teeth.

Mandibular

The lower arch in the mouth is referred to as the mandibular arch. This is named for the bone of the lower arch, which is called the mandible. The mandible is the only movable bone in the skull. The mandibular arch holds the lower 16 of the 32 permanent teeth, and the lower 10 of the 20 primary teeth. The curvature formed by the maxillary and mandibular arches is known as the curve of Spee.

Quadrants

The mouth can be divided into smaller areas to make charting and communication easier. One such division is called a quadrant. The mouth is divided into four quadrants: Upper Right, Upper Left, Lower Left, and Lower Right. Each quadrant holds eight teeth.

Anterior Teeth

These teeth are located at the front of the mouth. They consist of the central and lateral incisors and the cuspids (canines). Anterior teeth are designed for cutting and tearing of food. These teeth have incisal edges. There are six anterior teeth in each arch in both the primary and permanent dentitions.

Posterior Teeth

These teeth are located at the back of the mouth. They consist of premolars (bicuspids) and molars. Posterior teeth are designed for chewing and grinding of food just prior to swallowing. These teeth have biting surfaces that have grooves, pits, and fissures to aid in chewing, which are known as the occlusal surfaces. There are ten posterior teeth in each arch in the permanent dentition and only four posterior teeth per arch in the primary dentition.

Names of the Teeth

Central Incisors

These teeth are located at the midline of the face, at the anterior of the mouth. They are the teeth that are most visible when smiling. These teeth are used for cutting and tearing of food.

Lateral Incisors

These teeth are located next to the centrals, at the anterior of the mouth, and are smaller in size than the centrals. These teeth are also used for cutting and tearing of food.

Cuspids

These teeth are located at the corners of both arches and are the longest rooted teeth in the mouth. Cuspids are sometimes referred to as canines or "eye-teeth" because of their pointy shape. They are anterior teeth and are considered to be the cornerstone of the arches.

Premolars or Bicuspids

These teeth are located in the posterior of the mouth and used for chewing and grinding of food. They are smaller than the molars and can be single or double rooted, depending on the individual. There are two premolars in each quadrant: a first premolar and a second premolar.

Molars

These teeth are located in the posterior of the mouth and are used for chewing and grinding of food. There are three molars in each quadrant: first molar, second molar, and third molar (wisdom teeth). These teeth are multi-rooted and can have as many as four roots.

Tooth Surfaces

Mesial

This is the surface of the tooth closest to the midline. It is located interproximally, or in between the teeth.

Distal

This is the surface of the tooth that is the furthest distance away from the midline. It is located interproximally, or in between the teeth.

Lingual

This is the surface of the tooth closest to the tongue.

Facial/Buccal

This is the surface of the tooth closest to the face or cheek. Facial is the term used for the anterior teeth. Buccal is the term used for the posterior teeth. The two names designate the same area of the tooth but are site-specific to the area of the mouth.

Occlusal/Incisal

This is the surface of the tooth used for chewing or cutting of food. Occlusal is the term used for the chewing surface of posterior teeth, and incisal is the term used for the cutting edge of the anterior teeth. The two names designate the same area of the tooth but are site-specific to the area of the mouth.

Tooth Numbering Systems

Numbering systems are utilized as a means of communication and identification among dental team members. Documentation and insurance companies require a consistent format of charting procedures. There are three numbering systems that are utilized in dentistry.

Universal Numbering System

The Universal Numbering System is the most common in the United States and is approved by the American Dental Association (ADA). Teeth are numbered from 1 to 16 on the upper arch, beginning with the patient's upper-right quadrant. Teeth are numbered from 17 to 32 on the lower arch, beginning with the patient's lower-left quadrant. The primary dentition is charted using letters instead of numbers. The primary teeth are lettered A–T.

ISO Numbering System

The International Standards Organization (ISO) numbering system is accepted by the World Health Organization (WHO) and used internationally. This numbering system assigns each quadrant a number—for example, UR quadrant = 1. Next, each quadrant numbers the teeth 1–8. The charting would look like this: 1, 8. This would be read as: upper-right third molar. This is true for both primary and permanent charting.

Palmer Notation System

This numbering system assigns a number and bracket to each tooth. For the primary dentition, a letter and a bracket are assigned to each tooth. The bracket designates the quadrant in which the tooth is located, depending upon its position. This system is common for charting in orthodontics.

Anatomic Features of the Teeth

Teeth should have contours, contacts, and embrasures. Contours of the teeth refer to the curving of the tooth. This can be either concave (curved inward) or convex (curved outward). Contacts are the areas where two surfaces of the teeth touch, which is also referred to as interproximal. Embrasures are the V-shaped space just below or just above the contact points of two teeth.

Tooth Morphology

Tooth morphology is the study of the shape of teeth.

Anterior Permanent Dentition

The anterior teeth have a distinct shape. They are generally smaller than the posterior teeth, have a straight flat edge, and have concave lingual surfaces. These teeth are designed and shaped in this manner to aid in the process of chewing and swallowing food. Anterior teeth also provide the patient with an esthetically pleasing smile.

Posterior Permanent Dentition

The posterior teeth are the powerhouse teeth in the mouth. They are generally larger in size than the anterior teeth; have wide chewing surfaces with pits, fissures, and grooves; and are multi-rooted. These teeth are designed and shaped in this manner to prepare food for being swallowed and digested.

Primary Dentition

The primary dentition consists of 20 "baby" teeth. These teeth are the incisors, the cuspids, and the molars. Children do not have premolars or bicuspids. These teeth erupt when the primary, or baby, first molar is lost. These teeth are usually not very large and are similarly shaped to those in the permanent dentition.

Oral Embryology and Histology

Oral embryology is the study of the prenatal development of the oral cavity. Histology is the study of the function and structure of tissues.

Oral Embryology

Oral embryology is the study of prenatal oral development, from zygote to embryo to fetus.

Prenatal Development

Preimplantation: This stage occurs the week following fertilization. The ovum implants itself, and the cells begin to multiply to begin forming body systems. The teeth are one of the first structures to begin formation.

Embryonic: This stage occurs from week two to week eight of the pregnancy. At about six weeks, the teeth begin to form at a more consistent rate. The zygote is now called an embryo.

Fetal: This stage occurs from week nine to birth, at approximately 40 weeks. The teeth continue to develop and form through gestation.

Life Cycle of a Tooth

Every tooth passes through stages of growth. The bud, cap, and bell stages are the growth periods of a tooth. Teeth grow very similarly to the way a baby grows. They are contained in a sac and continue to move through the growth periods prior to eruption.

Oral Histology

Oral histology is the study of the function and structure of the teeth as well as the tissues surrounding them. Each tooth consists of a crown and root. The surrounding tissues are called the periodontium and support the tooth in its socket.

Layers of the Tooth

Teeth have three layers. The first layer is the enamel. This is a protective layer that is stronger than bone. Enamel is the hardest structure in the body. The second layer is the dentin. Dentin is softer than enamel and will decay very rapidly. Dentin is the only layer of the tooth that can regenerate, or rebuild, itself, known as secondary dentin. The third layer of the tooth is the pulp. The pulp is the "heart" of the tooth. It supplies oxygen, blood, nutrients, and vitamins to the tooth. If the pulp becomes damaged or injured, it is possible that it will die or begin the process of dying. The tooth will need a root canal if this occurs.

Head and Neck Anatomy

A dental assistant should be knowledgeable in the anatomy of the head and neck. Bones, muscles, glands, nerves, and sinuses all play a role in dental health.

Bones of the Skull

The human skull is divided into the cranium and the face. The cranium consists of eight bones that protect the brain. The face has 14 bones.

Features of the Face and Neck

The face muscles are responsible for our facial expressions and play important roles in chewing, digestion, and speaking. Facial landmarks include the nostrils, known as anterior nares.

Salivary Glands

Saliva lubricates, cleans the mouth, and begins the digestion process. There are three major salivary glands and numerous minor salivary glands. The three major glands are the parotid salivary, the submandibular, and the sublingual.

Parotid Salivary Gland
- It is located in the cheeks, just below the ears.
- It is the largest of the three major salivary glands.
- It secretes approximately 25% of the saliva in the mouth.
- The Stensen's duct delivers the saliva to the mouth from the gland.
- The Stensen's duct opens on the buccal surface of the maxillary first molars.

Submandibular Salivary Gland
- It is the size of a walnut, located in the deep floor of the mouth.
- It secretes approximately 60% of the saliva in the mouth.
- The Wharton's duct delivers saliva to the oral cavity.

Sublingual Salivary Gland
- It is located in the floor of the mouth just under the tongue.
- It is the smallest of the three major salivary glands.
- It provides approximately 10% of the saliva in the mouth.
- The Bartholin's duct delivers saliva to the oral cavity.

Blood and Nerve Supply

Arteries and veins carry blood to the neck and face. The internal carotid artery carries blood to the brain, and the exterior carotid artery carries blood to the face and mouth. There are 12 pairs of cranial nerves.

Sinuses

Sinuses are air-filled cavities in the face and skull that produce mucus. There are several sinus cavities: ethmoid sinuses, sphenoid sinuses, maxillary sinuses, and frontal sinuses. The sinuses can become blocked, which can cause discomfort for the patient similar to a toothache.

Dental Caries Process

Dental caries are known as tooth decay and are often called "cavities" by patients. This is an infectious process. Caries is caused by a bacterial infection and is contagious. The bacteria are found in dental plaque. The bacteria can be transmitted from person to person. The condition of the mouth must have the following present for caries to form: Lactobacillus (LB) bacteria, Mutanstreptococci (MS) bacteria, a diet high in fermentable carbohydrates (sugars), and a susceptible tooth.

Caries Process

The caries process takes approximately two years, but it can be halted or disrupted.

Stages of Carious Lesions
- Incipient: This is the very start of tooth decay. The decay has not yet reached the dentinal layer.
- Overt: The decay has reached the dentinal layer, and there is a visible hole in the tooth.
- Rampant: There are overt carious lesions present in many teeth in the mouth at the same time. This is common in patients with poor oral hygiene.

Diagnosis of Caries

A dentist will check for dental caries at each exam appointment. There are two main ways in which a dentist can detect caries: radiographs and dental explorers.

Radiographs

Radiographs, or X-rays, are one of the best tools a dentist has to detect caries interproximally. Today, many dentists use digital radiographs that eliminate the need for film.

Dental Explorers

The explorer is used to check the surfaces of the teeth. The explorer will stick to any suspicious area.

Periodontal Disease Process

Today, 75% of Americans have some form of periodontal disease.

Causes of the disease

The causes of periodontal disease are dental plaque and calculus. Bacteria in dental plaque cause inflammation and destroy tissue. The tissues will pull away from the plaque and bacteria, creating a periodontal pocket. More plaque and bacteria fills the periodontal pocket and hardens. Calculus is hardened plaque, and it is also called tartar. It builds up on the surface of the teeth, irritating the surrounding tissues and perpetuating the disease cycle.

Types of Periodontal Disease

Type I: Gingivitis

Gingivitis is the inflammation of the gingiva, which can be caused by lack of oral hygiene, hormonal imbalance, or illness. It is totally reversible at this stage.

Type II: Early Periodontitis

There has been a progression from gingivitis into the non-reversible start of periodontal disease. Early periodontitis is the beginning of the periodontal disease process. At this stage, the patient will experience bleeding and maybe some generalized or localized swelling of the gingiva. Pockets may have increased in size.

Type III: Moderate Periodontitis

This is the middle stage of the disease process. There has been further progression of the disease. At this point, surgery may be recommended by the dentist or specialist. Bleeding has increased, pockets have grown in size, and the patient may be experiencing bad breath and/or swelling.

Type IV: Advanced Periodontitis

The supporting structures of the mouth are being destroyed by the disease. There has been more damage and destruction to the periodontium. The patient is experiencing pain, increased bleeding, tooth mobility, swelling, and extreme bad breath. The patient will lose his or her teeth.

Signs and Symptoms

There are several signs and symptoms of periodontal disease. These include loose teeth, pain when chewing, gums that bleed easily when brushing or flossing, redness, swollen gingiva, bad breath, soreness, and tenderness. In the early stages, periodontal disease is often painless and has minimal symptoms. Early detection through regular examinations is crucial.

Effects on Systemic Health

Periodontal disease has an effect on the entire human body. Whenever there is disease present in the human body, the immune system reacts. Periodontal disease causes the immune system to be on constant alert, thereby making the patient more susceptible to other illnesses by weakening the immune system. Periodontal disease has been scientifically linked with premature childbirth, heart disease and stroke, bacterial pneumonia, and diabetes.

Preventive Dentistry

The goal of dentistry is for the patient to keep his or her own teeth for life. This can be achieved through education by working together with the patient as a team regarding a preventative routine.

Patient Maintenance

Patients will be educated regarding the importance of cleanings and examinations every six months, sealants, and oral hygiene at home. The patient will establish an oral hygiene routine and schedule for maintaining dental health with help from the dental team.

Routine Cleanings

A dental prophylaxis should be performed every six months to maintain a proper cleaning schedule. This procedure may be performed by a dentist or dental hygienist.

Fluoride Treatments

Fluoride is a naturally occurring mineral found in many of the items that we use daily. Some community drinking water is fluoridated. Many types of toothpaste contain fluoride. Fluoride treatments are applied topically and allowed to contact tooth surfaces for a designated amount of time in the dental setting. Fluoride drops and supplements are prescribed by physicians and dentists to prevent tooth decay in babies and young children.

Sealants

This preventive measure is a form of flowable composite that is placed into the pits and fissures on the occlusal surfaces of posterior teeth. This technique has been proven to prevent decay on the occlusal surfaces (not interproximal) and is recommended as soon as the permanent teeth have erupted fully into the oral cavity.

Oral Healthcare Instructions

The dentist depends on the dental assistant to provide the patients with accurate, concise oral hygiene instructions. In some offices, the dentist may ask the assistant to present treatment plans as well. Dental assistants are often the dental healthcare provider the patient will look to for clarification of the treatment being recommended by the dentist. It is important for dental assistants to understand the procedures they are assisting in and how to explain each step to the patient in a calm, reassuring, and informative manner.

Nutrition

A patient's diet can have an impact on his or her dental health. Dental assistants are often tasked with discussing proper nutrition with the patient and/or the patient's family. There are many different ways to discuss the importance of nutrition in a dental setting.

Food Pyramid

The food pyramid was designed and is maintained by the Food and Drug Administration (FDA). The pyramid's aim is to help Americans know how many servings from each food group should be consumed for optimal health and nutrition. When discussing nutrition, it is important to refer to this guide.

Vitamins and Minerals

Vitamins are essential to good oral health as well as overall health. The best way to receive these vitamins is from nutritious food, but supplements can help as well. Minerals are essential for optimal health. Both vitamins and minerals occur naturally in the food and drink we consume. This is why it is important to have a good balance between fruits, vegetables, grains, dairy, oils, meats, and legumes.

Carbohydrates, Proteins, and Fats

Carbohydrates are products in foods that the body converts into energy. Proteins are essential to build and repair tissues. Fats protect the organs of the body and are utilized as sources of energy.

Water

Water is often referred to as "the forgotten nutrient." Humans cannot survive without water. Humans can go longer without food than without water. The oral cavity needs water to remain hydrated. The FDA recommends that adults have eight glasses of water per day. Water is also found in some foods we eat.

Eating Disorders

Eating disorders can affect both men and women of all ages, and are usually associated with self-image issues. The two leading eating disorders are anorexia nervosa and bulimia nervosa. In the oral cavity, dental healthcare providers can see the effects of these two disorders. The enamel layer is actually eaten away by the acids from the stomach each time patients cause themselves to vomit. The damage is quite obvious upon examination. The dental team is obligated to offer help to patients by referring them to a mental health professional.

Oral Pathology

Oral pathology is the study of the diseases of the oral cavity, and dental assistants need to be aware of any abnormalities to alert the dentist.

Diagnosis

Often, the patient will not realize there is an issue involving their soft tissue health. Upon examination, the dental healthcare provider will inspect the entire oral cavity. This is usually when an abnormality is discovered. The dentist then determines the best route for diagnosis. A biopsy is the most common method of diagnosis. Dental assistants cannot diagnose, but they do play an important role in helping the dentist to do so.

Lesions of the Oral Cavity

Oral lesions are abnormal tissue development in the mouth. These can include ulcers, abscesses, cysts, blisters, and plaques.

Classifications of Lesions

Lesions are classified by whether they extend above or below the oral mucosa. Ulcers, erosions, abscesses, and cysts are below the mucosal surface, while blisters and plaques are above that surface.

Soft Tissue Diseases

There are five major diseases of the oral soft tissues: leukoplakia, lichen planus, candidiasis, aphthous ulcers, and cellulitis. However, these are not the only soft tissue diseases.

Conditions of the Tongue

Inflammation of the tongue is called glossitis. Other conditions of the tongue include black hairy tongue, geographic tongue, and fissured tongue.

Oral Cancer

Oral cancer is more common than one would think. Like other cancers, the oral disease can be treated by radiation and chemotherapy or surgery.

Other Pathological Disorders

Symptoms of HIV/AIDS often include oral lesions. Other pathological disorders with oral symptoms include hairy leukoplakia, Kaposi's sarcoma, herpes simplex, herpes zoster, and human papillomavirus (HPV).

General Anatomy

Every dental assistant must understand the shape and structure of the human body as well as its functions.

Body Planes

Imaginary lines known as planes divide the body into sections from top to bottom and left and right.

Structural Components of the Body

There are four structural components of the body. These are cell, tissues, organs, and body systems.

Cells

The human body contains about 75 trillion cells. Each cell has a nucleus surrounded by cytoplasm wrapped in a membrane.

Tissues

Hard and soft tissues are formed by many millions of cells that perform a similar function. There are four types of tissue in the human body: epithelial, connective, muscle, and nerve tissues.

Organs

The different types of tissues come together to form organs. These include, but are not limited to: the eyes, ears, lungs, heart, and liver.

Body Systems

A body system is formed when a group of organs work together to allow the body to function.

General Physiology

Physiology is the biological science that studies how the human body functions, in particular the ten systems of the human body. These systems are skeletal, muscular, cardiovascular, nervous, respiratory, digestive, reproductive, integumentary, urinary, and endocrine.

Skeletal System

The skeletal system consists of 206 bones. The bones are connected by cartilage and joints.

Muscular System

The human body has more than 600 individual muscles, of which there are three types: striated, smooth, and cardiac.

Cardiovascular System

The cardiovascular system has three parts: the heart, the circulatory system, and the lymphatic system.

Nervous System

The human body is composed of the central nervous system and the peripheral nervous system. These are the communication systems of the human body.

Respiratory System

The respiratory system delivers oxygen to cells and expels carbon dioxide. The system consists of the nose, throat or pharynx, epiglottis, larynx, trachea, and lungs.

Digestive System

The digestive system is the arrangement of interactive body organs that break down food into nutrients for the body to absorb. The digestive process has five stages: ingestion, digestion, movement, absorption, and elimination. The system consists of nine major structures: mouth, pharynx, esophagus, stomach, small and large intestines, liver, gallbladder, and pancreas.

Reproductive System

The system includes the sexual organs that allow men and women to reproduce.

Integumentary System

The integumentary system is the outer covering of the body. Also known as the skin system, it consists of three layers: the epidermis, dermis, and subcutaneous fat. Skin appendages in humans include hair, nails, and glands.

Urinary System

This body system filters out unneeded liquids from the food we eat as well as toxic wastes and then excretes them. The system consists of four main organs: kidneys, bladder, ureters, and urethra.

Endocrine System

The endocrine system consists of a series of glands that secrete hormones directly into the circulatory system that regulates bodily functions.

▶ Practice Questions

Answer questions 1–8 using the following figure.

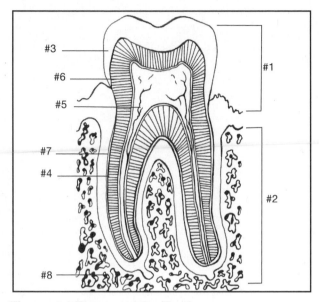

Figure 4.1 Tissues of the Tooth

1. What is #1?
    a. clinical crown
    b. anatomical crown
    c. root
    d. alveolar bone
    e. both a and b

2. What is #2?
    a. clinical crown
    b. anatomical crown
    c. root
    d. pulp
    e. apex

3. What is #3?
    a. enamel
    b. dentin
    c. cementum
    d. pulp
    e. alveolar bone

4. What is #4?
   a. pulp
   b. apex
   c. cementum
   d. root
   e. dentin

5. What is #5?
   a. enamel
   b. dentin
   c. cementum
   d. pulp
   e. alveolar bone

6. What is #6?
   a. pulp
   b. apex
   c. cementum
   d. root
   e. dentin

7. What is #7?
   a. enamel
   b. dentin
   c. cementum
   d. pulp
   e. alveolar bone

8. What is #8?
   a. pulp
   b. apex
   c. cementum
   d. root
   e. alveolar process

9. Using the Universal Numbering System, which tooth is the maxillary right first molar?
   a. 1
   b. 3
   c. 14
   d. 19
   e. 30

10. Using the ISO numbering system, how is the mandibular left second molar charted?

    a. 4,7

    b. 4,6

    c. 2,7

    d. 3,7

    e. 8,7

11. How many major salivary glands are there?

    a. six

    b. three

    c. two

    d. four

    e. five

12. The larynx is also known as the

    a. throat.

    b. esophagus.

    c. voicebox.

    d. Adam's apple.

    e. both a and b

13. What is the name of the bone on the lower arch?

    a. maxilla

    b. mandible

    c. masseter

    d. TMJ

    e. both b and c

14. How many sets of teeth does a human being have in a lifetime?

    a. one

    b. two

    c. three

    d. four

    e. none of the above

15. When is the term *mixed dentition* used?

    a. when there are only permanent teeth present in the mouth

    b. when there are only primary teeth present in the mouth

    c. when there is a combination of primary and permanent teeth in the mouth

    d. when primary teeth are falling out, but no permanent teeth are present yet

    e. when permanent teeth are erupting, but no primary teeth are being exfoliated

16. What are the names of the two types of saliva?

    a. serous, mucous

    b. serous, spit

    c. lubrication, enzymes

    d. demineralization, remineralization

    e. subcutaneous, minerals

17. How many surfaces does each tooth have?

    a. two

    b. three

    c. four

    d. five

    e. six

18. In dentistry, what are front teeth called?

    a. maxillary

    b. mandibular

    c. anterior

    d. lateral

    e. posterior

19. What is the *curve of Spee*?

    a. the curve of the occlusal plane

    b. the curve of the midsagittal plane

    c. the curve of the midline

    d. the curve of the Frankfurt plane

    e. both a and d

20. What is an *embrasure*?

    a. a triangular space above the contact just before the gumline

    b. a triangular space below the contact near the chewing surface of the tooth

    c. a space in the vestibule

    d. a space in between tooth #9 and #10

    e. a space where the teeth occlude

21. What is the other name for the nostril?

    a. anterior naris

    b. tragus

    c. philtrum

    d. ala of the nose

    e. none of the above

22. What is the longest rooted tooth in the permanent dentition?
    a. central incisor
    b. first molar
    c. first bicuspid or premolar
    d. cuspid
    e. third molar

23. What is the name of the extra (or fifth) cusp of the maxillary first molar?
    a. fossa
    b. mamelon
    c. furcation
    d. Cusp of Carabelli
    e. Cusp of Cingulum

24. How many teeth are in development when a baby is born?
    a. 15
    b. 50
    c. 44
    d. 20
    e. 32

25. What is the name of the top surface of the tongue?
    a. ventral
    b. lingual
    c. dorsal
    d. taste buds
    e. buccal

26. Which teeth found in the permanent dentition are not found in the primary dentition?
    a. cuspids, first bicuspids or premolars, second bicuspids or premolars
    b. first molars, first bicuspids or premolars, second bicuspids or premolars
    c. second and third molars
    d. first bicuspids or premolars, second bicuspids or premolars, third molars
    e. cuspids and third molars

27. What are the smallest teeth in the permanent dentition?
    a. maxillary lateral incisors
    b. mandibular central incisors
    c. mandibular lateral incisors
    d. maxillary cuspids
    e. mandibular cuspids

28. The clinical crown of the tooth is:
   a. the portion under the gum tissue.
   b. the portion we see upon examination.
   c. the roots of the tooth.
   d. the entire tooth.
   e. both b and d

29. When does drifting occur?
   a. when a tooth is missing
   b. when there is no contact for an opposing tooth
   c. when there is a fossa present
   d. when there is a large cingulum
   e. both a and b

30. Type I periodontal disease is known as
   a. refractory periodontitis.
   b. advanced periodontitis.
   c. recurring caries.
   d. gingivitis.
   e. acute periodontitis.

31. What three factors must occur at the same time for caries to develop?
   a. susceptible tooth, poor oral hygiene, bacteria
   b. susceptible tooth, bacteria, fermentable carbohydrates
   c. bacteria, fermentable carbohydrates, non-fluoridated water
   d. bacteria, saliva, fermentable carbohydrates
   e. saliva, susceptible tooth, bacteria

32. What is an incipient carious lesion?
   a. rampant caries
   b. recurrent caries
   c. first stage of caries
   d. gingivitis
   e. overt caries

33. What is broken down during the periodontal disease process?
   a. periodontium
   b. alveolar mucosa
   c. cementum
   d. dentin
   e. oral mucosa

34. What percentage of Americans are currently living with one form of periodontal disease present in their mouth?
   a. 10%
   b. 25%
   c. 40%
   d. 50%
   e. 75%

35. What eating disorder is characterized by self-starvation?
   a. fasting
   b. bulimia
   c. anorexia nervosa
   d. dieting
   e. both b and c

36. What is/are often referred to as "the forgotten nutrient"?
   a. water
   b. minerals
   c. vitamins
   d. proteins
   e. fats

37. Which pathologic term describes an inflammation of the tongue?
   a. candidiasis
   b. cellulitis
   c. leukoplakia
   d. glossitis
   e. geographic tongue

38. Patients who have undergone radiation or chemotherapy treatments often experience "dry mouth," or a reduction in saliva flow. What is the dental term for this?
   a. sarcoma
   b. xerostomia
   c. hyperplasia
   d. anadontia
   e. parathesia

39. How many bones are in the human body?
   a. 206
   b. 225
   c. 200
   d. 215
   e. 230

40. What is the name of the body system that includes the skin?

    a. nervous system

    b. muscular system

    c. skeletal system

    d. integumentary system

    e. pulmonary system

Answer questions 41–43 using the following figure.

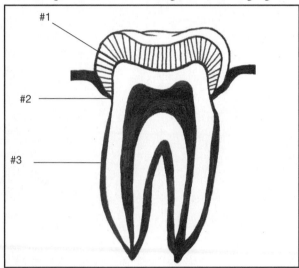

Figure 4.2 Tissue Junctions of the Tooth

41. What is #1?

    a. cementoenamel junction

    b. dentinocemental junction

    c. dentinopulpal junction

    d. dentinoenamel junction

    e. none of the above

42. What is #2?

    a. cementoenamel junction

    b. dentinocemental junction

    c. dentinopulpal junction

    d. dentinoenamel junction

    e. none of the above

43. What is #3?

    a. cementoenamel junction

    b. dentinocemental junction

    c. dentinopulpal junction

    d. dentinoenamel junction

    e. none of the above

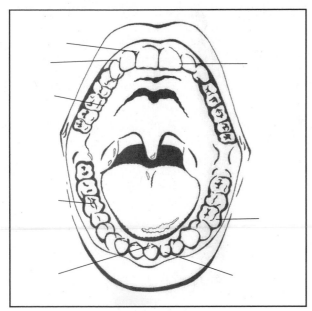

Figure 4.3 Surfaces of the Teeth

44. Identify the eight surfaces of the teeth in Figure 4.3 above.

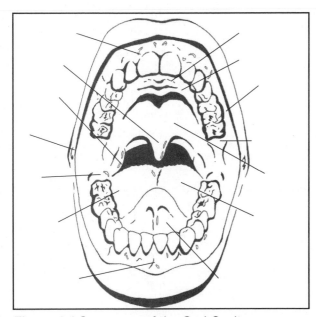

Figure 4.4 Structures of the Oral Cavity

45. Identify the 14 structures of the oral cavity in Figure 4.4 above.

▶ Practice Answers and Explanations

1. b. Anatomical crown. The anatomical crown is supragingival, above the gingiva and partially subgingival, below the gingiva. The clinical crown is the portion of the anatomical crown that is supragingival, above the gingiva and can be seen by a clinical examination.

2. c. Root. The root is what anchors the tooth into the alveolar bone.

3. a. Enamel. The enamel is the hardest tissue of the tooth and makes up the outermost layer of the crown.

4. c. Cementum. The cementum is the lining around the dentin in the root portion of the tooth. The cementum is attached to the periodontal ligament.

5. d. Pulp. The pulp is the innermost tissue of the tooth. It contains blood vessels and nerves and is sometimes referred to as the "heart" of the tooth.

6. e. Dentin. The dentin is the tissue underneath the enamel in the coronal portion of the tooth and under the cementium in the root of the tooth.

7. b. Dentin. The dentin is the tissue of which the root is mostly made. It is the largest layer of the tooth.

8. e. Alveolar process. The root of the tooth is embedded into the alveolar process or alveolar bone.

9. b. #3. The Universal Numbering System consists of #1–16 in the maxillary arch and #17–32 in the mandibular arch. The first molar in the maxillary right quadrant is #3.

10. d. The ISO Numbering System/International Standards Organization assigns a number to each quadrant in the permanent dentition and to each quadrant in the primary dentition. This quadrant number represents the first number. The second number relates to the tooth in the quadrant counting from the midline to the posterior of the mouth. There are eight teeth in each permanent dentition quadrant and five teeth in each primary dentition quadrant. Therefore, the permanent second molar is #7.

11. b. There are three major salivary glands in the human body. They are the parotid, the sublingual, and the submandibular glands.

12. c. The larynx is the scientific term for the voicebox. Without the larynx, humans could not speak.

13. b. The mandible is the bone of the lower arch. It is the only bone in the human skull that is movable.

14. b. There are two sets of teeth we call dentitions: the primary dentition and the permanent dentition.

15. c. A mixed dentition occurs in patients aged six to 12. During this age period, primary teeth are being exfoliated and permanent teeth are erupting, and both are present in the mouth at the same time.

16. a. There are two types of saliva in the human mouth: serous and mucous. Serous is considered normal saliva, and mucous, sometimes referred to as ropey saliva, is very thick.

17. d. There are five surfaces on every tooth. These surfaces are mesial, distal, occlusal/incisal, lingual, and buccal/facial.

18. c. The anterior portion of the mouth is located toward the face and consists of the central incisors, the lateral incisors, and the cuspids. The posterior portion of the mouth is located behind the anterior. It consists of the first and second bicuspids/premolars, and the first, second, and third molars.

19. a. The curve of Spee is also known as the curve of the occlusal plane. It forms a slight smile curve.

20. a. The triangular space above the contact just before the gumline is the embrasure.

21. a. The anterior naris is the scientific name for the nostril.

22. d. The cuspid is the longest rooted tooth in the permanent dentition and is located at the corner of the arch.

23. d. The Cusp of Carabelli is the name of the fifth cusp on the permanent maxillary first molar. It is located on the lingual surface.

24. c. There are 44 teeth developing when a baby is born.

25. c. The top of the tongue is referred to as the dorsal. The underneath side of the tongue is referred to as the ventral.

26. d. First bicuspids/premolars, second bicuspids/premolars, and third molars are not present in the primary dentition. The primary dentition consists of only five teeth in each quadrant: the central incisor, the lateral incisor, the cuspid, the first molar, and the second molar.

27. b. The smallest teeth in the permanent dentition are the mandibular central incisors. They are also the first permanent teeth to erupt into the mouth.

28. b. The clinical crown is the portion of the anatomical crown that is visible upon examination, above the gumline.

29. e. Drifting occurs when a tooth is missing and there is no contact for an opposing tooth. The two teeth on either side of the missing tooth drift toward the space, and the opposing tooth to the missing tooth supraerupts toward the space.

30. d. Periodontal disease is classified into five types. Type I is gingivitis. Types II through V are acute periodontitis, moderate periodontitis, advanced periodontitis, and refractory periodontitis.

31. b. In order for caries to develop, there needs to be a susceptible tooth, some bacteria, and fermentable carbohydrates.

32. c. The first stage of caries is incipient caries. This is when the caries begin to demineralize the enamel of the tooth.

33. a. Periodontal disease is the process of breaking down the periodontium. The periodontium consists of the gingiva, the epithelial attachment, the sulcus, the periodontal ligament, the cementum, and the alveolar bone. With periodontal disease, the periodontium is broken down, and there is a loss of tissue and destruction of the alveolar bone.

34. e. In America, 75% of the population have one form of periodontal disease.

35. c. Anorexia nervosa is an eating disorder that is characterized by self-starvation. Periodontal tissues are reduced, and the teeth are not as strong since the calcium intake is decreased by not eating.

36. a. Water is often referred to as the forgotten nutrient. The human body is approximately 80% water, which is needed to build tissues, regulate the temperature of the body, and lubricate the joints and mucous membranes. Saliva is made up of water, calcium, and phosphate, which can promote reminerialization of incipient caries.

37. d. Glossitis is the scientific term used to describe inflammation of the tongue.

38. b. When a patient undergoes radiation or chemotherapies and the salivary glands are affected, saliva can no longer be produced. The mouth becomes severely dry, and there is less blood supply sent to the tissues. This condition will aid in oral infection, delay any healing, and make it difficult to wear any dentures.

39. a. The human body consists of 206 bones.

40. d. The integumentary system includes the skin.

41. d. The dentinoenamel junction is where the enamel in the crown meets the underlying layer of dentin.

42. a. The cementoenamel junction is where the enamel that surrounds the crown meets the cementum that surrounds the root at the neck of the tooth.

43. b. The dentinocemental junction is where the dentin meets the layer of cementum on the root.

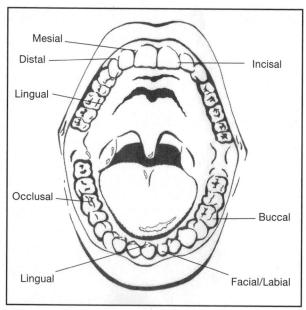

Figure 4.3 Surfaces of the Teeth

44. The eight surfaces of the teeth are shown in Figure 4.3 above.

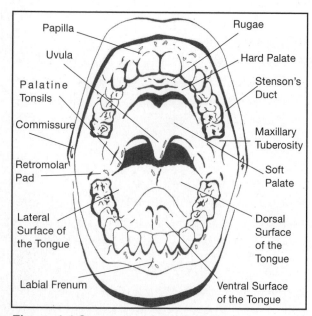

Figure 4.4 Structures of the Oral Cavity

45. The 14 structures of the oral cavity are shown in Figure 4.4 above.

5 ▶ Infection Control

CHAPTER OVERVIEW

Infection control is a vital part of dental assisting. Members of the dental healthcare team are exposed to many different diseases that may be transmitted throughout the dental office and beyond. It is important for all team members to realize their role in delivering patient care and chances of occupational exposure.

EACH DENTAL PROFESSIONAL has a responsibility to be aware of current infection control techniques and trends. Infection control is an area of dentistry that is constantly altering and evolving. Rules and regulations change yearly, and some states are more stringent than others. Infection control updates should be a regular part of a dental professional's continuing education. In fact, this is an Occupational Safety and Health Administration (OHSA) requirement.

KEY TERMS

antiseptic	blood-borne disease	chemical vapor sterilization
asepsis	blood-borne pathogens	cidal agents
autoclave	Centers for Disease Control	critical instruments
bioburden	and Prevention (CDC)	cross-contamination
biologic indicators	chain of infection	cross-infection

KEY TERMS (continued)

direct contact	percutaneous	spores
disinfectant	permucosal	standard precautions
disinfection	personal protection	static agents
disposables	equipment (PPE)	sterilization
dry heat sterilizer	process indicators	surface wipes
glutaraldehyde	route of entry	ultrasonic cleaner
iodophor	sanitization	universal precautions
Occupational Safety and	semi-critical instruments	virulence
Health Administration (OSHA)	sepsis	
other potentially infectious	sharps	
materials (OPIM)	sodium hypochlorite	

▶ Concepts and Skills

Infection control is broken down into four main areas:

- Disease Transmission
- Occupational Safety and Health Administration (OSHA)/Centers for Disease Control and Prevention (CDC)
- Disinfection
- Sterilization

In this chapter, we will present questions relating to each of these four areas of infection control. The following outline chronicles current information regarding each area of infection control.

Disease Transmission

Germs are the main causes of disease. Germs are also termed microorganisms and/or pathogens. When these germs multiply, they become diseases. Diseases can be transmitted only in a distinct pathway. This pathway is known as the chain of infection.

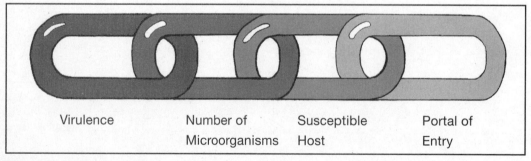

| Virulence | Number of Microorganisms | Susceptible Host | Portal of Entry |

Figure 5.1 Chain of Infection

Chain of Infection

The chain of infection contains four links: virulence, number of microorganisms, susceptible host, and portal of entry. All of these must be present for the individual to become infected with a disease. If one of these is missing, the disease cannot be transmitted.

Virulence

The virulence of an organism is its strength or ability to cause disease. The more virulent the organism, the more serious the disease. A virulent disease is also more difficult for the body to fight off and could be resistant to certain medications.

Number of Microorganisms

The number of microorganisms describes the amount of pathogens present. A large number of pathogens will overwhelm the body's immune system and diminish the body's ability to fight off the pathogens.

Susceptible Host

A susceptible host is someone who has a compromised immune system. This means that this person has a disease already, is currently undergoing treatment for a condition, has not been getting enough rest, and is run down or under stress. These things can suppress a person's immune system and cause her or him to be more susceptible to an illness or disease.

Portal of Entry

A portal of entry is the way in which an infection enters the body. An infection can enter the body through various modes.

Modes of Disease Transmission

An infectious disease is one that is contagious and can be transmitted from host to host via the chain of infection. Diseases are transmitted in one of the following five modes of transmission: direct; indirect; airborne; aerosol, spray, or spatter; or blood-borne transmission.

Direct Transmission

This route of transmission occurs when there is direct contact with infected blood, saliva, or other potentially infectious materials (OPIM). Personal protective equipment (PPE) is essential in preventing transmission.

Indirect Transmission

This route of transmission occurs when the dental healthcare professional comes in contact with a contaminated surface without the protection of PPE.

Airborne Transmission

This route of transmission occurs through methods of inhalation. For example, a patient sneezes, and another inhales some spores that may be present in the sneeze. Many serious diseases are spread via the air.

Aerosol, Spray, or Spatter

This route of transmission is a form of airborne transmission. Aerosol is generated by the use of the high-speed hand piece in the mouth. An aerosol mist is emitted from the oral cavity, which is contaminated with the patient's bacteria. Spray and spatter follow the same form, but are larger in size than an aerosol mist. These occur in the patient's mouth and splash out of the oral cavity, contaminating the surrounding area.

Blood-Borne Transmission

This route of transmission occurs only from blood-to-blood contact with an infected individual. Many diseases, such as HIV/AIDS and Hepatitis C, are transmitted this way. The most common method of transmission is through a needle-stick injury. Therefore, maintaining safe practices and procedures while paying attention to details helps prevent this type of transmission.

Disease Transmission in the Dental Office

All members of the dental healthcare team should be concerned about disease transmission in the dental office. Dental professionals call this cross-contamination. Cross-contamination refers to germs within or from the dental setting being transmitted to other areas of the dental office or carried out of the dental setting. This can occur in a number of ways, including patient to patient, healthcare worker to patient, patient to healthcare worker, and healthcare worker to community.

Patient to Patient

Cross-contamination can occur from patient to patient by not changing PPE between patients, by not properly disinfecting the treatment room, and by not properly sterilizing the dental instruments. The germs and bacteria are then introduced into a new host, causing a "sharing" or "crossing" of infection. It is imperative that dental assistants understand the importance of preventing cross-contamination.

Healthcare Worker to Patient

The patient and dental healthcare worker sit in very close proximity to one another. Therefore, it is possible for the dental healthcare worker to transmit microorganisms to the patient unintentionally. It is important to don fresh PPE for each patient. This includes a new pair of disposable gloves; a new disposable mask; and clean, disinfected safety glasses. Hand washing is always an important aspect of infection control.

Patient to Healthcare Worker

The patient can also transmit microorganisms to the dental healthcare team. The same precautions as above should be followed by the dental healthcare team to prevent the transmission of microorganisms.

Healthcare Worker to Community

The dental healthcare worker may unintentionally transmit contaminants from the dental setting into the community. Care should be taken by the dental healthcare worker to avoid this by changing into street clothes prior to leaving the office, and laundering contaminated clothes properly.

Occupational Safety and Health Administration (OSHA)/Centers for Disease Control and Prevention (CDC)

Occupational Safety and Health Administration (OSHA) and the Centers for Disease Control and Prevention (CDC) are federal agencies that are primarily responsible for infection control measures utilized in the United States. OSHA is a regulatory agency responsible for ensuring the safety and health of employees in the United States. OSHA has developed a set of standards to provide a safe workplace in the dental office. OSHA's main concern is the welfare of the employee, not the patient. The agency also conducts training and educational programs regarding OSHA implementation and regulations.

The CDC is an advisory agency tasked with the research and study of diseases of consequence to the American population. They make recommendations, or suggestions, regarding infection control after conducting intensive research on the topic. The CDC's main concern is the health and protection of the overall population through preventive measures and proper treatment.

Blood-Borne Pathogens Standard

OSHA developed the Blood-Borne Pathogens (BBP) Standard, which has become the most important law governing infection control in dentistry today. The BBP Standard discusses how the dental office deals with, and its plan for, exposure to blood-borne pathogens. There are several parts to this standard that are discussed in detail in OSHA's BBP Standard.

Universal Precautions

Universal precautions is a protocol followed by each dental office that mandates that all patients be treated as if they have a deadly disease, regardless of their health history.

Standard Precautions

Standard precautions is an expansion of universal precautions. Standard precautions outlines how the dental office will handle its infection control protocol for each patient. This means that the infection control protocol for each patient will be the same, no matter what.

Categories of Employees

OSHA has designed categories for each employee in the dental office based on his or her exposure risk to blood, saliva, or bodily fluids. Category I is the highest risk category, involving direct contact with blood, saliva, and other potentially infectious materials (OPIM). These dental healthcare members include the dentist, chairside dental assistants, and the hygienist.

Post-Exposure Protocol

Each dental office is required by OSHA to develop a written protocol outlining steps or measures to be taken after an exposure incident occurs. An example of an exposure incident is being stuck with a contaminated needle, being punctured by an instrument, or being cut with a bur.

Hepatitis B Immunization

OSHA requires that every dentist offer and pay for the Hepatitis B vaccination to all categories of employees who want to be immunized. The Hepatitis B vaccine is given in three doses over a specified period of time.

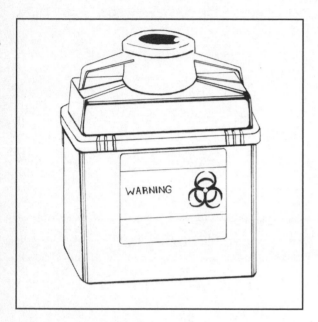

Figure 5.2 Sharps Disposal Container

Management of Sharps Waste

Sharps, such as needles, scalpels, broken glass from an anesthetic carpule, old burs, broken instruments, etc., must be disposed of in a biohazard, non-permeable, red plastic container. Each operatory or treatment room must have its own sharps container. The office contacts a hazardous material company to dispose of the sharps waste properly, following the laws of the state.

Personal Protective Equipment (PPE)

Personal protective equipment (PPE) is required by OSHA as a means of protection for the dental healthcare worker. The dentist must supply the proper PPE for the employee. PPE consists of scrubs (overcoat, jacket, and disposable protective gown), leather shoes, lab coat, mask, safety glasses/face shield, and gloves. PPE should be donned/performed in the following manner: lab coat, mask, safety glasses/face shield, wash hands, and gloves. PPE should be removed/performed in the following manner: gloves, wash hands, safety glasses, mask, lab coat, and second hand washing.

Classifications of Waste

There are many types of waste in a dental office. OSHA classifies waste as general waste, contaminated waste, hazardous waste, infectious waste, and biohazardous waste. Each must be disposed of properly.

Waste Management for the Dental Office
OSHA requires that all dental offices have a waste management plan. This is designed to protect the environment, follow state and federal laws, and ensure the safety of those who may come in contact with the materials in the garbage. Accurate disposal records must be kept.

Disinfection

Disinfection is the process of killing some microorganisms, but not all. Some bacteria will form into spore colonies to protect themselves from being destroyed. Disinfection does not kill spores.

Disinfection in the Dental Office

In the dental office, most hard surface areas are disinfected with disinfectant wipes or spray. Any area that may have been contaminated during a procedure will be disinfected. Some examples of areas that would need to be disinfected following treatment include the mobile cart, lines, counter tops, dental chair, light, and any other contaminated surfaces.

Use of Surface Barriers

Surface barriers are materials used to cover equipment and surfaces to prevent cross-contamination. Any surface that may be contaminated during treatment should be covered with a disposable plastic barrier. Some examples of surface barriers include light handle covers, syringe sleeves, and chair covers.

Single-Use Disposable Items

Today, many dental supplies used for patient treatment are single-use disposable items. Some examples include cotton rolls, gloves, prophy angles, 2 x 2 gauze, HVE tips, and so on.

Types of Gloves for Protection

There are four main types of gloves that a dental assistant may use for protection. These are examination gloves, utility gloves, overgloves, and sterile gloves.

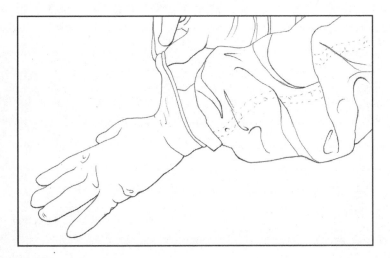

Figure 5.3 Non-sterile Examination Gloves

Examination Gloves

Examination gloves are latex, vinyl, or nitrile materials that are most often worn by members of the dental team. Examination or procedure gloves are inexpensive and disposable. They come in a variety of sizes and colors, and can be scented or flavored.

Utility Gloves

Utility gloves are similar to old-fashioned dishwashing gloves. They are used to break down a contaminated treatment room and to handle contaminated instruments. They would never be used when treating a patient. These gloves can be disinfected and/or sterilized in the autoclave.

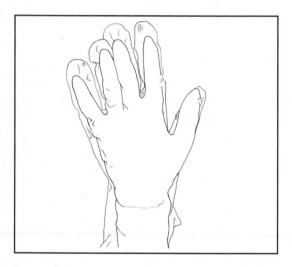

Figure 5.4 Overgloves Worn Over Latex Examination Gloves

Overgloves

Overgloves are used when an assistant must leave the treatment room, open a drawer during the procedure to retrieve a supply the dentist needs, or to make notes. These gloves are similar to food-handling gloves.

Sterile Gloves

Sterile gloves are utilized during surgical procedures involving the bone or periodontium. These gloves are supplied in a protective pouch. When the protective pouch is opened, the gloves can clearly be seen labeled for the right or left hand.

Disinfectants

Disinfectants are used to kill some of the microorganisms prior to sterilization. Dental assistants use disinfectants to wipe down treatment rooms or other contaminated surfaces following a procedure. The two most popular disinfectants utilized in the dental office are iodophors and gluteraldehydes.

Iodophors

Iodophors are used in the dental treatment rooms to disinfect the hard surface areas and equipment, but they have a tendency to stain. They are supplied in either a spray or a wipe.

Gluteraldehydes

Gluteraldehydes are interesting due to their ability to be both a sterilant and a disinfectant. In the dental office, gluteraldehydes are used as the holding bath or "cold sterile." Some instruments cannot withstand heat sterilization and must be sterilized in the cold sterile. For this to occur, the instrument must be immersed in the solution for ten hours. Anything less than that time, and the instrument is considered to be disinfected, but not sterilized.

Procedural Steps in Disinfection

All contaminated items are removed from the treatment room and properly disposed of or taken to the sterilization area in a closed, covered container. Begin disinfection using the desired method selected by the dental office. The wipes method of disinfection is most popular. Wipe the entire operatory thoroughly while wearing proper PPE. After the room is disinfected, wash hands, and place new barriers.

Sterilization

Sterilization is the process that completely destroys microorganisms (including bacteria and spores) on instruments, equipment, and surfaces.

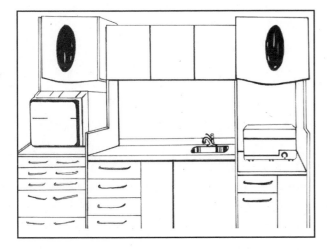

Figure 5.5 Sterilization Center

Instrument Classification

Dental instruments are grouped into three categories, according to their function: critical, semi-critical, and non-critical.

Critical Instruments

Critical instruments are those that contact or penetrate soft tissue or bone. These include scalpels, burs, scalers, and other dental tools that penetrate bone and tissue.

Semi-critical Instruments

Semi-critical instruments are instruments that come in contact with the oral cavity but do not penetrate soft tissue or bone. These include amalgam carriers, condensers, and other items that touch tissue and are contaminated by blood and saliva.

Non-critical Instruments

Non-critical instruments are those that pose the least risk of spreading infection because they do not come in contact with soft tissue, membranes, or broken skin. These include items such as the X-ray unit position indicator device or X-ray film holder (Snap-A-Ray).

Instrument Processing

Instrument processing involves seven steps: transport, cleaning, packaging, sterilization, storage, delivery, and quality assurance of all dental instruments. Personal protective equipment must be worn at all times during the sterilization process. All instruments are packaged after cleaning and before sterilization to group them in sets and to protect them from contamination after sterilization.

Methods of Sterilization

Four of the leading methods of sterilization are autoclave, chemiclave, flash sterilization, and cold sterilization.

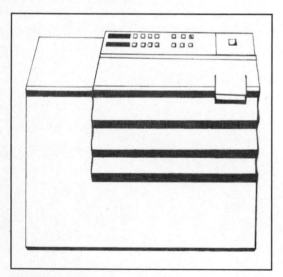

Figure 5.6 Steam Autoclave

Autoclave

An autoclave sterilizes instruments by converting water to steam and pressurizing it. This is known as steam under pressure. High heat and pressure kills any remaining microorganisms or spores. The average cycle of an autoclave is 30 minutes: 20 minutes at 250° F (121° C) at 15–20 pounds per square inch (psi) for sterilizing, and ten minutes venting time for drying.

Chemiclave

The chemiclave converts chemical vapor into steam and pressurizes it. The odor emitted is unpleasant, and the office should be equipped with a special vent for use with this type of sterilizer. The average cycle of a chemiclave is 30 minutes: 20 minutes at 270° F (132° C) at 20 psi for sterilizing, and ten minutes for drying.

Flash Sterilization

Flash sterilization is utilized in an office when a particular instrument is needed right away. The average cycle of a flash sterilizer is three minutes at 270° F (132° C) at 15 psi for unwrapped instruments. The instrument needs to be used right away since it is unwrapped.

Forms of Sterilization Monitoring

Whatever type of sterilizing is used, it must be monitored to ensure that the dental instruments are properly sterilized. There are three forms of monitoring: physical, chemical, and biological.

Physical Monitoring

Physical monitoring of the sterilization process involves checking the readings on the indicators on the sterilizer, along with checking if the color-changing pouch or tape has in fact changed color to denote that a certain temperature level was reached.

Chemical Monitoring

Chemical monitoring of sterilization uses heat-sensitive chemicals that change color under certain conditions. Process indicators are placed outside the instrument packs, while process integrators are placed inside.

Biological Monitoring

Biological monitoring involves spore testing to establish whether the sterilization process was successful. Weekly testing is mandated by OSHA for every sterilization device utilized in the office. The spores utilized are bacillus stearothermophilus for steam and chemical vapor sterilizers, and bacillus subtilis for dry heat and ethylene oxide sterilizers.

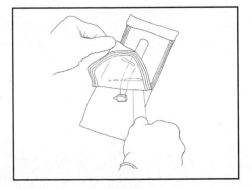

Figure 5.7 Hand-Piece Sterilization

Hand-Piece Sterilization

Dental hand pieces must be carefully sterilized to avoid cross-contamination.

Pre-cleaning Techniques

Before the actual sterilization begins, wipe down the hand piece with disinfectant wipes or alcohol-soaked gauze 2 x 2s to remove any bioburden. It is recommended that the hand piece be flushed for 20–30 seconds prior to disconnecting to remove any contaminated water. Hand pieces should never be immersed in any type of liquid. Follow the manufacturer's directions regarding lubrication of the dental hand piece.

Sterilization Techniques

There are only two ways to properly sterilize hand pieces: steam or chemical vapor sterilizers. As with other dental instruments, hand pieces should be packaged before being sterilized.

▶ Practice Questions

1. The condition of being free of pathogenic microorganisms is known as

    a. asepsis.

    b. sepsis.

    c. sterile.

    d. both b and c

    e. none of the above

2. Which of the following disinfectants is commonly known as "household bleach"?

    a. chlorine

    b. sodium hypochlorite

    c. iodophors

    d. gluteraldehyde

    e. both b and d

3. What is the length of one autoclave cycle?

    a. 15 minutes

    b. 1 hour

    c. 30 minutes

    d. 45 minutes

    e. none of the above

4. How does the autoclave sterilize instruments?

    a. steam under pressure

    b. vapors under pressure

    c. chemicals under pressure

    d. dry heat

    e. both a and d

5. What does a chemiclave sterilizer run on?

    a. tap water

    b. vapo-sterile solution

    c. distilled water

    d. general purpose cleaner

    e. bottled water

6. Which of the following is an example of a semi-critical instrument?
   a. amalgam condenser
   b. bur
   c. bone chisel
   d. Snap-A-Ray X-ray holder
   e. scalpel

7. Which of the following is an example of a critical instrument?
   a. scalpel
   b. gingival margin trimmer
   c. bur
   d. both a and c
   e. all of the above

8. Which of the following is an example of a non-critical instrument?
   a. mouth mirror
   b. explorer
   c. Snap-A-Ray X-ray holder
   d. perio probe
   e. both a and c

9. How should alginate impressions be disinfected?
   a. autoclaving
   b. soaking in disinfectant
   c. spraying with disinfectant and wrapping in a moist paper towel
   d. immersing in the ultrasonic cleaner
   e. both b and c

10. What is bioburden?
   a. blood, saliva, and/or OPIM
   b. debris not visible to the human eye
   c. bacteria found in the sterilization room
   d. material that cannot be removed from surfaces or instruments
   e. both a and d

11. What does the ultrasonic cleaner do?

    a. loosens debris from instruments

    b. adheres debris to the instruments

    c. safely and more effectively cleans than hand-scrubbing instruments

    d. not used in the dental office

    e. both a and c

12. Gluteraldehydes are used for

    a. cold sterilization.

    b. immersion disinfection purposes.

    c. penetration of blood, saliva, and OPIM.

    d. surface disinfection in dental treatment rooms.

    e. a, b, and c

13. How often should biological monitoring of sterilization equipment be done?

    a. daily

    b. weekly

    c. monthly

    d. yearly

    e. none of the above

14. Which infection poses the greatest risk of patient-to-dental professional transfer?

    a. HIV

    b. Hepatitis B

    c. measles

    d. common cold

    e. flu

15. What is the term for treating every patient as if he or she were potentially infectious?

    a. standard precautions

    b. universal precautions

    c. no precautions

    d. awareness

    e. both a and b

16. What is the term for following a specific routine for sterilization and disinfection?

    a. standard precautions

    b. universal precautions

    c. pathogenic precautions

    d. both a and c

    e. none of the above

17. Which of the following is an example of PPE?
   a. saliva ejector
   b. rubber dam
   c. mask
   d. gloves
   e. both c and d

18. Which of the following agencies issues regulations in regards to employee safety?
   a. Environmental Protection Agency (EPA)
   b. Centers for Disease Control and Prevention (CDC)
   c. Occupational Safety and Health Administration (OSHA)
   d. National Institute of Occupational Safety and Health (NIOSH)
   e. both c and d

19. What is the most critical PPE?
   a. gloves
   b. lab coat
   c. mask
   d. eyewear/face shield
   e. leather shoes

20. What is the proper order for donning/performing PPE?
   a. lab coat, wash hands, gloves, eyewear, mask
   b. lab coat, mask, eyewear, wash hands, gloves
   c. lab coat, eyewear, mask, wash hands, gloves
   d. wash hands, lab coat, mask, eyewear, gloves
   e. mask, lab coat, eyewear, wash hands, gloves

21. Which of the following is an example of a percutaneous injury?
   a. needle stick
   b. accidentally being cut with an instrument
   c. aerosol spatter during a procedure
   d. splashed with a substance in the eyes or mouth
   e. both a and b

22. A chairside dental assistant falls under which category of occupational exposure?
   a. Category I
   b. Category II
   c. Category III
   d. Category IV
   e. none of the above

23. Utility gloves are utilized in a dental office for which of the following tasks?
    a. setting up the operatory
    b. disposing of sharps
    c. handling instruments while preparing for sterilization
    d. disinfecting the operatory following patient care
    e. both c and d

24. What is the procedure for preparing the high-speed hand piece for sterilization?
    a. placed into the ultrasonic cleaner prior to bagging
    b. disassembled and lubricated
    c. flushed, wiped down with alcohol or disinfectant, and bagged
    d. soaked in disinfectant
    e. both a and c

25. PPE worn during each procedure is determined by the dentist.
    a. True
    b. False

26. Overloading the sterilizer can cause sterilization failure.
    a. True
    b. False

27. The ultrasonic cleaner works by using light waves.
    a. True
    b. False

28. Cold sterilization is achieved in six hours.
    a. True
    b. False

29. High-level disinfection kills all bacterial spores.
    a. True
    b. False

30. It is not mandatory for a dentist/employer to offer the Hepatitis B Vaccine (HBV) to a new employee.
    a. True
    b. False

▶ Practice Answers and Explanations

1. a. The definition of asepsis is being free of pathogenic microorganisms.

2. b. Sodium hypochlorite is the main ingredient in common household bleach.

3. c. The typical length of time for processing instruments using the autoclave is 30 minutes.

4. a. The chamber of an autoclave fills with water that is converted into steam when the chamber pressurizes.

5. b. A chemiclave differs from an autoclave in that water is not used. Instead, a chemical solution is pressurized, thereby sterilizing the instruments.

6. a. A semicritical instrument is one that comes in contact with soft tissue or bone but does not penetrate. An amalgam condenser comes in contact with the tooth but does not penetrate.

7. d. A critical instrument is an instrument that penetrates soft tissue or bone. Both a scalpel and a bur can penetrate soft tissue or bone. A gingival margin trimmer is used as a hand-cutting instrument on enamel or dentin and therefore does not penetrate soft tissue or bone.

8. c. A noncritical instrument is one that comes in contact with only intact skin. A Snap-A-Ray is an X-ray film-holding device that does not penetrate soft tissue or bone.

9. c. Alginate impressions are very sensitive. They need to be handled properly. Spraying with a disinfectant and then wrapping in a moist paper towel is the proper disinfecting technique.

10. a. Bioburden is made up of the patient's blood, saliva, and other potentially infectious materials (OPIM).

11. e. The ultrasonic cleaner is used to pre-clean instruments. It loosens debris from the instruments using sound waves and is safer and more effective than scrubbing the instruments by hand.

12. e. Gluteraldehydes are very versatile in the dental office. They can be used for immersion disinfection and sterilization. They are strong enough to penetrate blood, saliva, and OPIM if exposed the proper length of time.

13. b. Biological monitoring is also known as spore testing. These tests are performed weekly to ensure proper sterilization function. A harmless spore strip is inserted into the sterilizer during a cycle, and then mailed to a laboratory where it is examined under a microscope. The technician is checking for sterilization.

14. b. Of all the blood-borne diseases, Hepatitis B is the most likely to be transmitted. It is transmitted through the air and is easily transmitted from patient to healthcare worker and from patient to patient.

15. b. Universal precautions is the act of treating all patients as if they are potentially infectious. This is an OSHA regulation.

16. a. Standard precautions is the act of developing a routine of dealing with disinfection and sterilization procedures within the dental office. A standard of care is developed where the dental assistant follows the same routine for each patient regarding the set-up and break down of the operatories, disinfection, and sterilization procedures.

17. e. PPE consists of lab coat, mask, eyewear, and gloves.

18. c. OSHA's primary concern is the safety of the employee. The agency issues regulations to protect the employee from contracting an illness.

19. a. Gloves are the most critical PPE since the hands enter the patient's mouth and are exposed to blood, saliva, and OPIM. The mask, eyewear, and lab coat are important but not as critical as the gloves.

20. b. The proper order of donning/performing PPE is lab coat, mask, eyewear, wash hands, and gloves. The gloves are donned last since they are the PPE that will be entering the patient's mouth.

21. e. "Percutaneous" means through the skin. A needle or a sharp instrument can injure the healthcare worker by cutting the skin. Splash and spatter is considered to be a permucosal injury since it contacts the mucous membranes. PPE and observing care help prevent these injuries.

22. a. Occupational exposures are categorized depending on the location in the office where the professional works. Category I includes all healthcare workers who come into direct contact with blood, saliva, or OPIM. Professionals included in this category are the dentist, the chairside dental assistant, and the dental hygienist.

23. e. Utility gloves are recommended by OSHA, to be utilized when disinfecting dental operatory and when preparing contaminated instruments for sterilization. The hands are better protected during a critical exposure time.

24. c. Prior to sterilization, the high-speed hand piece should follow a pre-cleaning protocol. The hand piece should be run or flushed by stepping on the rheostat for 20 seconds prior to disconnecting it from the dental unit. This is done to eliminate any contaminated water from remaining in the hand piece. Next, the hand piece is brought into the sterilization area, and the outside of it is wiped down with either a disinfectant wipe or a 2 x 2 gauze soaked in alcohol. This is done to remove any bioburden since it is never recommended to immerse a hand piece in liquid of any kind. Finally, it is bagged and sterilized.

25. **False.** OSHA , not the dentist, determines the PPE worn by all dental professionals.

26. **True.** Manufacturers often recommend not overloading the sterilizer. It is believed that the instruments are not sterilized properly.

27. **False.** The ultrasonic cleaner removes bioburden via sound waves. The sound waves gently shake the instruments to remove the debris.

28. **False.** Cold sterilization is the use of gluteraldehyde in a holding container. In order for sterilization to be achieved, the instruments must be exposed to the solution for ten hours. Cold sterilization is used for instruments that cannot withstand heat or chemical sterilization.

29. **False.** Disinfection kills some but not all spores. Sterilization kills all spores.

30. **False.** According to OSHA regulations, a new employee must be offered the HBV series within ten days of employment. Failure to do so is a violation of OSHA regulations and puts the employee at risk.

CHAPTER

6 ▶ Chairside Assisting

CHAPTER OVERVIEW

The chairside dental assistant must be familiar with every aspect of the dental operation. Dental offices can be organized in various ways, but there are certain essential requirements such as the reception and front desk area and the treatment rooms. This is also true of the dental equipment throughout the dental office. For example, dental assistants are responsible for the correct positioning of the dental chair and light. Assistants must work closely with dentists to deliver the highest quality dental care.

THE DENTAL OFFICE has many exciting areas in which to be a team member. Chairside assisting is an example of one such area. Assistants are utilized to their fullest capabilities. They must possess extensive knowledge in order to truly be effective at the chair. Dentists appreciate assistants who can anticipate their needs as operators and help them treat their patients. Efficient chairside assistants will increase the overall production of dental practices by aiding dentists in completing their procedures more quickly and more effectively.

KEY TERMS

alveolitis	four-handed dentistry	nitrous oxide
anesthetic	HVE (high-volume evacuator)	occlusion
biohazard	lesion	orthodontics
bioburden	malocclusion	operating zones
cavity	mandibular	overbite
crossbite	maxillary	pedodontics
endodontics	mobility	periodontal disease

KEY TERMS (continued)

periodontics	subgingival	traumatic intrusion
prosthodontics	sublingual	ultrasonic scaler
reversible pulpitis	subsupine	vasoconstrictor
saliva ejector	supine	
six-handed dentistry	supragingival	

▶ Concepts and Skills

Knowledge of the following concepts and skills are necessary to become a licensed, highly skilled, and efficient chairside dental assistant. Chairside assisting is divided into ten main topics:

- Layout of a Dental Office
- Equipment in the Operatory (Treatment Room)
- Chair Positions
- Light Positions
- Clock Concept of Operating Zones
- Delivery of Dental Care
- Local Anesthetics and Analgesics
- Dental Support Aides
- Other Duties of Dental Assistants
- Dental Specialties

Layout of a Dental Office

A dental office can be organized in many ways. Some dentists prefer to work out of many operatories, while others will choose to work out of two treatment rooms. All offices will have the areas listed below. An informed assistant should be cross-trained to assist the dentist in the best way possible.

Reception Area

Patients enter this area first when arriving at the dental office. First impressions are important. This area can be decorated in any way the dentist chooses, but it should be welcoming and calming. It is important to straighten up the reception area continually throughout the day.

Front Desk

The front desk handles the business operations of the dental office. The assistant at the front desk is responsible for making appointments, answering the phone, insurance billing, patient invoicing, treatment-plan presentation (in some offices), and handling all financial matters.

Operatory or Treatment Rooms

This is where all dental services are performed. The dentist will typically work out of several rooms, while the hygienist works out of one assigned treatment room.

Laboratory

This area has many uses. Dental appliances can be fabricated here or sent to an outside lab if the dentist chooses. Lab cases can be stored here, and, if needed, this area can serve as overflow storage for back stock. There is specialized equipment found in the lab, such as a dental lathe and model trimmers.

Sterilization Area (Central)

This area is often referred to as "Central" because most dental offices are arranged to situate the sterilization area in the middle of the office, and all operatories feed into this area. Instruments are processed here using an autoclave or a similar type of sterilizer.

Team Lounge

This area serves as a private area for the dental team members. Purses, lunches, and other personal belongings should be stored here during the workday.

Dentist's Private Office

This area is where the dentist will be able to have privacy while reviewing and signing patient charts and for other private matters.

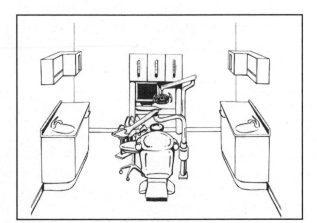

Figure 6.1 Dental Treatment Area

Equipment in the Operatory (Treatment Room)

The operatory, or treatment room, is the heart of the dental operation. It must be designed for efficiency and safety. The equipment in the operatory is divided into ten areas: light, dental chair and controls, portable unit, operator's equipment, table top, rheostat, assistant's stool, operator's stool, operatory sink, and operatory computer.

Light

Each operatory is equipped with an overhead light to aid the dental team with illumination into the oral cavity. Some lights have a dimming switch to use while placing light-sensitive materials. Changing the position of the light is the responsibility of the dental assistant.

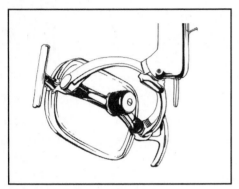

Figure 6.2 Operating Light

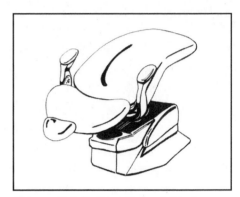

Figure 6.3 Patient Dental Chair

Dental Chair and Controls

There are many types of dental chairs from which the dentist can choose. Since sit-down dentistry is most common today, most chairs are built for that purpose. Controls can be located in any area of the chair the dentist chooses. Currently, the most common way to control a dental chair is via foot controls. These controls can be pre-programmed to the positions the dentist prefers. The patient dental chair is contoured for the patient's comfort. Newer models come with a massager and heat. The chair can be positioned in one of three ways: upright (used for taking impressions, exposing dental radiographs, and seating and dismissing the patient), supine (patients are reclined on their back), and subsupine (used for emergency situations).

Portable Unit

The portable unit consists of the high-volume evacuator (HVE), the saliva ejector, and the air/water syringe (triplex syringe).

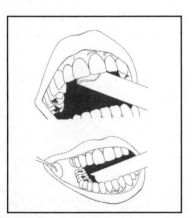

Figure 6.4 High-Volume Evacuator

High-Volume Evacuator (HVE)

This is a high-speed suction device used by the assistant for removing debris, particles, and large amounts of water very quickly from the oral cavity.

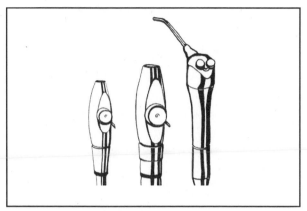

Figure 6.5 Saliva Ejector, HVE, Air/Water Syringe

Saliva Ejector

This is a slow-speed suction device used by assistants for removing saliva only.

Air/Water Syringe (Triplex Syringe)

This device is capable of performing three functions. It can blow air, spray water, or "blast" a combination of air and water. The assistant utilizes this device while handling the HVE or saliva ejector.

Operator's Equipment

The dentist's equipment includes two types of hand pieces—high-speed and low-speed—as well as the air/water syringe.

High-Speed Hand Piece

This is commonly known as the drill. This piece of equipment is used by the dentist to prepare the tooth to receive a restoration.

Low-Speed Hand Piece

This piece of equipment is used by the dentist, along with the high-speed hand piece, to remove soft decay, polish a restoration, or complete a prophy.

Table Top

This is where the assistant will place the instruments on the tray or in their cassette for the specific procedure. The table top is also known as the "mobile cart."

Rheostat

This "foot pedal" controls the dental hand pieces.

Figure 6.6 Assistant's Stool

Assistant's Stool

This chair is designed specifically for the way an assistant sits at the dental chair. The stool is equipped with wheels and castors, a comfortable cushion, a lever to adjust the height, a foot ring, and often a belly bar for abdominal support.

Operator's Stool

This chair is designed specifically for the operator and the way she or he is positioned at the dental chair. This stool has a low adjustable backrest, a comfortable cushion, a lever to adjust both the backrest and height, and wheels and castors. There is never a ring on an operator's stool. The dentist should be able to sit with his or her feet flat on the floor. For maximum visibility, the dental assistant's stool should be four to six inches above that of the operator.

Operatory Sink

Each treatment room has at least one sink. Typically, there will be a sink on both the operator's side and the assistant's side.

Operatory Computer

Today's operatory is usually equipped with a computer that runs dental office software. It can be utilized for one or all of the following:

- accessing the patient's electronic chart
- digital X-rays

- intraoral images
- treatment plan for the patients

Chair Positions

Dental chairs are the centerpiece of the operatory. They are adjustable to accommodate patients of all shapes and sizes. The three main positions are upright, supine, and subsupine.

Upright

The patient enters and leaves the dental chair in the upright position.

Supine

Dental treatment is performed in this position. The supine position places the patient flat on his or her back, with the head in line with the knees.

Subsupine

Dental treatment can be performed in this position if the dentist desires. The subsupine position places the patient's head below her or his knees. This position also places the patient's head directly in the operator's lap. This is used for emergencies.

Light Positions

The operating light is an essential part of the equipment in the treatment room. It must be placed correctly to illuminate the area to be treated. There are two main light positions: maxillary and mandibular.

Maxillary Position

The light is positioned over the patient's chest. Once the light is switched on, the beam should be directed toward the maxillary by gently pulling the light forward to the patient's chin and then tipping it upward.

Mandibular Position

The light is positioned over the patient's chest. Once the light is switched on, it should be pulled forward until it is directly over the patient's mouth. The beam should be shining directly onto the mandibular teeth.

Clock Concept of Operating Zones

The dentist and assistant must work in harmony as a coordinated team. Operating zones define what activities take place in which areas. These zones are defined based on the hands of a clock. There are four defined zones: static zone, assistant's zone, transfer zone, and operator's zone. These zones differ for right-handed and left-handed operators.

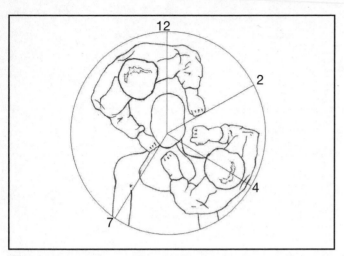

Figure 6.7 Operating Zones for a Right-handed Dentist

Right-Handed Operator

The four clock zones (based on clock positions) for the right-handed operator are as follows:

- 12–2 = Static Zone
- 2–4 = Assistant's Zone
- 4–7 = Transfer Zone
- 7–12 = Operator's Zone

12–2 = Static Zone

This is the clock zone where very little occurs.

2–4 = Assistant's Zone

This is the clock zone where the assistant sits while assisting for chairside procedures.

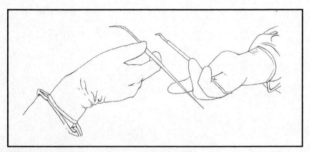

Figure 6.8 Instrument Exchange

4–7 = Transfer Zone

This is the clock zone where instrument transfer takes place. The assistant hands instruments and medicaments from the instrument tray to the operator through this zone.

7–12 = Operator's Zone
This is the clock zone where the operator sits and performs all dental procedures.

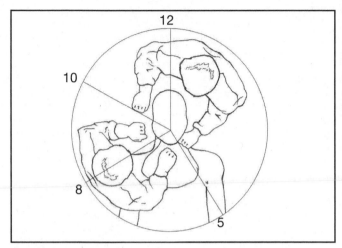

Figure 6.9 Operating Zones for a Left-handed Dentist

Left-Handed Operator

A left-handed dentist also has the four operating zones, but they are reversed.

- 12–5 = Operator's Zone
- 5–8 = Transfer Zone
- 8–10 = Assistant's Zone
- 10–12 = Static Zone

The descriptions of these zones are the same as those for the right-handed operator. However, the clock times are switched.

Delivery of Dental Care

Four-handed dentistry involves the operator and *one* assistant working together at the chair, while six-handed dentistry involves the dentist and *two* assistants working together at the chair. One assistant is the chairside assistant, and the other is the roving assistant. The chairside assistant is responsible for patient safety and for maintaining a clean, debris-free environment in the oral cavity. The roving assistant is responsible for instrument transfer, mixing of materials, and the pace of the procedure.

Techniques of Four-Handed Dentistry

Four-handed dentistry is also known as team dentistry because the dentist and the assistant work closely together in a coordinated manner.

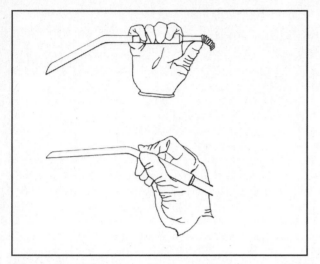

Figure 6.10 Thumb-to-Nose and Pen Grasp of HVE

Instrument Grasps

Various grasps are utilized by the operator depending upon the instrument of choice. These grasps include pen grasp, palm grasp, modified pen grasp, and modified palm grasp. There are two main HVE grasps: thumb-to-nose grasp, and pen grasp. In the thumb-to-nose grasp, the assistant holds the HVE in this grasp for maximum control of the HVE. The hand is wrapped around the HVE, with the thumb pointed toward the patient's nose. In the pen grasp, the assistant utilizes this grasp primarily for assisting with dental treatment performed in the anterior area of the oral cavity.

Fulcrum

Fulcrum is a resting point for the operator's working hand. A fulcrum allows for stability and control while utilizing an instrument or dental hand piece in the patient's mouth.

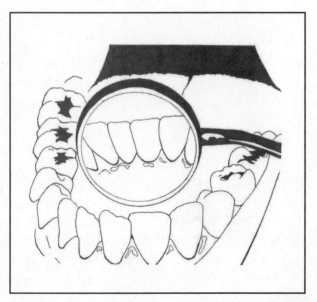

Figure 6.11 Using a Mouth Mirror for Indirect Vision

Direct and Indirect Vision

The operator utilizes both direct and indirect vision while performing dental treatment. Direct vision is when the operator has a direct line of sight to the area of the mouth on which she or he is working. Indirect vision is when the operator looks into a mouth mirror to visualize the area of the mouth being worked on. The assistant is responsible for spraying air on the mouth mirror to keep the dentist's line of vision clear.

Instrumentation

Generalized: In a general dental office, one will find a wide variety of dental instrumentation from each specialty. There will be a limited amount of specialized instrumentation, depending on how often the general dentist performs that specialty procedure. Some instrument setups found in a general dental office are basic setup, restorative set-up, crown and bridge setup, and emergency setup.

Specialized: In a specialty office, one will find instruments specific to that specialty. For example, an orthodontic office will have a specific instrument setup for cementation of bands, bonding of brackets, adjustment of arch wire, changing of elastics, and removal of orthodontic appliances.

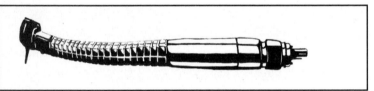

Figure 6.12 High-Speed Hand Piece

Hand-Piece Identification and Utilization: High-speed hand pieces are all one unit, spray water, and have a fiber-optic light. They rotate at 450,000 rpm, are used for preparation of teeth for restorations, and are slightly angled. Hand pieces are designed to spray water to wash away debris and to keep the tooth cool and prevent overheating. Slow-speed hand pieces have multiple parts and attachments, with a motor in the base. Attachments include straight, contra-angle, and prophy-angle.

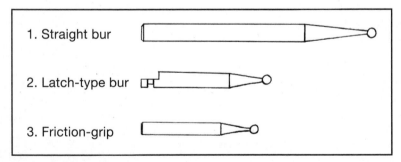

Figure 6.13 Types of Burs and Parts of the Bur

Bur Identification and Utilization: Dental burs are drill bits used in hand pieces. There are two main types of burs—carbide and diamond. The three bur shanks are straight, friction grip, and latch type. The three parts of the bur are the shank, neck, and head. The head of the bur cuts the tooth structure, and comes in many shapes. Burs are inserted into hand pieces to perform dental treatment.

Hand Instruments

Hand instruments are classified according to their use. Hand-cutting instruments are those used by the dentist to cut actual tooth structure (usually dentin). Hand-carving instruments are used to "carve anatomy" into the restorative material (amalgam). Exploratory instruments, also known as exam instruments, are used to perform an intraoral examination. This set includes the mouth mirror, explorer, cotton forceps, and a periodontal probe. The mouth mirror is used to retract the cheeks, lips, and tongue, as well as to reflect light and provide indirect vision.

Another category of hand instruments are accessory in nature. Crown and bridge scissors, articulating paper holders, and dappen dishes are a few examples. Articulating paper holders secure the colored marking paper used to identify high spots on a newly placed restoration (amalgam, composite, crowns, bridges, dentures, or partials).

Local Anesthetics and Analgesics

All dental assistants must be knowledgeable about anesthetics and analgesics.

Topical Anesthetic

The topical anesthetic numbs the gum and nerves to allow the dentist to administer the local anesthetic to the patient with the least irritation or pain. The most common form of topical anesthetic is gel.

The mandibular block injection is placed in the retromolar pad area in order to anesthetize the fifth cranial trigeminal nerve. Because the maxilla is more porous than the bone of the mandible, infiltration anesthesia is used. The operator injects the anesthetic around the area of the root above the target tooth/teeth. A vasoconstrictor is found in some anesthetics in varying ratios (1:20,000; 1:50,000; 1:100,000; and 1:200,000). This chemical gives a deeper anesthesia and lasts longer than plain anesthetics. Caution should be used for medically compromised patients (cardiac or hypertensive patients) with the use of vasoconstrictors. Parasthesia is the prolonged effect of the anesthetic and may be caused by expired anesthetic solution, anesthetic apparatus prepared in advance (metal ions from the needle leach into the solution), or if the nerve is damaged or nicked during the anesthetic process. Parasthesia may be permanent or subside after several days, weeks, or months.

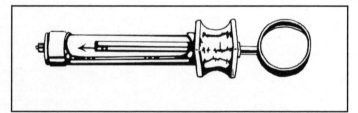

Figure 6.14 Local Anesthetic Aspirating Syringe

Assembly of Syringe

Dental assistants cannot administer local anesthetics, but they must be knowledgeable about them and be able to prepare the syringe for the dentist. This preparation involves aspirating the syringe, inserting the carpule, engaging the harpoon, selecting the proper size needle, and transfering the syringe to the dentist.

Needle Lengths and Usage

Needles come in two lengths: short or long. Long needles are used for mandibular injections, while short needles are used for maxillary injections.

Carpules

Carpule labels have a wealth of information: name of the anesthetic, the concentration, expiration date, manufacturer's name, and so on. The assistant should always double-check the expiration date and color code, and inspect the carpule for signs of damage.

Disassembly of Syringe

To disassemble the syringe, remove the needle, place it in a sharps container, disengage the harpoon, remove the carpule, and dispose of it properly. Remember to sterilize the syringe after use.

Proper Disposal of Sharps

Dispose of all used needles in a sharps container.

Nitrous-Oxide Sedation

Nitrous-oxide sedation is a gas mixture of oxygen and nitrous oxide administered through an inhalation technique. This is generally the responsibility of the dentist. However, in some states, assistants with expanded function credentials may also perform this function. Following the procedure, the patient should be flushed with 100% pure oxygen ten minutes prior to the end of the procedure. The patient should never be left alone while on nitrous oxide. The patient should be awake and responsive. Prior to leaving the office, the patient should be as alert as he or she was on entering the office. Note that the nitrous-oxide and oxygen tanks and gas lines are color coded. Nitrous oxide is blue and oxygen is green. There are hazards associated with exposure to nitrous oxide and it should never be administered to pregnant women or patients with breathing difficulty. A scavenger system is mandatory to protect dental personnel from ambient gases released by the patient upon exhaling.

Dental Support Aides

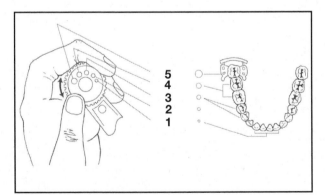

Figure 6.15 Rubber Dam Punch Hole Sizes

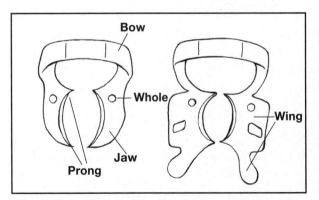

Figure 6.16 Parts of the Dental Dam Clamp

Rubber Dam

The rubber dam is utilized for retraction, moisture control, isolation, and patient management. The entire dam system includes the frame, punch, rubber dam material, template, napkins, lubricant, forceps, and clamps.

The dental dam frame holds the material taut and secures it extraorally. The dental dam clamp comes in varying sizes and may be winged or wingless. The clamp secures the dental dam material around the tooth. The dental dam punch makes the holes in the dental dam material that isolate the tooth/teeth. The #1 hole (smallest) is used for mandibular anteriors, #2 for maxillary anteriors, #3 for premolars, #4 for molars, and #5 for bridges or as the anchor tooth. The material between the holes is called the septum. This is cut using crown and bridge scissors when removing the dental dam material after the procedure. The various-sized holes correlate to the different teeth in the arch. One hole is used for endodontic treatment, while 6–8 teeth are recommended for multiple-tooth isolation. The dental dam forcep is used to open and release the clamp in order to place and remove the clamp from the tooth.

Other Moisture-Control Aides

These include dry angles (or dry aids) and cotton rolls.

Tofflemire Retainer with Matrix Band

The main parts of this retainer include the outer nut, inner nut, spindle, diagonal slot vise, and guide channels. It is used to build a temporary wall or matrix to replace lost tooth structure while the filling material is being placed. There are two types of matrix bands: universal and MOD. Other types of matrix systems include automatrix, omni matrix, and palodents.

Other Duties of Dental Assistants

Before dental procedures even begin, the dental assistant must welcome the patient into the operatory and make him or her comfortable. It is customary for the dental assistant to take the patient's pulse and blood pressure. Normal resting pulse rate is between 60 and 100 beats per minute. Blood pressure consist of two numbers, the higher one being the systolic and the lower the diastolic. Normal blood pressure is considered to be 120 over 80.

Clinical and Periodontal Charting

It is important for the dental team to keep good records, and charting is an essential part of that. Traditional records were kept on paper charts, but today, more and more dental offices are computerizing charts.

Black's Cavity Classifications

Black's Cavity Classifications describes the location of the decay on the tooth. It includes six classes according to the location of the cavity. The

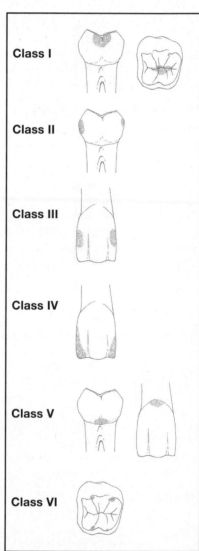

Figure 6.17 Black's Cavity Classifications

system also suggests the best way of restoring the tooth. For example, in perio charting, Class II indicates moderate mobility.

In orthodontics, patients are screened by their occlusion. Once established, the orthodontist will classify the type of malocclusion according to Angle's classification. Class I is normal, Class II is distocclusion where the maxillary teeth stick out beyond the mandible in an abnormal degree, giving the appearance of buck teeth. Class III is known as mesiocclusion and the mandible juts out anterior to the maxilla. For example, an occlusion with tongue thrusting is a Class II.

Tooth Preparation

During a composite procedure, the steps of tooth preparation basically mirror that of an amalgam restoration. Once the tooth is prepared with orthophosphoric acid (etchant) and the bonding agent is placed, a clear plastic mylar strip (or celluloid strip) is placed to act as a matrix. The clear matrix allows for operator visibility, as well as for the curing light to polymerize the composite material. The composite will not stick to or become discolored from the mylar material.

Tooth Staining

Staining of the teeth can come from several sources. Stains are categorized according to their location and source. Extrinsic stains occur on the outside of the tooth structure, while intrinsic stains are integrated into the tooth itself. Exogenous stains occur from sources outside of the tooth (smoking, drinking coffee and colas, etc.). Extrinsic stains are removed during the coronal polishing portion of a dental prophylaxis, or by using bleaching techniques.

Dental Specialties

Each specialty uses highly specialized instrumentation and procedure setups. There are nine dental specialties, as listed below:

- **endodontics**—treatment and diseases of the dental pulp
- **periodontics**—treatment of the diseases of the supporting structures, gingiva, and alveolar bone of the oral cavity
- **pediatric dentistry**—treatment of children from birth through adolescence
- **orthodontics and dentofacial orthopedics**—treatment and correction of all forms of malocclusion
- **prosthodontics**—restoration of oral function by restoring natural teeth or replacing missing teeth with a prosthesis (denture, partial, bridge, or implant)
- **oral and maxillofacial surgery**—diagnosis and surgical treatment of diseases, injuries, and defects of the oral and maxillofacial regions
- **oral and maxillofacial pathology**—diagnosis and treatment of abnormalities of the soft tissues and surrounding oral region
- **oral and maxillofacial radiology**—production and interpretation of X-ray images
- **dental public health**—promotes dental health in the community; prevents and controls dental diseases via educational means

Oral and maxillofacial surgeons extract teeth, biopsy lesions (abnormalities), correct anatomical defects, and place dental implants, to name a few procedures. For instance, rongeurs are used to contour the alveolar bone to eliminate sharp edges prior to the fabrication of a complete or partial denture. After an extraction, some patients experience alveolitis, also commonly known as a "dry socket." This occurs due to the loss or lack of development of a healthy blood clot in the alveolar socket. A surgical dressing is placed in the alveolus until adequate healing has occurred.

Pediatric dentists treat children from newborn through adolescence. Older patients with special needs may continue to be treated by the pediatric dentist. Patients with physical or mental disorders can be treated in a hospital under the care of a pediatric dentist with hospital privileges. All others are seen in the pediatric dental office. Aside from the regular dental procedures, pediatric dentists also treat many emergencies seen in children. For instance, traumatic intrusion occurs when a tooth has been forced inward by a fall or sports injury. Avulsion occurs when the tooth is completely knocked out of the alveolar socket.

In the specialty of endodontics, the dentist treats diseases of the pulp and surrounding tissues. Pulpal irritation can be classified as reversible pulpitis or irreversible pulpitis. In reversible pulpitis, the dentist places a sedative medicament over the pulpal floor in order to give the pulp time to heal and calm down. If this works, further treatment is not necessary at this time. Irreversible pulpitis occurs when the pulp becomes infected or dies due to trauma or decay. Root canal therapy is then performed by the dentist unless the patient chooses an extraction.

During the course of a root canal, the dentist cleans out and enlarges the canal(s) of the tooth. This is done using small instruments such as broaches, reamers, and files. Once the chamber is uniform in size and enlarged enough to accept the final filling material, the doctor will irrigate the canal(s) with a mixture of sodium hypochlorite and water. This step will "sterilize" the canal by removing any tissue particles or debris from the small chamber of the canal. The canal is thoroughly dried with paper points prior to the placement of the gutta percha filling material. The gutta percha is cemented into the canal with a sealer cement.

Specialty Procedures

Below is a list of common procedures performed by each specialty:

- **endodontics**—root canals, specialized diagnosis, post placement
- **periodontics**—root planning, perio hygiene, graphs, gingivectomy, gingioplasty, osseous surgeries
- **pediatric dentistry**—coronal polishing, stainless-steel crowns, pulpotomies, fluoride treatments, restorations, space maintainers
- **orthodontics**—invisalign, placement of full appliance, appliance adjustment, retainers, positioners, debanding and banding, palatal expander placement
- **prosthodontics**—implant crowns, crowns and bridges, full dentures, partial dentures, denture abutments
- **oral and maxillofacial surgery**—simple and surgical extractions, multiple extractions, facial reconstruction, removal of tumors and oral lesions, postoperative appointments
- **oral and maxillofacial pathology**—exfoliative biopsy, incisional biopsy, excisional biopsy, growth of cultures, microscopic evaluations
- **oral and maxillofacial radiology**—production and interpretation of X-ray(s) for diagnosis and treatment of diseases of the upper jaw and face
- **dental public health**—outreach programs, volunteer clinics, school educational programs, elderly outreach

As you can see, there is much that chairside assistants must know. Each of the previously mentioned skills and knowledge can be expanded upon and further developed. In addition to those skills and knowledge, the chairside assistant must also be familiar with and well versed in numerous other skills (see below), which will be covered in subsequent chapters of this book:

- **dental materials**—armamentarium and manipulation of cements, liners, impression materials, restorative materials, and so on
- **dental radiology**—the exposure, processing, mounting, and evaluation of dental films, including regard for patient safety while exposing X-rays
- **infection control**—treatment-room setup; PPE; aseptic technique during procedures; sterilization of instruments; and the disinfection of treatment room, equipment, and supplies
- **additional duties**—knowing and understanding state and federal laws regulating dental assisting duties; the importance of ethical behavior; the anatomy of the oral cavity; and how to cope with medical emergencies

► **Practice Questions**

1. What is the operator zone for a right-handed dentist?
   a. 2–4
   b. 1–6
   c. 7–12
   d. 12–2
   e. none of the above

2. What is the assistant's zone for a right-handed operator?
   a. 9–11
   b. 12–2
   c. 2–4
   d. 4–7
   e. none of the above

3. What is the transfer of instruments between the operator and the assistant called?
   a. six-handed dentistry
   b. four-handed dentistry
   c. two-handed dentistry
   d. none of the above
   e. both b and c

4. In which grasp can the HVE be held?
   a. modified pen
   b. reversed modified pen
   c. thumb-to-nose
   d. both a and c
   e. none of the above

5. When positioned at the chair, where should the assistant be relative to the operator?
   a. 3–5 inches lower
   b. parallel
   c. 2–5 inches higher
   d. 4–6 inches higher
   e. none of the above

6. What is the chair position called when patients are flat on their backs?
   a. upright
   b. semi-supine
   c. subsupine
   d. supine
   e. none of the above

7. In what form is the most common topical anesthetic supplied?
   a. liquid
   b. gel
   c. pill
   d. spray
   e. none of the above

8. In what area is a block injection given?
   a. mental nerve
   b. incisive nerve
   c. mental foramen
   d. trigeminal nerve
   e. both b and d

9. What is an injection given on the maxilla called?
   a. block
   b. infiltration
   c. mental
   d. incisive
   e. both b and c

10. How should needles be disposed?
   a. regular garbage
   b. trash marked biohazard
   c. the sharps container
   d. none of the above
   e. both b and c

11. What does a vasoconstrictor cause?
   a. blood vessels to narrow
   b. blood vessels to expand
   c. blood vessels to burst
   d. increase in length of duration
   e. both a and d

12. How is parasthesia defined?
   a. injection into the muscle
   b. swelling of blood in the tissues
   c. injury to the nerve causing permanent numbness
   d. both a and b
   e. both a and c

13. Nitrous oxide is a combination of what two gases?
    a. oxygen and helium
    b. nitrogen and carbon dioxide
    c. oxygen and nitrogen
    d. nitrogen and helium
    e. both c and d

14. What color is an oxygen tank?
    a. blue
    b. green
    c. yellow
    d. black
    e. both a and b

15. What color is a nitrous-oxide tank?
    a. blue
    b. green
    c. yellow
    d. black
    e. both a and b

16. How is nitrous oxide administered?
    a. inhalation
    b. transdermal
    c. sublingual
    d. both a and b
    e. both a and c

17. What is the use of the largest hole in the rubber dam punch?
    a. maxillary incisors
    b. mandibular premolars/bicuspids
    c. mandibular cuspids
    d. the anchor tooth
    e. maxillary molars

18. In which specialty of dentistry is single-tooth isolation used?
    a. prosthodontics
    b. orthodontics
    c. periodontics
    d. endodontics
    e. pedodontics

19. What is the size of a posterior dental rubber dam?

    a. 4 x 4

    b. 5 x 5

    c. 3 x 3

    d. 6 x 6

    e. both b and d

20. Which dental-dam punch-hole number is used for placement on a premolar/bicuspid?

    a. 1

    b. 2

    c. 3

    d. 4

    e. 5

21. In the removal of a dental dam, with what is the septum cut?

    a. interproximal knife

    b. surgical scissors

    c. a beavertail burnisher

    d. crown and bridge scissors

    e. both a and d

22. How many teeth should be punched in an average rubber dam?

    a. 1

    b. 5

    c. 6–8

    d. 8–10

    e. both a and b

23. What is the normal resting pulse rate for an adult?

    a. 60–100 beats per minute

    b. 40–65 beats per minute

    c. 50–100 beats per minute

    d. 100–150 beats per minute

    e. 120 beats per minute

24. When taking blood pressure, which is the systolic reading?

    a. lower number

    b. higher number

    c. it is not a number

    d. middle number

    e. none of the above

25. One of the assistant's main responsibilities at the chair, besides the patient's safety, is the portable unit. What makes up the portable unit?
   a.   HVE, saliva ejector, light
   b.   HVE, saliva ejector, air/water syringe
   c.   HVE, light, hand pieces
   d.   instruments, disposables, saliva ejector
   e.   both c and d

26. How are cavities occurring in the pit and fissures on the occlusal surfaces classified?
   a.   Class I
   b.   Class II
   c.   Class III
   d.   Class IV
   e.   Class V

27. How are cavities occurring along the interproximal and incisal edge of anterior teeth classified?
   a.   Class I
   b.   Class II
   c.   Class III
   d.   Class IV
   e.   Class V

28. Which hand piece sprays water?
   a.   contra-angle
   b.   slow-speed
   c.   high-speed
   d.   prophy angle
   e.   both b and c

29. What is the purpose of the water spray from a hand piece?
   a.   prohibiting the bur from overheating
   b.   adding moisture to the patient's mouth
   c.   prohibiting the tooth from overheating
   d.   keeping the work area clean
   e.   both b and c

30. What is the function of the rheostat?
   a.   allows the hand piece to rotate
   b.   allows the hand piece to stop rotating
   c.   allows the patient to be in a supine position
   d.   changes the bur for the operator
   e.   both a and b

31. Which of the following is NOT a benefit of using the HVE?
   a. keeps the area free from debris
   b. retraction of tongue
   c. allows light into the mouth
   d. retraction of the soft tissues
   e. eliminates the use of the rubber dam

32. Which of the following is not a hand-cutting instrument?
   a. hoe
   b. chisel
   c. gingival margin trimmer
   d. discoid-cleoid
   e. hatchet

33. What is the use of a mouth mirror?
   a. reflecting light and retracting the cheek
   b. retracting the cheek and retracting the tongue
   c. retracting the cheek, retracting the tongue, and indirect vision
   d. indirect vision
   e. all of the above

34. How should the patient be seated when taking an alginate impression of the maxillary arch?
   a. supine position
   b. subsupine position
   c. upright position, with head tilted slightly forward
   d. upright position, with head tilted back
   e. slightly reclined with chin tilted downward

35. When assisting a Class III restoration, what type of matrix is used?
   a. clear plastic strip
   b. T-band
   c. universal
   d. Palodentt
   e. both a and c

36. Which of the following statements is correct about at-home bleaching using a bleaching tray?
   a. It is effective on extrinsic stains.
   b. It is effective on intrinsic stains.
   c. It is recommended for non-vital teeth.
   d. It produces permanent results.
   e. both a and b

37. On what part of a newly placed restoration or sealant will articulating paper leave colored marks?

    a. indentations

    b. high spots

    c. overhangs

    d. gingival third

    e. buccal groove

38. What part of a Tofflemire matrix retainer tightens the band securely within the retainer?

    a. inner knob

    b. outer knob

    c. spindle

    d. channel guide

    e. both a and c

39. What are the three parts of a bur?

    a. shank, neck, head

    b. shank, shaft, head

    c. shaft, insert, head

    d. shank, insert, neck

    e. shaft, neck, head

40. In which styles are burs supplied?

    a. carbide and metal

    b. diamond and plastic

    c. carbide and diamond

    d. latch-type and friction grip

    e. both c and d

41. What is an all-encompassing term for an abnormality in the oral cavity?

    a. lesion

    b. antigen

    c. antibody

    d. plaque

    e. mucosa

42. What is the instrument called that is used to contour alveolar bone to eliminate sharp edges?

    a. surgical scissors

    b. bone files

    c. rongeurs

    d. chisel

    e. elevator

43. What is alveolitis more commonly called?

   a. excessive bleeding

   b. pack the sockets

   c. dry socket

   d. impaction

   e. periocoronitis

44. Where can pediatric patients with certain physical and mental disorders be treated?

   a. at the hospital

   b. in the pediatric office

   c. at the home

   d. both a and b

   e. a, b, and c

45. If a patient has traumatic intrusion, what does this mean?

   a. The tooth has been knocked out of the mouth completely.

   b. The tooth has been forced inward.

   c. The tooth has been luxated.

   d. The tooth has been avulsed.

   e. The tooth has been untouched.

46. What type of occlusion will tongue thrusting produce?

   a. Class I

   b. Class II

   c. Class III

   d. crossbite

   e. overbite

47. What fast and effective instrument that sprays water to cool and flush an area can be used instead of manual hand scaling?

   a. electrosurgery unit

   b. ultrasonic scaler unit

   c. surgical scalpel

   d. universal curette

   e. slow-speed hand piece with prophy-angle

48. While perio charting, the chairside assistant charts conditions involving the soft tissues as well as pocket readings. What class indicates moderate mobility?

   a. Class I

   b. Class II

   c. Class III

   d. Class IV

   e. both a and b

49. When is endodontic treatment not suggested?
   a. when diagnosis is reversible pulpitis
   b. when a tooth has severe periodontal problems
   c. when diagnosis is irreversible pulpitis
   d. both a and b
   e. a, b, and c

50. During endodontic treatment, with what are the canals irrigated?
   a. glutaraldehyde
   b. sterile saline solution
   c. sodium hypochlorite
   d. sodium bicarbonate
   e. gutta percha

▶ Practice Answers and Explanations

1. c. The operating zone for a right-handed dentist, according to the clock concept, is 7–12.

2. c. The assistant's zone for assisting a right-handed operator, according to the clock concept, is 2–4.

3. b. The operator has two hands, and the assistant has two hands. Therefore, it is termed four-handed dentistry.

4. d. Modified pen and thumb-to-nose are the two possible grasps utilized by the assistant for the HVE.

5. d. The assistant must be seated 4–6 inches higher than the operator to establish visibility.

6. d. Supine position is when a patient is lying back and his or her body is parallel to the floor.

7. b. Gel-form topical anesthetic is the most common and popular way to administer topical anesthetic to a patient.

8. d. A block injection is given distal of the retromolar pad in the area where the long buccal nerve, the lingual nerve, and the inferior alveolar nerve intersect. This intersection is called the trigeminal nerve.

9. b. An infiltration injection is always administered on the maxillary arch due to the numerous nerves that surround the roots of every tooth.

10. c. Needles of any kind are always disposed of in the impervious red sharps container, per OSHA regulations.

11. e. A vasoconstrictor is an ingredient present in local anesthetic that causes the blood vessels to constrict and lessen the blood flow, as well as increase the working time or duration of the local anesthetic.

12. c. Parasthesia is a side effect of local anesthetic caused by the anesthetic needle injuring the nerve during administration of the local anesthetic. Depending on the severity of the injury to the nerve, it can cause varying degrees of numbness to the patient's face.

13. c. Nitrous-oxide gas is a mixture of oxygen and nitrogen.

14. b. Oxygen tanks are always colored green.

15. a. Nitrous-oxide tanks are always colored blue.

16. a. A nose mask is placed over the patient's nose. The patient is instructed to breathe deeply through the nose. Therefore, this analgesic is administered via inhalation.

17. d. The anchor tooth, also known as the clamped tooth, requires the largest hole punched in the rubber dam material in order to stretch over the clamp and prevent moisture leakage.

18. d. In endodontics, the focus is on one particular tooth. Due to the use of certain endodontic medicaments, it is best to utilize single-tooth isolation with the rubber dam.

19. d. According to manufacturers' recommendations, 6 x 6 size rubber dam material is best used for posterior isolation. For anterior isolation, 5 x 5 rubber dam material is best.

20. c. Rubber dam hole size 3 is the recommended hole size to be punched for a premolar/bicuspid.

21. d. Crown and bridge scissors are used to cut the interdental septum of the rubber dam material, cutting away from the gingival tissue to avoid injury to the patient.

22. c. In standard restorative procedures, it is customary to expose the entire quadrant of teeth (6–8) when placing a rubber dam.

23. a. The normal resting pulse rate for an adult is 60–100 beats per minute.

24. b. The systolic reading is always the higher number, which is the heart muscle taking in oxygenated blood (e.g., systolic/diastolic or 120/80).

25. b. The portable unit is located on the assistant's side of the chair and consists of the HVE, saliva ejector, and air/water syringe.

26. a. Black's Cavity Classifications help dental personnel specify locations of decay. Class I refers to decay that is located on the occlusal surfaces of posterior teeth.

27. d. Class IV refers to decay located along the interproximal involving the incisal edges of anterior teeth. This is another of Black's Cavity Classifications.

28. c. The high-speed hand piece rotates at 470,000 rotations per minute (RPM), which causes extreme heat on a tooth. This is the only hand piece that sprays water.

29. c. To avoid injury to the pulp, a cool water spray is emitted from the high-speed hand piece, which prohibits the tooth from overheating and killing the pulp.

30. e. The rheostat, or foot pedal, is the control for the dental hand pieces. The hand pieces will not function unless the rheostat is activated.

31. e. The HVE is beneficial in many areas of the oral cavity. It provides additional light into the oral cavity via retraction of the tongue and soft tissues while keeping the area free of debris. However, the HVE will not eliminate the need for or use of the rubber dam.

32. d. A discoid-cleoid is a carver, not a hand-cutting instrument. A carver carves freshly placed amalgam, while a hand-cutting instrument cuts tooth structure manually.

33. e. A mouth mirror is used for reflecting light, retracting the cheek and tongue, and providing indirect vision for the operator.

34. c. When taking an alginate impression of the maxillary arch, a patient should be seated in the upright position, with his or her head tilted slightly forward to avoid possible gagging on the alginate material.

35. a. The use of a clear plastic mylar strip as a matrix for composite placement is preferred to allow the curing light to penetrate and cure the material. The use of the other choices given would prohibit the adequate curing of the material.

36. a. Extrinsic stains are stains that occur on the external surfaces of the tooth and can be removed via various dental procedures, such as home bleaching.

37. b. Articulating paper is utilized to ensure the operator has restored the patient's bite properly following the placement of a restoration. Therefore, articulating paper will leave colored marks on any high spots on the new restoration.

38. a. The inner knob of the Tofflemire retainer is used to secure the band tightly within the retainer. The outer knob is used to adjust the size of the band once it is placed over the tooth.

39. a. There are three portions to a bur. The shank is the portion that fits into the hand piece and can be friction grip or latch type. The neck is the portion that connects the shank to the head of the bur. The head is the actual cutting portion of the bur.

40. e. Burs are supplied in carbide metal or diamond. Carbide metal is used for cutting restorations and removing decay. Diamond burs are used for gross reduction of enamel in procedures such as crown and bridge. Both types are supplied in either friction grip or latch type, depending on the hand piece being used.

41. a. A lesion is a generalized term used in dentistry to describe any abnormality in the oral cavity.

42. c. A ronguers is used to trim and contour the alveolar bone exclusively. It is often used in surgical settings, such as periodontal or oral surgeries.

43. c. Alveolitis, or dry socket, is an infection of the alveolar bone that became exposed to bacteria in the mouth after the blood clot covering the bone post-extraction was dislodged.

44. d. Pediatric dental patients with physical or mental complications can be treated successfully at either the private pedodontic office or using an operating room with hospital privileges, depending upon the severity of the patient's disorder.

45. b. Traumatic intrusion is the forcing of the permanent or primary tooth back into the socket. This usually occurs accidentally with small children; however, it can also happen to any patient involved in a traumatic accident.

46. b. Class II malocclusion is referred to as buck tooth appearance or a distocclusion. The maxillary teeth appear more mesial than the mandibular. The tongue is a very strong muscle that can push the teeth into this position.

47. b. The ultrasonic scaler is a fast and effective way of removing excess cements from supragingival surfaces. It is also used by hygienists to remove calculus from all surfaces of a patient's tooth.

48. b. Class II mobility indicates moderate mobility while perio charting. Class I is slight mobility, Class III is advanced mobility, and Class IV is severe mobility. These classes are indicators of periodontal disease.

49. a. Reversible pulpitis is a condition in which the pulp can heal itself, or the dentist may be able to place a medicament to encourage the pulp to heal. An endodontic procedure is not indicated at this point due to the possibility of the reversal of the inflammation.

50. c. Sodium hypochlorite is a mixture of bleach and water. Irrigation of the canals is indicated to help kill any remaining infection that may be present in the root canals.

Dental Materials

CHAPTER OVERVIEW

The area of dental materials is one that is constantly evolving and changing. New techniques, products, and armamentarium are being developed daily. Part of being an effective dental assistant is to be educated and remain up to date on these new trends. Dental materials are used every day in the dental setting for a wide variety of procedures and processes.

K NOWING HOW TO manipulate, store, and handle dental materials is critical for chairside assisting. A well-rounded understanding of the choice of material and its use is beneficial for the patient and the operator. The dentist will determine the type of material needed based on the extent of the decay, the condition of the patient's oral cavity, the location of the dental defect, and the cost factor for the patient. Additionally, each area of dentistry will have its own unique materials that may be used only in that specialty.

KEY TERMS

acid etchant	auto-cure	custom acrylic provisional
alginate	base	custom tray
alloy	catalyst	dual-cure
amalgam	composite	etchant

KEY TERMS (continued)

exothermic	microleakage	sealant
framework	partial denture	sedative
full denture	periodontal dressing ("perio pak")	smear layer
galvanic		spatulate
gold	permanent cement	stent
gutta percha	polymerization	temporary cement
homogeneous	poly vinyl siloxane	trituration
immediate denture	prophy paste	vacuum former ("suck down" machine)
implant	provisional	
light-cure	radiopaque	viscosity
liner	relining	
luting	retention	

▶ Concepts and Skills

This chapter will include questions that focus on dental materials, covering seven main concepts:

- Bases and Liners
- Bonding Procedures
- Restorative Dental Materials
- Dental Cements
- Impression Materials
- Laboratory Materials
- Laboratory Equipment
- Accessory Materials

Bases and Liners
Bases and liners are used just prior to the filling of a prepped tooth to protect the pulp (base) or to stimulate secondary dentin growth (liner).

Bases
Dental bases are layers placed under the restoration to protect, insulate, and sedate the pulp. Two of the most popular bases are glass ionomer, and zinc oxide eugenol (ZOE).

Glass Ionomer
Glass ionomer is probably the most popular base because of its specialized functions:

- It releases fluoride ions.
- It bonds to enamel and dentin.

- It is radiopaque (blocking radiation, such as from X-rays).
- It is compatible with all dental restorative materials.

Zinc Oxide Eugenol (ZOE)

Zinc oxide eugenol is one of the most popular dental bases for the following reasons:

- It is sedative (soothing) to the pulp.
- It insulates the pulp from thermal forces.
- It protects the pulp.
- Oil of cloves in the eugenol produces a calming effect on the pulp.
- It is not compatible under resin-based restorations because the oil of cloves interferes with the bonding of the resin.

Liners

Dental liners are thin layers that protect the pulp from irritation. One of the most popular liners is calcium hydroxide.

Calcium Hydroxide

Calcium hydroxide is one of the most popular dental liners for the following reasons:

- It promotes secondary dentin as a measure to protect the pulp.
- It is placed only on dentin (on the walls and floor of the preparation area).
- It is compatible with all types of restorative materials.
- Some brand names include Dycal, Life, and Vitrebond.

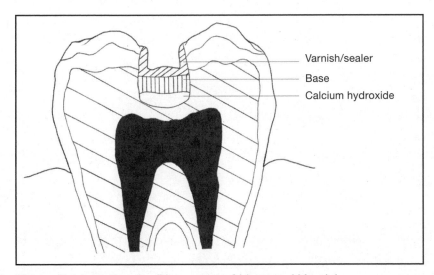

Figure 7.1 Location for Placement of Liner and Varnish

Varnishes

Dental varnish is a type of sealer that seals the dentinal tubules and flows easily but evaporates quickly. It should not be used under glass ionomer or resin restorations. Varnish is always applied after the liner.

Bonding Procedures

Restorations can be bonded to both enamel and dentin. Bonding materials prepare the tooth structure to accept a new restoration, sealant, or to bond for various orthodontic procedures. When a tooth is being prepared with the hand piece and bur, the oily layer that the tooth secretes is known as the smear layer. There are numerous techniques and manufacturers of these bonding systems, which are discussed below.

Acid Etchant ("Conditioner")

An acid etchant, or "conditioner," uses phosphoric or maleic acid (liquid or gel) to help form a bond between the restoration and the tooth. It can be used on enamel or dentin. Acid etching removes the smear layer just prior to bonding of new restorative material. Phosphoric acid is placed on the tooth structure for 15–20 seconds, then rinsed thoroughly and dried. The tooth structure should appear chalky. This process creates enamel tags that allow the resin-based materials to bond.

Application of Various Bonding Agents

Bonding agents have evolved over the past decade and have revolutionized the application and retention of composite and porcelain materials. The use of bonding creates a micromechanical retention between the restoration and tooth structure. A primer prepares the tooth for the resin materials and can also be a desensitizing agent. An adhesive creates a layer on which to place the resin material. The primer and adhesive can also be applied in one step. However, bonding systems by different manufacturers should not be used interchangeably. Dry field must be maintained via isolation techniques like rubber dam, cotton roll, or dry angle. Self-cure, light-cure, and dual-cure are types of adhesives.

Dental Sealants

Dental sealants protect teeth, particularly posterior teeth, from decay by coating the pits and fissures with resin sealant. Sealants are placed on the occlusal surfaces of posterior teeth. There is a specific order to apply the sealant: coronal polish, cotton roll isolation, acid etch-rinse-dry, primadry—then, sealant material is placed and cured. A properly placed sealant should last ten years. Pit and fissure sealants are flowable composite dental materials.

Restorative Dental Materials

Restorative dental materials can be either permanent or temporary. Once the dental disease is removed from the tooth, the tooth is restored to its functioning state using a restorative material. In addition to restoring function, restoring aesthetics is an important part of the material chosen. Restorative materials can be either direct or indirect. Medicaments are added in a certain order: liner, etch, primer, bond, then composite.

Direct Restorations

Direct restorations are completed in one dental visit. The material is placed in a pliable state, then hardened and polished. Examples of direct restorative materials are amalgams, composites, and glass ionomers.

Amalgam

Traditional amalgam ("silver fillings") restorations are an example of direct restoration. Amalgams are adhered with chemical bonding or physical retention and used primarily for posterior restorations. The mixing of the mercury and alloy powder that make up the amalgam is known as trituration. The sequence for a Class II amalgam restoration is: prep tooth, place liner or base, place Tofflemire matrix, place amalgam. Instruments are used in a specific order: amalgam carrier, condenser, carver, burnisher, and articulating paper. Amalgam has the following advantages and disadvantages:

- Amalgam is a mixture of alloy (two or more metals such as silver, tin, copper, and zinc) combined with mercury.
- Its safety is questioned by some. For example, clinical personnel are cautioned never to touch amalgam with bare hands; to use sufficient ventilation; and to discard it in a closed, covered, impervious container. It must be treated as hazardous waste.
- Amalgam can lead to recurrent decay, microleakage, tarnishing, fracturing teeth with expansion, and tattooing.
- It is aesthetically inferior to other materials.
- It is affordable.
- It is long lasting.
- It can be used on patients with poor oral hygiene.

Composite

Composite or resin restorations are often referred to as "tooth-colored fillings," and are another example of direct restorations. Composites have gained in popularity due to their esthetics. They can be "bonded" to the enamel and dentin, which actually helps strengthen the remaining tooth structure. The tooth preparation for a composite may be less invasive than an amalgam due to the bonding technique utilized. Glass is added to the composite material for strength. Composite material is layered incrementally and each is light cured in large restorations. (Remember that prolonged exposure to the curing light can damage the retina, so avoid staring directly at it.) Composite restorations have various classes. For example, a Class III restoration would use a mylar strip. Composites are easily polished but not with a low-speed hand piece. Flash refers to excess composite or bond material. A discoid cleoid is never found on a composite tray. A composite has the following qualities:

- It is currently the most popular choice of restorative material.
- It is aesthetically pleasing.
- It comes in many shades.
- It bonds chemically to the teeth.
- It can be anticariogenic (preventing tooth decay by releasing fluoride).
- The two types of composite materials are: filled, when strength is needed; and unfilled, for sealants and similar uses.
- Composites are cured in three ways: by using the curing light (light-cured), by mixing the base and catalyst (self-cured), or a combination of both (dual-cured).
- Polymerization is the process of hardening.
- It is not as strong as an amalgam.
- It is more expensive than an amalgam.

Glass Ionomer

A third type of direct restoration is glass ionomer. Glass ionomer properties can be altered, which allows them to be formulated as restorations, liners, cements, and bonding agents. When mixing glass ionomer, always follow the manufacturer's instructions. For example, GC Fuji suggests combining one scoop powder and one drop liquid; mix in one half of the powder for five to ten seconds, and then the second half of the powder for ten to 15 seconds.

A glass ionomer has the following advantages:

- It is very versatile. It can be used for liners, core build-ups, restoratives, and cements.
- It is aesthetically pleasing.
- It is anticariogenic (preventing tooth decay by releasing fluoride).
- It bonds chemically to the enamel and dentin of the teeth.
- It comes in many shades.
- It is radiopaque (visible on X-rays), which is a distinct advantage over calcium hydroxide.
- It is compatible with all dental restorative materials.

Indirect Restorations

Indirect restorations are completed in two or more dental visits, although CEREC (Chairside Economical Restoration of Esthetical Ceramics) units create a porcelain crown in one visit. Other restorations are actually fabricated in the dental lab. These restorations are referred to as cast restorations. Cast restorations are made from impressions taken of the patient's mouth and then sent to the lab. Sometimes, crowns have to be returned to the lab for perfecting, but not in the case of slightly high occlusion. Examples of indirect restorations are gold crowns, porcelain crowns/porcelain fused to metal crowns, and other indirect restorations (three-quarter crowns, inlays, onlays, and veneers).

Gold Crowns

Gold crowns have many advantages. These are used where aesthetics are not the primary concern and if the inter-arch space does not allow sufficient room for porcelain. Also, if the patient clenches or grinds, gold will not suffer fracture strain. Gold crowns have the following qualities:

- The gold in these crowns is combined with other metals for strength.
- They resist the harsh environment of the oral cavity.
- They are available in four types.
- They are fabricated in the dental lab.
- They are cemented with permanent cement.
- They are healthy for the gum tissue.

Porcelain Crowns/Porcelain Fused to Metal Crowns

Porcelain crowns and porcelain fused to metal crowns are most commonly used in fixed prosthodontics. The versatility of porcelain allows for the following advantages:

- They are most often used in dentistry.
- They are aesthetically pleasing.
- They are fabricated in the dental lab.
- They are cemented with permanent cement.
- They match natural surrounding teeth.

Other Indirect Restorations

Other indirect restorations include three-quarter crowns, inlays, onlays, and veneers. Inlays are fabricated extraorally and cemented in place. Onlays are similar to inlays, but they must include at least one cusp. For example, a restoration that extends over the cusps of posterior teeth leaving the facial and lingual aspects of the tooth intact is an onlay. These restorations may be made with porcelain or made of full gold.

Stainless-Steel Crowns

Stainless-steel crowns come in a variety of sizes and must be contoured and trimmed to fit the tooth. Adult gingival tissues do not tolerate stainless-steel crowns, which is why they are reserved mainly for use on children. They are utilized as permanent coverage on primary teeth or as temporaries on permanent teeth. Once trimmed, stainless-steel crowns are lined with cement and seated in place.

Retraction Cord

During the crown procedure, it is necessary to retract the gingival tissue prior to the final impression. This is done utilizing a gingival retraction cord. The cord comes in a variety of sizes, the largest of which is size 3. Retraction cords have the following qualities:

- They are utilized for temporary retraction of gingival tissues surrounding a prepped tooth so that an accurate impression of the margin can be attained.
- They can be braided or unbraided.
- They can be impregnated with hemostatic solution to control bleeding (epinephrine or vasoconstrictor are not to be used for patients with heart conditions).
- Some states limit this expanded function to a dental assistant only placing a non-impregnated retraction cord.
- Other methods, such as foaming agents and adjuncts, are utilized to retract gingival tissue.

Provisional (Temporary) Crowns

After the tooth has been prepared for a crown or bridge, the tooth needs coverage for comfort, protection, and aesthetic purposes. A provisional, or temporary, crown is prepared and placed for the interim while the final crown is fabricated in the dental laboratory. There are two types of provisional crowns: custom acrylic temporary crowns and preformed temporary crowns.

Custom Acrylic Temporary Crowns: These types of crowns can be made from powder and liquid (trim) or from a cartridge that combines a base and a catalyst in a mixing tip.

Preformed Temporary Crowns: These types of crowns have a polycarboxylate anterior and an aluminum shell posterior. Celluloid crowns are made of clear plastic material and are primarily used for anterior teeth.

Dental Cements

Dental cements are classified according to their properties and, therefore, their uses in dentistry. Type I cements are used for the placement of a restoration for long-term or short-term purposes. Type II are restorative materials. Type III are those materials utilized as bases and liners. Dental cements are either temporary or permanent.

Temporary Cements

Sometimes, there is a need for selecting a dental cement for short-term or sedative purposes. Generally, temporary cements last about six months. The operator will listen to the patient's chief complaint and choose the cement accordingly. Temporary cements have the following qualities:

- They are utilized for cementing provisional (temporary) restorations.
- In some cases, they are utilized for temporarily cementing permanent restorations when the tooth is experiencing symptoms.
- They can have sedative properties.
- Assistants should follow the manufacturer's instructions on whether to mix cements on paper or cooled glass, or with an automix extruder.

Brand Names of Temporary Cements

The most commonly used temporary cements are as follows:

- Temp Bond, which is supplied in two tubes: base and catalyst
- ZOE (zinc oxide eugenol), which comes in powder and liquid form

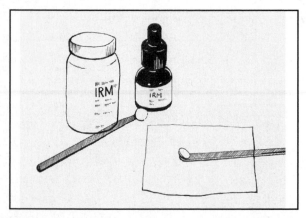

Figure 7.2 Intermediate Restorative Materials (IRM) Set-up

Permanent Cements

When seating a final cast restoration, the luting agent will act as an adhesive to hold the restoration to the tooth structure. Permanent cements are used to attach the permanent crown, which is placed in the patient's mouth, and he or she is instructed to bite down on an orangewood stick/cotton roll. A crown and bridge cementation tray set-up would include instruments such as a low-speed hand piece, plastic instrument, temporary cement, and cement spatula, but not a gingival margin trimmer. Permanent cements have the following qualities:

- They are utilized for permanently cementing cast restorations.
- They are long-lasting.
- They do not interfere with the proper fit of cast restorations.
- They can be anticariogenic.
- Assistants should follow the manufacturer's instructions on whether to mix cements on paper or cooled glass, or with an automix extruder.

Brand Names of Permanent Cements

The most commonly used permanent cements are as follows:

- Ketac Cem (glass ionomer), which comes in powder and liquid and/or applicaps
- Panavia (resin cement), which is light-cured and used for bonding all porcelain restorations
- Durelon (polycarboxylate), which comes in powder and liquid
- Fleck's (zinc phosphate cement), which comes in powder and liquid and is mixed on a glass slab since it has an exothermic reaction

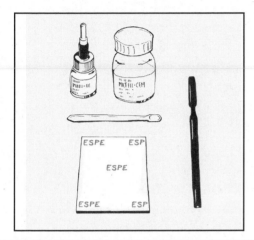

Figure 7.3 Ketac Cem Glass Ionomer Cement

Impression Materials

Impressions are taken in order to create reproductions of patients' teeth and tissues. Assistants should follow the manufacturer's instructions on whether to hand-mix these on a paper pad or to automix them in an extruder. When pouring an impression with dental plaster, the material is added slowly, with steady increments from one side of the impression. A positive reproduction of the impression is created in a model. Models may be used for several different purposes, including study models, prosthodontic models, and lab procedure models. There are two types of impression materials: preliminary (alginate), and final.

Preliminary Impression Materials (Alginate)

Preliminary impressions are used to create study models for "non-permanent" types of appliances. In some states, this is considered an expanded function for dental assistants. The most common material utilized for a preliminary impression is irreversible hydrocolloid, which is also known as alginate. It may be hand mixed or available for use in the Pentamix system. Preliminary impression materials have the following qualities:

- They are used for opposing impression during crown and bridge procedure.
- They are used for fabrication of diagnostic study models, bleach trays, occlusal guards, and some denture procedures.
- They come in powder and liquid forms.
- Some brands have automix cartridges.
- They can be flavored for patient comfort.

- They come in fast set or regular set.
- They are inexpensive.

Final Impression Materials

Final impressions must provide an extremely accurate reproduction of the tissues and teeth. The final impression must be taken by the dentist, but the assistant is responsible for mixing and dispensing the material into the impression tray. Final impression materials have the following qualities:

- They are utilized for master impression of the prepped tooth, and then sent to the lab for fabrication of a cast restoration.
- They are durable and resist tearing.
- Elastomeric impression materials are a type of final impression material.

Brands of Elastomeric Impression Materials

There are several brands/types of elastomeric impression materials: Polyether (Impregum), Polysulfide (Coe Flex), Polyvinyl Siloxane (Extrude and Express), and Bite Registration.

Polyether (Impregum): This is supplied in two tubes: base and catalyst. It is used in a Pentamix machine, which is a newer technology that "automixes" the impression material and dispenses the product much like a soft-serve ice cream machine. It eliminates the risk of improper mixing technique or exceeding the mixing time.

Polysulfide (Coe Flex): This is supplied in two tubes: base and catalyst.

Polyvinyl Siloxane (Extrude and Express): This uses a two-gun or a putty-wash technique.

Bite Registration: This technique is utilized for making a replica of the relationship of maxillary arch to the mandibular arch. It is sent to the lab with the final impression and opposing impression. Polyvinyl Siloxane bite registration material is used. It is supplied in a paste or cartridge system. This method is very accurate and is still used today.

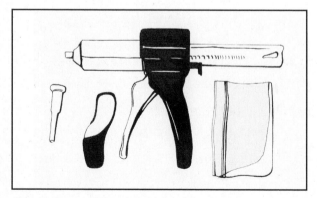

Figure 7.4 Bite Registration Materials

Trays

Impression materials must be delivered into the oral cavity utilizing an impression tray. Medium- or heavy-bodied impression material is known as tray material. Depending on the impression material or the area to be duplicated, the assistant and operator have several choices of the tray type selected: traditional metal trays, disposable trays, triple trays, or custom acrylic trays.

Traditional Metal Trays

Traditional metal trays come in perforated or solid, full arches or quadrant. They are autoclaved and reused. They are usually reserved for use with alginate.

Disposable Trays

Disposable trays come in perforated or solid, full arches or quadrant. These trays are single-use only. Usually, a tray adhesive is used.

Triple Trays

Triple trays are used only for final impressions and bite registrations. They are used as a time-saving technique by taking the final impression and bite registration at the same time.

Custom Acrylic Trays

Custom acrylic trays are made especially for the patient's arch. These trays are commonly used in prosthetic procedures.

Laboratory Materials

The gypsum product selected for the reproduction of dental models depends on the purpose of the model use. Dental laboratories tend to use stronger materials, while dental offices will use plaster and orthodontic stone for their purposes. There are several types of laboratory materials: plaster (model plaster), stone, and high-strength stone (die stone).

Plaster (Model Plaster)

Plaster or model plaster is used for making diagnostic casts and pouring preliminary impressions.

Stone

Stone is used when a stronger model is needed or for working models for dentures, night guards, bleaching trays, surgical stents, and so on.

High-Strength Stone (Die Stone)

High-strength stone or die stone is utilized by dental lab technicians for fabrication of cast restorations. It is the strongest stone.

Laboratory Equipment

There are several types of laboratory equipment used in a dental lab: lathe, model trimmer, vacuum former, vibrator, waxes, and tools.

Lathe

A lathe is used for polishing temporary crowns or casting gold restorations.

Model Trimmer

A model trimmer is used for trimming models when separated from impression materials.

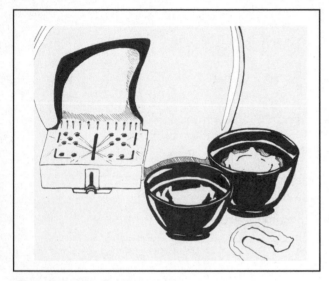

Figure 7.5 Model Trimmer

Vacuum Former

A vacuum former is used for the fabrication of bleach trays.

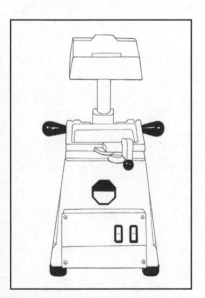

Figure 7.6 Vacuum Former

Vibrator

A vibrator is used to help eliminate air bubbles in freshly mixed plaster or stone.

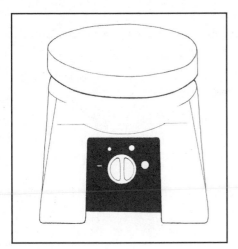

Figure 7.7 Vibrator

Waxes

Waxes are used for bite registration, customizing impression trays, wax rims, wax-up models, sticky wax, and so on.

Laboratory Instrumentation

Instruments used in a dental lab include lab knives, spatulas, mixing bowls, mixing pads, glass slabs, rag wheels, buffers, sand blasters, polishing discs, and so on.

Accessory Materials

In root canal therapy (RCT), the filling material placed in the canals is gutta percha, which is a type of rubber from the Palaquium gutta tree of Malaysia.

Periodontal dressings are used to cover and protect a surgical site while the tissue heals. They are supplied as a light-cured material, a eugenol-based material, and as a non-eugenol-based material.

Tooth whitening, also known as bleaching, is becoming one of the most popular ways of improving the appearance of teeth. Products are available in toothpaste, oral rinses, strips, and chewing gum for personal use. In-office materials are stronger and more effective. The main bleaching agents in in-office vital bleaching procedures are hydrogen peroxide and carbamide peroxide. In the professional treatment solutions, they come in concentrations of 30 to 35%.

▶ Practice Questions

1. When completing a large composite restoration, how should the composite material be placed into the prepared tooth?
   a. all at once
   b. in small increments by the layering technique, light-curing with each increment
   c. rolling into a ball
   d. with the dental hand piece
   e. both a and b

2. What is the proper order for placing these medicaments in a tooth prep for composite restorations?
   a. etch, primer, bond, liner, composite
   b. etch, liner, primer, bond, composite
   c. liner, primer, etch, bond, composite
   d. liner, etch, primer, bond, composite
   e. primer, bond, etch, liner, composite

3. What is used when completing a Class III composite restoration?
   a. a Tofflemire matrix
   b. an AutoMatrix
   c. a mylar strip
   d. a celluloid strip
   e. both c and d

4. Which of the following is NOT used to polish a composite restoration?
   a. finishing bur
   b. hollenback carver
   c. brownie and greenie rubber points
   d. low-speed hand piece
   e. finishing strips

5. What is the name of the unit that will harden the layers of composite in the prepared tooth?
   a. overhead light
   b. curing light
   c. bright light
   d. dim light
   e. none of the above

6. When a composite material is cured, it is said to be:
   a. marketed to patients.
   b. acid etched.
   c. hardened or set.
   d. more viscous.
   e. wet and softened.

7. Why is a rubber dam recommended when placing a composite restoration?
   a. The tooth will be less contaminated with saliva and moisture.
   b. Cotton roll isolation alone is not adequate enough.
   c. A composite is always completed prior to a root canal.
   d. The ADA demands the use of a rubber dam.
   e. both c and d

8. What does the term "flash" mean with regard to a composite restoration?
   a. a stuck piece of floss
   b. excess composite or bond material
   c. a picture taken when the procedure is complete
   d. the omission of the acid etch step
   e. none of the above

9. Which instrument is NOT used to prep the tooth and remove decay for an amalgam restoration?
   a. high-speed hand piece
   b. low-speed hand piece
   c. hatchet
   d. discoid-cleoid
   e. spoon

10. What is the purpose of a base?
   a. to stimulate secondary dentin growth
   b. to insulate the pulp from hot and cold
   c. to release fluoride
   d. to seal the dentinal tubules
   e. none of the above

11. What is the proper procedure for mixing a glass ionomer lining cement?
   a. Mix one scoop powder and one drop liquid so you can roll it into a ball.
   b. Mix equal amounts from each tube on a small mixing pad.
   c. Mix one scoop powder and one drop liquid, mix in one half the powder for five to ten seconds, and then the second half of the powder in ten to 15 seconds.
   d. Mix one scoop powder and three drops liquid, and mix all together for ten seconds until you have a "stringy" consistency.
   e. Always use a glass slab to keep the material cool.

12. Which of the following best describes cavity varnishes?
  a. seal the dentinal tubules
  b. flow easily but evaporate quickly
  c. should not be used under a glass ionomer or resin restoration
  d. both a and b
  e. all of the above

13. Which medication stimulates secondary dentin?
  a. amalgam
  b. composite
  c. calcium hydroxide
  d. zinc oxide eugenol
  e. both c and d

14. Which ingredient in glass ionomer is released slowly into the tooth structure?
  a. phosphor
  b. calcium
  c. fluoride
  d. oil of cloves
  e. zinc

15. Which ingredient in zinc oxide eugenol (ZOE) soothes the tooth structures?
  a. calcium hydroxide
  b. oil of cloves
  c. fluoride
  d. zinc phosphate
  e. both b and d

16. Which of the following are gypsum materials?
  a. lab plaster
  b. orthodontic stone
  c. Class I stone
  d. die stone
  e. all of the above

17. Which cement is preferred when cementing a temporary aluminum crown?
  a. polycarboxylate
  b. zinc oxide eugenol
  c. zinc phosphate
  d. non-eugenol temporary cement
  e. both b and d

18. What type of cement is preferred when cementing a temporary polycarbonate crown?
   a. polycarboxylate
   b. zinc oxide eugenol
   c. zinc phosphate
   d. non-eugenol temporary cement
   e. both b and d

19. How long is a temporary cement expected to last?
   a. two months
   b. three months
   c. six months
   d. nine months
   e. one year

20. What is the correct sequence for placing a Class II amalgam restoration?
   a. prep tooth, place Tofflemire matrix, place liner or base, place amalgam
   b. prep tooth, place liner or base, place Tofflemire matrix, place amalgam
   c. prep tooth, place amalgam, place liner or base, place Tofflemire matrix
   d. prep tooth, place liner or base, place amalgam, place Tofflemire matrix
   e. place Tofflemire matrix, prep tooth, place liner or base, place amalgam

21. What is the correct order of use of instruments for placing an amalgam restoration?
   a. amalgam carrier, condenser, burnisher, carver, articulating paper
   b. amalgam carrier, carver, burnisher, condenser, articulating paper
   c. amalgam carrier, condenser, articulating paper, carver, burnisher
   d. amalgam carrier, condenser, carver, burnisher, articulating paper
   e. amalgam carrier, articulating paper, condenser, burnisher, carver

22. Which dental material is used in pediatric dentistry as a barrier to protect pits and fissures of posterior teeth?
   a. stainless steel crown
   b. amalgam
   c. composite
   d. sealant
   e. polycarbonate

23. What is the correct order of operation for a sealant procedure?
   a. sealant material placed and cured, acid etch-rinse-dry, coronal polish, cotton roll isolation
   b. cotton roll isolation, coronal polish, acid etch-rinse-dry, sealant material placed and cured
   c. coronal polish, acid etch-rinse-dry, cotton roll isolation, sealant material placed and cured
   d. coronal polish, cotton roll isolation, sealant material placed and cured, acid etch-rinse-dry
   e. coronal polish, cotton roll isolation, acid etch-rinse-dry, primadry, sealant material placed and cured

24. What is the name of the filling material placed in the canals of RCT teeth?
  a. gutta percha
  b. sealant
  c. Cavit
  d. ZOE
  d. amalgam

25. Periodontal dressings are used to cover and protect a surgical site while the tissue heals. How are they supplied?
  a. a light cured material
  b. a eugenol based material
  c. a non-eugenol based material
  d. both b and c
  e. all of the above

26. When is a bite registration taken?
  a. before the tooth is prepped
  b. after the tooth is prepped
  c. does not matter; can be done anytime
  d. only on crown preps for molars and bicuspids
  e. both a and d

27. After filling the permanent crown with cement, the crown is placed on the patient's tooth and the patient is instructed to bite on:
  a. dental floss.
  b. gauze.
  c. an orangewood stick/cotton roll.
  d. a plastic instrument.
  e. both c and d

28. A crown would NOT have to be sent back to the lab to be perfected in which of the following cases?
  a. open contact
  b. slightly high occlusion
  c. open margin
  d. incorrect shade
  e. none of the above

29. Which of the following instruments/items do NOT belong on a crown and bridge cementation tray set-up?
  a. low-speed hand piece
  b. gingival margin trimmer
  c. plastic instrument
  d. temporary cement
  e. cement spatula

30. What is a restoration called that extends over the cusps of posterior teeth, but the facial and lingual aspects of the tooth are left intact?
   a. an onlay
   b. an inlay
   c. a full crown
   d. a provisional crown
   e. a veneer

31. Which of the following are NOT used as final impression materials for crown and bridge procedures?
   a. alginate
   b. polysulfide
   c. polyether
   d. polyvinylsiloxane
   e. none of the above

32. What is the largest size gingival retraction cord?
   a. size 000
   b. size 00
   c. size 0
   d. size 2
   e. size 3

33. What is another name for medium- or heavy-bodied impression material?
   a. syringe material
   b. wash material
   c. tray material
   d. alginate material
   e. none of the above

34. How long should etch material be left on a tooth?
   a. 25 seconds
   b. 30 seconds
   c. 15–20 seconds
   d. ten seconds
   e. no more than 35 seconds

35. Approximately how many years should a properly placed sealant last?
   a. ten years
   b. 15 years
   c. 20 years
   d. 25 years
   e. 30 years

36. What does the term *trituration* mean?
   a. mixing
   b. blending
   c. polymerizing
   d. setting
   e. curing

37. What causes damage to the retina?
   a. exposure to mercury
   b. not wearing personal protective equipment
   c. prolonged and frequent staring into the curing light
   d. overexposure to radiation from dental X-rays
   e. none of the above

38. Pit and fissure sealants are what type of dental material?
   a. packable composite
   b. in the alloy family of dental materials
   c. flowable composite
   d. an aesthetically pleasing material
   e. none of the above

39. After fabricating a custom acrylic temporary for a patient, what piece of lab equipment would be used to polish, smooth, and shine the new temporary?
   a. model trimmer
   b. vacuum former
   c. lathe
   d. peri pro developer
   e. none of the above

40. What is a smear layer?
   a. an oily layer the tooth secretes after being prepped with the hand piece and bur
   b. a layer added to the restoration by a dental material
   c. something that is needed in order for composite to bond to the tooth
   d. a layer of the tooth
   e. none of the above

41. Which of the following impressions is used for obtaining a perfect, accurate reproduction of the margin?
   a. bite registration
   b. final or master impression
   c. alginate impression
   d. wax bite impression
   e. none of the above

42. On which surfaces of which teeth are sealants placed?
    a. interproximal; posterior
    b. buccal; posterior
    c. lingual; anterior
    d. occlusal; posterior
    e. none of the above

43. Which of the following is an example of an elastomeric impression material?
    a. hydrocolloid
    b. poly vinyl siloxane (PVS)
    c. polysulfide
    d. polyether
    e. b, c, and d

44. What type of restoration is a dental sealant considered to be?
    a. permanent
    b. temporary
    c. preventive
    d. final
    e. preliminary

45. How is the material added when pouring an impression with dental plaster?
    a. slowly, with steady increments from one side of the impression
    b. quickly, with large increments from one side of the impression
    c. with one large swipe of plaster placed into the impression
    d. slowly, with steady increments from both sides of the impression
    e. none of the above

46. What is the name of the piece of lab equipment on which impressions are placed when being poured up?
    a. lathe
    b. model trimmer
    c. vibrator
    d. articulator
    e. triad machine

47. What is used to soften the bleach tray material when fabricating a bleach tray?
    a. vacuum former
    b. model trimmer
    c. vibrator
    d. triad machine
    e. articulator

48. What type of wax is used when taking a bite impression?

    a. utility wax

    b. baseplate wax

    c. casting wax

    d. bite registration wax

    e. none of the above

49. What type of particles are added to a filled composite material? Why?

    a. paper; strength

    b. glass; material

    c. glass; strength

    d. paper; material

    e. none of the above

50. What percentage of hydrogen or carbamide peroxide is included in in-office bleach material (bleach material that is applied in the dental office)?

    a. 5%–10%

    b. 10%–15%

    c. 15%–20%

    d. 20%–30%

    e. 30%–35%

▶ Practice Answers and Explanations

1. b. Composite should always be layered due to shrinkage upon curing. The layering technique prevents voids in the fill of the restoration.

2. d. A precise series of steps must be followed while preparing and placing a composite restoration into the tooth for a proper, long-lasting bond.

3. c. A Class III restoration is located on the anterior interproximal surfaces. While placing the composite restoration, a mylar strip must be placed in between the prepared tooth and the tooth next to it to avoid bonding the two interproximal surfaces together. A mylar strip allows the ultraviolet light from the curing unit to access and penetrate the uncured composite material.

4. b. A hollenback carver is used in amalgam procedures to carve the interproximal surfaces of a freshly placed amalgam restoration. It does not polish a composite restoration.

5. b. A curing light emits ultraviolet light, which causes polymerization to occur in the resin-based materials.

6. c. In dental terminology, cured means to set or harden. This occurs with many of the light-sensitive and/or resin-based materials.

7. a. Composites and other resin-based materials are typically very sensitive to moisture. It is recommended by composite manufacturers that a rubber dam be utilized while placement of this type of material is occurring. Saliva, water, and moisture from the patient's breath can all contaminate the bond strength of the composite restoration. The rubber dam aids in preventing this.

8. b. The term flash refers to excess bonding and composite materials remaining on the tooth structure following the curing process. Since bonding and composite materials are tooth colored, excess material is difficult to see. Flash is usually located during the polishing process.

9. d. A discoid-cleoid is a carving instrument used on the occlusal surface of freshly placed amalgam. It is not classified as a hand carver or a rotary instrument capable of tooth preparation or decay removal.

10. b. A base is placed on the floor of a tooth preparation to soothe and insulates the pulp from hot and cold temperatures.

11. c. Always follow the manufacturer's instructions when mixing any dental material. The instructions will be included with each package.

12. e. Cavity varnishes seal the dentinal tubules, are liquid so they flow easily, evaporate quickly, and should not be placed under a glass ionomer or a resin restoration because they inhibit the bond strength of the material.

13. c. Calcium hydroxide is known in dentistry as a liner that stimulates secondary dentin. It is placed on the floor of the cavity preparation just above the pulp.

14. c. One of the benefits of using glass ionomers is that they contain fluoride, which makes them anticariogenic. This continual release of fluoride strengthens the enamel and dentin.

15. b. Oil of cloves is an ingredient in ZOE that is very soothing to the pulp.

16. e. Gypsum materials are various types of plasters and stones with varying strengths, which are utilized for different purposes in dentistry.

17. e. Either ZOE or non-eugenol temporary cement would be acceptable when cementing an aluminum temporary restoration. The permanent restoration may be an all-porcelain crown and, in that case, temporary cement with no eugenol should be used. Answers **a** and **b** are both permanent cements, and should not be used for temporary restorations.

18. e. Either ZOE or non-eugenol temporary cement would be acceptable when cementing a polycarbonate temporary restoration. The permanent restoration may be an all-porcelain crown and, in that case, temporary cement with no eugenol should be used. Answers **a** and **b** are both permanent cements, and should not be used for temporary restorations.

19. c. According to the manufacturer, temporary cement is designed to last up to six months. However, most temporary cements are used for only two weeks until the permanent cast restoration is made by the lab.

20. b. This is the correct sequence for placing an amalgam restoration.

21. d. This is the sequence of instrumentation for an amalgam restoration.

22. d. Sealant material is a preventive measure used to prevent occlusal decay.

23. e. This is the correct sequence for placement of a sealant.

24. a. Gutta percha is the only dental material available that will flow into the canals of root-canal-treated teeth when heated.

25. e. Periodontal dressings are supplied as light-cured materials; they can be eugenol-based and non-eugenol-based.

26. b. A bite registration is taken after the tooth is prepped to demonstrate to the lab the amount of clearance from the prepped tooth to the surrounding natural teeth and anatomy of the occlusion.

27. c. The patient needs to apply intraoral force to the permanent crown during cementation to ensure the restoration has seated all the way to the margin. An orangewood stick or cotton roll is helpful in exerting proper intraoral forces along the cast restoration.

28. b. A slightly high occlusion can be adjusted by the dentist at the chair. The other examples would need to be repaired at the lab with the expertise of the lab technician.

29. b. A gingival margin trimmer is a hand-cutting instrument used during tooth preparation. It does not have a place on a crown and bridge cementation setup.

30. a. An onlay is a cast restoration that covers the cusps of the tooth but leaves the facial and lingual aspects of the tooth intact.

31. a. Alginate is not used as a final impression material because it is not an accurate elastomeric material. Final impressions must be extremely accurate.

32. e. The largest size retraction cord is a size 3. It is used in large sulcular areas.

33. c. Heavy- or medium-bodied impression material is also known as "tray" material because it is placed in a tray by the assistant just prior to placement in the mouth.

34. c. Acid etch, also known as tooth conditioner, should be placed on the prepared tooth for 15–20 seconds. If left longer, the acid etch could over-etch the tooth structure, causing sensitivity. If rinsed off too soon, it will cause compromised bond strength, and the restoration could fail.

35. a. Currently, ten years is the approximate life span of a properly placed sealant. The sealant will be examined at each six-month recall.

36. a. Trituration is the process of mixing. Amalgam capsules are placed into a triturator or amalgamator to combine the mercury and alloy powder to make the amalgam restoration.

37. c. It is not advised to look at the curing light when curing a resin-based material. Prolonged and frequent staring at this light over time will cause damage to the retina.

38. c. Sealant material is a form of flowable composite. This makes application easier, as it will flow into the fissures and grooves on the occlusal surfaces of posterior teeth.

39. c. The lathe is a machine to which a rag wheel is attached. The lathe spins in a circular motion and uses lab pumice to create a polished, smooth, and shiny appearance to the new temporary crown.

40. a. The smear layer is secreted by the dentinal tubules when they have been cut by the hand piece and bur. The dentin is trying to repair itself. This smear layer is removed by etching prior to placement of a resin-based material.

41. b. A final or master impression is obtained with elastomeric impression material and is capable of giving the best reproduction of the prepared margin.

42. d. Sealants are placed on the occlusal surfaces of posterior teeth into the pits and fissures.

43. e. PVS, polyether, and polysulfide are the three elastomeric impression materials used in dentistry for final impressions.

44. c. Sealants are a preventive restoration to prevent decay from occurring on the occlusal surfaces of posterior teeth.

45. a. Slow but steady increments from one side of the impression is the proper way to pour plaster into the impression and lessen the number of air bubbles in the set model.

46. c. A vibrator is used to lessen the amount of air trapped in the plaster or stone mixture just prior to pouring into an impression.

47. a. A vacuum former, also known as a "suck down" machine, is used to soften the bleach tray material by heating the material slowly. It then provides a rush of air to seal the material around the model, creating a custom bleach tray for the patient.

48. d. Bite registration wax is the wax of choice when using wax for this purpose. Alternatively, bite registration can also be taken with a PVS elastomeric material.

49. c. Glass particles, silicate, and quartz are all additives placed in filled resins. They add extra strength to the composite material itself. The operator will choose a filled or unfilled resin, based on his or her preferences. One is not better than the other.

50. e. An in-office bleach procedure will always have a higher percentage concentration than the take-home variety. This provides the dental office the opportunity to produce rapid results within an hour or two. The take-home bleach concentration ranges from 5% to 20% and up.

CHAPTER

▶ Dental
Radiology

CHAPTER OVERVIEW

Dental radiographs are images produced on film exposed to X-rays and then developed into a negative image o the inside of the oral cavity. These radiographs enable the dentist to look inside the patient's mouth and see internal structures as if they were transparent. Anatomic structures that cannot be seen by the naked eye are made visible with a radiograph.

THE DENTAL ASSISTANT is trained to obtain both intraoral (film placed inside the patient's mouth) and extraoral (film placed outside the patient's mouth) radiographs. There are two types of intraoral radiographs, which record images of the teeth and the supporting structures. The radiographs show the outline, dimension, and positions of the teeth. The supporting structures viewed are the alveolar bone, the lamina dura, the periodontal ligament, and the membrane space. Radiographs can reveal restorations with amalgam overhangs, restorations that are failing, recurrent decay on a tooth, interproximal caries, calculus levels, crestal bone levels, internal pulp pathology, anatomy and pathology in the root area, and surrounding bony structures and occlusal relationships.

Radiation is used to produce radiographs (X-ray films) and can be biologically damaging. Every exposure has the ability to damage living tissue. Therefore, the operator and patient must be properly protected, and stringent infection control techniques must be followed. The operator must also follow proper exposing and processing techniques for the safety of all.

KEY TERMS

absorb	bitewing radiograph	overlapping
absorption	cathode	penumbra
aluminum filter	dosimeter	photon
ammonium thiosulfate	electron	primary radiation
anatomic landmark	film	scatter radiation
area monitoring	filter	X-radiation
barrier	fixer	

▶ Concepts and Skills

Radiology is a central tool in dental diagnosis and treatment. This topic is broken down into nine concepts and skills:

- Intraoral Radiographic Technique
- Processing Intraoral Radiographs
- The Generation of X-rays in the X-ray Tube Head
- Characteristics of the Image
- Radiation Biology and Protection
- Radiographic Presentation of Lesions
- Extraoral Radiography
- Digital Imaging
- Patient Management

We will present questions relating to each of these areas of dental radiology. The outline below chronicles current information regarding exposing, processing, mounting, and interpreting both intraoral and extraoral radiographs.

Intraoral Radiographic Technique

There are two intraoral X-ray techniques used in dentistry. The oldest technique is the bisecting angle technique, and the newer is the paralleling technique, which is widely taught in all dental schools.

The film is sealed in a packet to protect it. If this is placed backward in the mouth, the result is an image of low density with a herringbone pattern on the film.

The speed of the film is determined by the size of the silver halide crystals and is classified A through F, F being the fastest.

Types of Intraoral Surveys

The examination of a complete area with radiographs is referred to as a survey. Intraoral surveys could include a full-mouth series of films or a localized area, such as a maxillary cuspid view.

Bitewings

The bitewing radiograph shows both the maxillary and mandibular teeth in occlusion. Bitewings can either be taken horizontally or vertically. The main purpose of a bitewing is to examine the interproximal surfaces, mesial and distal, and the height of the crestal bone level. Other purposes include detection of overhanging restorations, pathology of the pulp, and detection of location of calculus. Bitewings are usually taken once or twice a year depending on the patient's caries rate and level of oral home care. A bicuspid/premolar bitewing radiograph should be placed to include the distal half of the mandibular cuspid. The standard film size used for bitewings is size 2. Size 0 or 1 can be used for children with primary teeth. Size 3 is specially made for an extra long bitewing; however, it is seldom used.

Periapicals

The periapical radiograph shows the most accurate image of crowns, roots, and supporting structures of a particular area of the oral cavity. Supporting tissues examined in a periapical radiograph include the alveolar bone, lamina dura, periodontal ligament, periodontal membrane space, and 2–3 mm of supporting tissue beyond the apex of the tooth. Periapicals are used to examine the anatomy and pathology of a particular area and generally use size 1 or 2 film. Size 1 film would most likely be used to radiograph the incisors and cuspids of adult patients.

Occlusal Films

Occlusal films examine the complete arch of teeth, maxillary or mandibular, all in one view. The occlusal film, a size 4 film, is much larger than a bitewing or periapical film. This film is used to locate objects present in the oral cavity, along with locating supernumerary teeth (extra teeth), impacted teeth, root tips of extracted teeth that were left behind, tumors, and cysts. Other uses of the occlusal film include the examination of the maxillary sinuses, large sections of the jaw, and to determine the presence of any jaw fractures or pathologies such as cysts and malignancies. The two main techniques for exposing an occlusal film are topographical and cross-sectional.

Basic Principles of Intraoral Survey

The intraoral survey, full mouth X-ray (FMX) series, consists of 18 to 20 individual films showing the entire oral cavity. The full mouth series consists of bitewings and periapicals. Areas of the oral cavity are grouped together and films are taken of each quadrant, usually only every three to five years. Occlusal films are another intraoral film; however, they are not included in a full-mouth series.

Paralleling Technique

The paralleling technique is widely used in dental radiology because it produces a quality, anatomically correct image so that no retakes are needed. Having no retakes or minimal retakes reduces the patient's exposure to radiation. The paralleling technique is an exposure technique in which the film is placed parallel to the long axis of the tooth and the central beam is directed at a right angle to both the tooth and the film.

Infection Control

Infection control must be followed in exposing radiographs. PPE—gloves, mask, lab coat, and eyewear—is always worn by the operator. Protective barriers are placed on the exposure button, the X-ray unit buttons, and on the X-ray tube head and position indicating device (PID).

Disposable film holders are used along with reusable film holders that are sterilized. The treatment room is disinfected, but no antiseptic agents are used. Infection control measures must be followed while processing the films. However, immersing a contaminated exposed film packet in a disinfecting solution will destroy the image.

Processing Intraoral Radiographs

Conventional intraoral radiographs require a process that brings out the latent image, making it visible.

Latent Image

A latent image is an unseen image that is on the film from the exposure time to the time that the image appears on the film. This invisible image is made when the X-radiation in the X-ray tube head strikes the silver halide crystals on the film.

Film Composition

Dental X-ray film is covered with an emulsion on both sides of the film. The emulsion consists of a mixture of silver halide crystals in a gelatin base. These halide crystals change when they are exposed to radiation. When the film is processed, the developer and fixer chemicals react with these exposed and unexposed silver halide crystals to produce an image.

Chemicals Involved in Processing

The three forms of processing chemicals are ready-to-use, concentrate, and powder. The concentrate form is most commonly used in dental offices.

Developer

The developer reacts with the exposed silver halide crystals and is responsible for creating the black or dark tones on the image. The reducing agents in the developer are metol and hydroquinone.

Fixer

The fixer reacts with unexposed silver halide crystals and removes them from the film, which causes a white or clear area. The fixing agent is ammonium thiosulfate.

Water

Water is used in the processing of dental X-rays to rinse and remove any developer or fixer chemicals on the film.

Automatic Film Processing

Automatic processing systems can develop intraoral films in four to five minutes or less. There is much less room for operator error as the temperature and developing and fixing time are controlled by the processor and not the operator. Some automatic processors have a daylight loader attached to them so that a darkroom is not necessary. The solutions in the automatic processors are much warmer than in manual processing. The solutions are approximately 85–105° F (30–40° C). The films move through the processor on rollers. Maintenance of the automatic processor is very important. Solutions must be replenished daily and changed every two to six weeks, depending on the rate of use. The processor rollers must be cleaned each time the solutions are changed. Chemicals must be disposed of according to local regulation, and documentation should be filed. There is less chance of error using automatic processors.

Manual Film Processing

Films may be processed manually in a darkroom with an X-ray utility "red" safety light over the traditional tank. Intraoral films are clipped to a film rack and processed on the rack. Accurate temperature of the developer and fixer solutions and timing is mandatory to obtain a diagnostic image. Optimum developing time and temperature for manual processing is four-and-a-half to five minutes at 68° F (20° C). Increasing the time that the films are in the developer and increasing the temperature of the developer cause a denser, darker image. Fixing time is usually twice the developing time. The films are then washed for at least 20 minutes in a fresh running water tank, then hung to dry. The process includes developing, rinsing, fixing, washing, and drying.

Mounting Films

There are 18–20 individual films mounted into a full mouth survey mount. A dot (pimple, not a dimple) is utilized to determine the front side of the film. This is known as labial mounting. Anatomical landmarks are used to aid in mounting. Note that on an edentulous patient, the maxillary tuberosity and the outer corner of the eye would serve as the landmarks of the maxillary molar radiograph.

Helpful hints include:

- Maxillary molars have three roots.
- Mandibular molars have two roots.
- Maxillary central incisor films show the median palatine suture, a radiolucent line between the maxillary central incisors.
- Anterior films are orientated vertically.
- Posterior films are orientated horizontally.
- Maxillary films have large radiolucent areas: nasal fossa and maxillary sinuses.
- Maxillary molar films show the maxillary tuberosity.
- Mandibular molar films show the retromolar pad and the external oblique ridge.
- The overall appearance of the full mouth survey is in an upward curve (smile).
- Radiolucent structures, such as dental pulp, permit the passage of X-rays and thus appear dark on the film. On the other hand, radiopaque materials, such as gold and amalgam, block the penetration of X-rays and therefore appear lighter on the film.
- If the operator uses too much vertical angulation, the result is an X-ray image that is shorter than the actual tooth; this is known as foreshortening.
- The correct vertical angulation in a bitewing radiograph is +10 degrees.

Duplicating Films

Intraoral film is available in double-pack films, which creates two originals simultaneously. However, duplicating is completed using a duplicating film. Duplication is completed in a darkroom using a duplicator that shines a bright ultraviolet light onto the films that then produces an image onto the duplicating film.

The Generation of X-rays in the X-ray Tube Head

X-rays are produced in the tube head and are the result of high-speed electrons stopping or slowing. The electron kinetic energy is changed into electromagnetic energy by Bremsstrahlung radiation. The X-ray photons produced in the tube head have many different wavelengths. Photons striking a living organism break molecules into smaller pieces, disrupt molecular bonds, and form new ones within molecules and between new molecules.

Properties of X-rays

X-rays are energy that travels in a wave-like motion. They penetrate matter, produce fluorescence in some materials, cause ionization of matter, and produce a latent image on the film. Ionization is the loss of electrons from a substance.

Parts of the Dental X-ray Tube

There are five main parts in a dental X-ray tube: anode-tungsten target, cathode-tungsten filament, aluminum filter, lead collimator, and position indicating device (PID). Each is discussed in turn. The X-ray tube creates the X-ray production conditions of: a source of electrons, high voltage for electron speed, and a target that can stop the electrons.

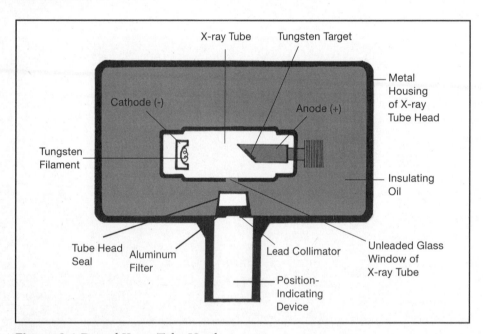

Figure 8.1 Dental X-ray Tube Head

Anode-Tungsten Target

This is the positively charged end of the X-ray tube head. The kilovoltage (kV) setting controls the current in the anode or the quality.

Cathode-Tungsten Filament

This is the negatively charged side of the X-ray tube head where the electrons are boiled off of the tungsten filament. The milliampere (mA) setting controls the number of electrons or quantity.

Aluminum Filter

This filter is located in the position indicating device (PID) between the PID and the X-ray tube head. This filter removes the long wave—low energy wavelengths that are not needed to produce X-rays.

Lead Collimator

Also referred to as the lead disc, the lead collimator restricts the spread of the X-ray beam to no more than 2.75 inches (70 mm) at the patient's face. Lead is used because it is resistant to the penetration of ionizing radiation.

Position Indicating Device (PID)

The position indicating device (PID) is also referred to as the cone. The PID is used for aiming the central beam toward the patient's face and anatomical landmarks.

Production of X-rays

Thermionic emission occurs at the tungsten filament in the cathode. A cloud of electrons is boiled off the filament. The negatively charged electrons are attracted to the tungsten target in the anode, the positive side of the tube. When the electrons collide with the target, energy in the form of X-rays and heat is produced. Ninety-nine percent of the energy is heat and only 1% of the energy produced is X-rays. The X-rays then escape the tube head through the aluminum filter and collimator and travel down the PID to strike the matter and the film.

Characteristics of the Image

There are four characteristics of an X-ray image. These are: contrast, density, detail, and geometric distortion. Each is discussed in turn. The dentist requires properly processed radiographs with minimal distortion to be diagnostically acceptable. For example, a film that has been exposed to radiation twice, known as double exposure, is of no use.

Contrast

This refers to the varying shades of gray present in the image. Contrast is dependent upon density and can be influenced by processing. Contrast is difference in densities. It is controlled by the voltage (kV) setting.

Density

Radiographic density is the degree of darkness in the image. Density depends on the total amount of radiation that the film receives, the thickness of the bone, the developing/processing conditions, and the distance between the X-ray tube head and the patient. Density is controlled by the amperage (mA) setting.

Detail

Detail is the sharpness and clarity of the image. Detail is affected by patient movement or X-ray tube head movement. Any movement during the exposure of an X-ray will cause the image to appear blurry and out of focus.

Geometric Distortion

By increasing the object-to-film distance, a penumbra will be present. A penumbra is the lack of sharpness that surrounds the shadow. This results in an inaccurate duplication of the tooth since it is geometrically distorted. Also, if the patient makes any slight movement, the result will be a blurry image.

Radiation Biology and Protection

Radiation is extremely dangerous. So, it is essential that dental assistants have a complete knowledge and understanding of how it works, and the proper protection from harmful rays for both the patient and dental staff. Five topics covered are: cellular and molecular changes, radiation measurement, operator protection, patient protection, and the benefits and risks of radiographs. There are several factors that determine radiation injury: total dose, dose rate, area exposed, age, sensitivity of the individual, and cell and tissue sensitivity.

Cellular and Molecular Changes

The energy of the X-ray beam is transferred to the matter that it passes through. This is called absorption. The molecules are affected by the X-rays. A molecule can break into smaller molecules, form new bonds with other molecules, form new bonds within itself, or be disrupted. Reproductive cells, bone marrow, small lymphocytes, and internal mucosa are the cells most sensitive to radiation. Muscle and nerve cells are the least sensitive. The harmful effects of radiation are cumulative and sometimes do not show up immediately. The latent period is the period of time from when the tissue is exposed to radiation to the first signs of biologic damage.

Radiation Measurement

Rad is the term that is used to describe the absorbed radiation dose. The International System of Units (SI) uses the unit gray (Gy). One gray is equal to 100 rad (1 rad is equal to 0.01 gray). Rem is the equivalent or effective radiation dose. The SI unit is sievert (Sv). One sievert is equal to 100 Rem (1 Rem is equal to 0.01 sievert). Roentgen (R) is the term that describes radiation exposure. Generally, exposure of 1 R will result in an absorbed dose of 1 rad, or 0.01 Gy.

Operator Protection

The exposure MPD limit for an occupational worker is the maximum permissible dose, or MPD. For an occupational worker, MPD is 5.0 Rem per year.

The operator must be behind a barrier while exposing films. If no barrier is available, the operator should be at least six feet away from the patient and in an area that is between 90° and 135° to the primary beam of X-ray. Radiation measuring devises such as film badges, film rings, and dosimeters should be worn by the operator to measure radiation exposure. Film holders should be utilized, and an operator should never hold a film for the patient.

Patient Protection

When it comes to exposure to radiation, the ALARA concept should be followed. ALARA stands for As Low As Reasonably Achievable. X-rays should be prescribed by the doctor and not taken as a matter of routine. X-ray machines rated at over 70 kilovoltage peak (kVp) must use a one inch (2.5 cm) aluminum filter. The collimator is the lead disc that restricts the size of the X-ray beam to 2.75 inches (70 mm) at the patient's face. Long cone PIDs (12–16 inches long) should be utilized as they cause less spread of the X-ray beam. Patients should wear a thyroid collar and lead apron impregnated with 0.25 mm of lead to shield out radiation.

Benefits and Risks of Radiographs

When addressing the patient's concerns regarding dental X-rays, it is important to explain the benefits versus the risks. Dental radiographs taken using the prescribed precautions pose little risk to the patient. Radiographs should only be taken when the benefits far outweigh the risks.

Radiographic Presentation of Lesions

Doctors use radiographs to locate and view the extent of many lesions. Lesions are growths that are not coordinated with a body system, and therefore serve no useful purpose. Not all lesions are malignant. Some lesions that can be seen in a dental X-ray include periapical infection, caries or decay, trauma, periodontal disease, oral lesions, and dental abnormalities. This allows for the early detection of precancerous or cancerous lesions.

Without the benefit of dental radiographs, the dentist does not have the tools necessary to detect growths that cannot be seen with a clinical examination. Early detection can save lives.

Extraoral Radiography

Extraoral films are placed outside of the patient's mouth. They are much larger than intraoral films and are utilized to view large areas of the skull and jaw. Extraoral radiography includes panoramic radiography, as well as views of the temporomandibular joint (TMJ), maxillary sinuses, and a cephalometric view.

Panoramic Radiography

A panoramic film is placed into a cassette that contains an intensifying screen on either side of the film. The intensifying screen is made up of phosphor, which emits blue or green light onto the film when X-rays are exposed to it. The panoramic film has less detail than an intraoral periapical or bitewing.

Note that a patient placed in a panoramic unit with chin too low will result in X-ray images with an exaggerated curve of Spee. Prior to placing an implant, the panoramic technique is preferred when exposing intraoral films.

Technique

The patient must remove all appliances in her or his mouth and any facial jewelry, large necklaces, earrings, hearing aids, and glasses as they will interfere with the radiograph and show a ghost image. The patient is draped with a lead apron that covers both front and back of the body to the waist. No thyroid collar is utilized as it would block the X-rays. The patient is instructed to bite down on a bite tab and the operator then exposes the film. The film in the cassette and the panoramic tube head rotate around the patient to obtain the radiograph. The patient is instructed to place his or her tongue on the roof of the mouth and hold very still. The operator must align the patient's Frankfort plane parallel to the floor and the patient's midsagittal plane perpendicular to the floor.

Temporomandibular Joint (TMJ) Views

There are many extraoral radiographs available that view the temporomandibular joint (TMJ) at different views. Submentovertex projection views the joint from under the patient's chin looking up at the TMJ. The panoramic projection can view the TMJ; however, sometimes the glenoid fossa is not in clear view. The anthrogram views the soft tissues of the TMJ. Magnetic resonance imaging (MRI) can also be used to view soft tissue. Other TMJ views include the transcranial, transpharyngeal, tomographic, and transorbital.

Maxillary Sinuses Views

The maxillary sinuses can be viewed in the water's view extraoral radiograph.

Cephalometric View

Commonly used by orthodontists to measure arch size changes, this extraoral view is a lateral profile of the entire skull.

Digital Imaging

More and more dental practices are moving away from traditional film radiography toward digital imaging. Both hardware and software for digital imaging are widely available. There are many advantages to digital radiography. There is less radiation and no chemicals are needed. Over the long term, digital radiographs cost less, and there is no processor maintenance. Images can be manipulated, which allows for better patient understanding when these tools are used while explaining interpretation. Easy duplication allows radiographs to be sent electronically to referred doctors and when filing insurance claims.

Direct Imaging

Charged couple devices (CCDs) are used in direct imaging. They are made of a silicon chip embedded with an electronic circuit. CCDs come in area array detectors and linear array detectors. The area array detectors are used with intraoral digital X-rays and video cameras. They are the size of an intraoral dental film size—0, 1, and 2. The electronic signals that are received by the CCDs are displayed on a computer screen. They are exposed to X-rays. Linear array detectors are used with digital panoramic imaging.

Indirect Imaging

Scanners are used to obtain an image or digitize an existing radiograph.

Phosphor Storage Plates

Phosphor storage plates are made in the same size as number 0, 1, and 2 size intraoral films. They are placed in plastic barriers, then put in the patient's mouth and exposed to X-rays. The plate is then placed into a device that reads the light signal stored on the plate, and the image is displayed on a computer monitor. This uses the same technique as intraoral X-rays, but with less radiation and with digital processing.

Patient Management

The dental assistant must not only be properly skilled and trained to produce clinically acceptable radiographs, but also be able to communicate with patients. Patients who are informed and educated are more likely to cooperate and comply.

Pediatric Radiographic Technique

Exposing dental radiographs on children can be challenging. Children have a tendency to move and sometimes gag. Some basic tips include:

- Explain in simple terms what you are about to do.
- Show the child the film, the camera, and the film holder, and let him or her touch the film prior to placing it in the child's mouth.
- Work quickly and communicate the importance of holding perfectly still so that no retakes will be needed.
- Use the smallest film that can record the most accurate image. Smaller films mean less gagging.
- Utilize occlusal films since they induce less gagging and show all teeth in one arch.
- Praise the child for helping you so much and thank him or her for being such a great helper.

Edentulous Radiographic Technique

Patients with no teeth will need to have radiographs taken to determine bone quality, height, and quantity, and to visualize anatomic structures such as the foramen and the maxillary sinuses and pathologic anomalies. Because of the absence of the teeth, proper film placement is determined by the location of anatomical structures on the face.

Techniques used are the bisecting the angle and paralleling. Cotton rolls can also be used to help hold the film in place.

Endodontic Radiographic Technique

The paralleling technique is the best technique available to obtain an accurate anatomical image. The rubber dam clamp and endodontic files may be in the way and not allow for proper film placement. Using a film holder, the patient may be allowed to hold the film using a Snap-A-Ray or hemostat. The bisecting technique is employed so that the film may be placed parallel to the long axis of the tooth. The X-ray beam is directly perpendicular to the imaginary line that bisects the angle formed by the recording plane of the dental X-ray film and the long axis of the tooth. The tooth being treated should be centered on the film, and 5 mm of bone beyond the apex should be present on the film.

Bisecting the Angle Technique

This technique is used when the paralleling technique cannot be used. In other words, if the film holder cannot be employed, as with edentulous patients, small children, and so on, the bisecting angle technique must be used. The film is placed directly against the teeth to be radiographed. The central beam is directed perpendicular to the line that bisects the angle made by the tooth and the film.

Anatomic Variations

Some patients present the operator with a variety of anatomic variations such as palatal tori, mandibular tori, crowded and/or misaligned teeth, narrow palate, and ankyloglossia (tongue tie). Film placement can be altered to accommodate these variations.

▶ **Practice Questions**

1. The harmful effects of radiation on human tissues are
   a. immediately exhibited.
   b. insignificant.
   c. usually acute.
   d. cumulative.
   e. painful.

2. The protective lead apron must be impregnated with how much lead?
   a. 0.20 mm
   b. 0.22 mm
   c. 0.25 mm
   d. 0.30 mm
   e. 0.35 mm

3. You have a patient who has read articles describing the hazards of medical/dental radiation and is not sure about letting you take X-rays on her. Based on what you now know, how could you explain the procedure in a way that would be reassuring?
   a. You are using a lead apron and lead thyroid shield.
   b. You are using the long cone paralleling technique.
   c. You take radiographs only when a need is indicated by clinical examination, not based on an arbitrary time schedule.
   d. both a and b
   e. all of the above

4. What do filters do in the X-ray beam?
   a. increase density and short waves
   b. reduce density
   c. reduce exposure time
   d. correct the size of the beam
   e. reduce patient radiation dose and remove the long waves

5. The X-ray photons generated by the dental X-ray machine have
   a. the same energy and wavelengths.
   b. many different wavelengths.
   c. only a few energies capable of penetrating dense tissue.
   d. many different speeds.
   e. none of the above.

6. What is the recommended collimation of the radiation beam at the patient's skin surface?
   a. 1.5 inches
   b. 2.75 inches
   c. 3.75 inches
   d. 2.75 cm
   e. both b and d

7. What does the ALARA concept stand for?
   a. as low as reasonably achievable
   b. as little as radiation is allowable
   c. as low as radiation is around
   d. as long as reasonably allowable
   e. none of the above

8. Which of the following devices is an example of personnel monitoring?
   a. film badge
   b. pocket dosimeter
   c. film ring
   d. both a and c
   e. a, b, and c

9. The transfer of energy as it passes through matter is called
   a. reproduction.
   b. cumulative.
   c. mutation.
   d. absorption.
   e. energize.

10. What is it called when a lead disc is used for the elimination of the peripheral portion of the X-ray beam?
   a. filtration
   b. collimation
   c. elongation
   d. ionization
   e. absorption

11. Which molecular changes occur in a living organism being struck by photons?
   a. Molecules break into smaller pieces.
   b. New bonds form within molecules.
   c. Molecular bonds are disrupted.
   d. New bonds form between new molecules.
   e. all of the above

12. What is the correct vertical angulation used when taking a bitewing radiograph?
- **a.** 0 degrees
- **b.** +10 degrees
- **c.** −10 degrees
- **d.** +30 degrees
- **e.** +5 degrees

13. In the bisecting the angle technique, where is the vertical angle of the central beam directed?
- **a.** parallel to the film
- **b.** perpendicular to the line bisecting the angle made by the film and the side of the tongue
- **c.** parallel to the long axis of the tooth
- **d.** perpendicular to the line bisecting the angle made by the long axis of the tooth and the film
- **e.** both b and d

14. What is true of a full-mouth X-ray series?
- **a.** always has periapical and bitewing films
- **b.** has a minimum of 20 films
- **c.** can be replaced by a panoramic film
- **d.** varies in need and number of films according to selection criteria and mouth size
- **e.** both a and d

15. In dental radiography, what infection control procedures are included?
- **a.** sterilization
- **b.** disinfection
- **c.** antiseptic agents
- **d.** both a and b
- **e.** all of the above

16. What is the safest position for an operator while exposing an intraoral film?
- **a.** behind the head of the X-ray unit
- **b.** behind a lead barrier
- **c.** at a 45° angle to the opposite side of the patient's head
- **d.** both b and c
- **e.** all of the above

17. What does immersing the contaminated exposed film packet in a disinfecting solution do?
- **a.** disinfects it
- **b.** destroys the image
- **c.** takes too long
- **d.** makes the images clearer
- **e.** none of the above

18. What needs to happen when exposing a full-mouth set of radiographs?
   a. The PID need not be covered with a barrier if gloves are worn.
   b. A film dispenser should be used.
   c. Unexposed film should be kept on the counter in the room.
   d. The exposure button should be covered with a plastic barrier.
   e. none of the above

19. Where in the X-ray head does thermionic emission take place?
   a. tungsten target
   b. tungsten filament
   c. step-down transformer
   d. PID
   e. both a and b

20. Which radiographic technique records the most accurate image of crowns, roots, and supporting structures of a selected area of the oral cavity?
   a. bitewing film
   b. panoramic film
   c. periapical film
   d. occlusal film
   e. extraoral film

21. The bicuspid/premolar bitewing radiograph should be placed to include which of the following anatomic structures?
   a. all of the mandibular cuspid
   b. the distal half of the mandibular cuspid
   c. the distal half of the maxillary cuspid
   d. the mesial half of the maxillary first premolar
   e. the distal half of the mandibular first molar

22. What is the primary diagnostic use of a bitewing radiograph?
   a. Check for unerupted teeth.
   b. Register the appearance of supporting structures such as bone and soft tissue.
   c. Show a crown preparation, placement, and residual excess cement.
   d. Check the length of the canal for endodontic procedures.
   e. Check for interproximal decay and crestal bone levels.

23. The size-1 film would most likely be used to radiograph which of the following areas on an adult patient?
   a. incisors and cuspids
   b. maxillary bicuspids
   c. mandibular bicuspids if the floor of the mouth is too shallow
   d. mandibular bicuspids
   e. both a and c

24. What causes a herringbone pattern across a film with low density?
   a. static electricity
   b. film bending
   c. the film packet placed backwards
   d. double exposure
   e. a fingernail artifact

25. What determines the speed of the film?
   a. the size of the film
   b. the exposure time
   c. the size of the silver halide crystals
   d. the amount of radiation emitted from the X-ray machine
   e. both b and c

26. Which of the following sequences represents the correct developing and processing procedure for manual processing?
   a. develop, rinse, fix, wash
   b. develop, wash, fix, rinse
   c. fix, wash, develop, rinse
   d. develop, fix, wash, rinse
   e. wash, develop, fix, rinse

27. What is the name of the chemical in the fixer that clears the unexposed silver halide crystals?
   a. metol or hydroquinone
   b. sodium sulfite
   c. ammonium thiosulfate
   d. ammonium bicarbonate
   e. aluminum chloride or sulfide

28. Which chemical-reducing agent is present in the developer and is responsible for building the black and gray tones on a film?
   a. potassium bromide
   b. sodium carbide
   c. ammonium thiosulfate
   d. metol and hydroquinone
   e. ammonium glutaraldehyde

29. What does the term radiographic density describe?
   a. thickness of the emulsion on the film
   b. thickness of the subject (larger patient)
   c. amount of radiation in the X-ray beam
   d. degree of darkness or blackness on the film
   e. varying shades of gray

30. A double exposure occurs when
    a. the film is not exposed to radiation.
    b. the film is exposed to natural light.
    c. the same film is exposed to radiation twice.
    d. the film is overdeveloped.
    e. the film is developed with exhausted solution.

31. Which term describes the loss of electrons from a substance?
    a. braking radiation
    b. scatter radiation
    c. ionization
    d. background radiation
    e. both a and c

32. Which of the following materials is most resistant to the penetration of ionizing radiation?
    a. aluminum
    b. copper
    c. lead
    d. hard plastic
    e. silicon

33. What percentage of the energy generated by the collision between electrons from the cathode and the anode is actually converted to heat?
    a. 99%
    b. 90%
    c. 10%
    d. 2%
    e. 1%

34. If there are no teeth to serve as guides, which of the following landmarks indicates a maxillary molar area radiograph?
    a. incisive foramen
    b. mental foramen and corner of the mouth
    c. internal oblique ridge
    d. tuberosity and near the outer corner of the eye
    e. retromolar pad

35. What is the most likely cause of black spots on a set of bitewings?
    a. fixer splashed on them
    b. developer splashed on them
    c. water splashed on them
    d. fluoride solution on a glove transferred to the film
    e. both b and d

36. Which of the following appears radiolucent on a radiograph?
   a. enamel
   b. implant
   c. dental pulp
   d. amalgam
   e. gold

37. What causes light films?
   a. underdeveloping
   b. underexposure
   c. not enough mA or kV
   d. both a and b
   e. all of the above

38. How does a structure that is radiolucent appear on the radiograph?
   a. light
   b. dark
   c. gray
   d. blue
   e. clear

39. Which restorative materials appear radiopaque on a radiograph?
   a. amalgam
   b. composite
   c. gold crown
   d. both a and c
   e. all of the above

40. Which of the following is a helpful hint for mounting a full-mouth set of radiographs?
   a. Maxillary teeth usually have smaller crowns and shorter roots than mandibular teeth.
   b. The longer side of the film is usually vertical for posterior teeth and horizontal for anterior teeth.
   c. Maxillary molars usually have two roots, and mandibular molars usually have three roots.
   d. The overall appearance of the radiographic survey will have an upward curve like a smile.
   e. both a and d

41. What will too much vertical angulation (either positively or negatively) cause?
   a. foreshortening
   b. elongation
   c. cone cut
   d. overlapping
   e. blurriness

42. What is the primary use for occlusal dental radiographs?
   a. identify caries activity
   b. diagnose periodontal conditions
   c. locate foreign bodies
   d. examine lesions of the mucosa
   e. help determine the length of the root canal

43. What do intensifying screens do?
   a. absorb scatter radiation
   b. contain phosphors that emit blue or green light
   c. increase the amount of radiation needed
   d. increase the amount of exposure time needed
   e. magnify the amount of radiation

44. While taking a panoramic extraoral X-ray, where should the assistant instruct the patient to place his or her tongue?
   a. on the floor of the mouth
   b. on the roof of the mouth (palate)
   c. against the mandibular anterior teeth
   d. to the left side
   e. both a and c

45. Which of the following is not classified as a developmental dental abnormality?
   a. dens in dente
   b. taurodont
   c. periapical abscess
   d. mesiodens
   e. both b and c

46. A charged coupling device (CCD) is primarily made of what substance?
   a. calcium tungsten
   b. ammonium thiosulfate
   c. phosphor
   d. aluminum or lead
   e. silicon

47. If a patient is positioned in a panoramic unit with his or her chin too low, which of the following images might be seen on the resultant radiograph?
   a. wide blurry anterior teeth
   b. molars on one side more magnified than on the other side
   c. flattened curve of Spee
   d. exaggerated curve of Spee
   e. both a and d

48. What technique is best when exposing intraoral films prior to placing an implant?

    a. paralleling technique

    b. bisecting the angle technique

    c. panoramic technique

    d. occlusal technique

    e. both a and b

49. Match the component of the X-ray tube head with the correct letter in the following figure.

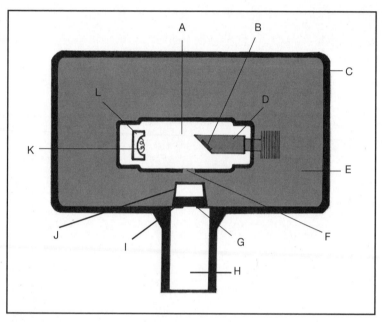

Figure 8.2 Dental X-ray Tube Head

Aluminum filter _____

Anode _____

Cathode _____

Insulating oil _____

Lead collimator _____

Metal housing of X-ray tube head _____

Position indicating device _____

Tube head seal _____

Tungsten filament _____

Tungsten target _____

Unleaded glass window of X-ray tube _____

X-ray tube _____

Answer questions 50–55 using the following figure.

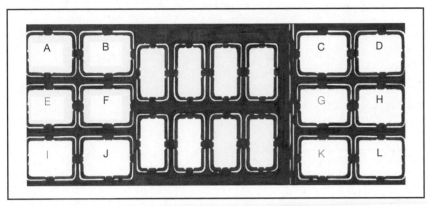

Figure 8.2 Full Mouth X-ray Mount

50. Choose the correct window for proper mounting of the film displayed in the figure below.

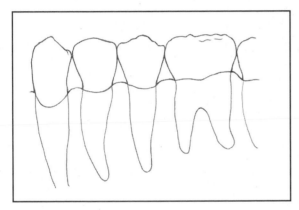

Figure 8.3 X-ray 1

Answer: _____

51. Choose the correct window for proper mounting of the film displayed in the figure below.

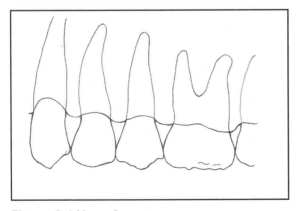

Figure 8.4 X-ray 2

Answer: _____

52. Choose the correct window for proper mounting of the film in the figure below.

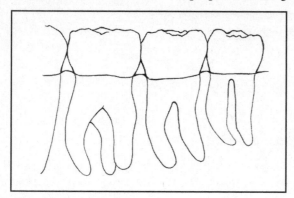

Figure 8.5 X-ray 3

Answer: _____

53. Choose the correct window for proper mounting of the film displayed in the figure below.

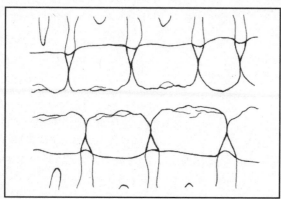

Figure 8.6 X-ray 4

Answer: _____

54. Choose the correct window for proper mounting of the film displayed in the figure below.

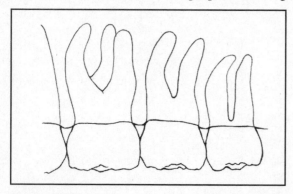

Figure 8.7 X-ray 5

Answer: _____

▶ Practice Answers and Explanations

1. d. The effects of repeated exposure to radiation are cumulative and can result in many different disorders such as cancer, cataracts, leukemia, and genetic abnormalities.

2. c. The lead apron must be impregnated with 0.25 mm of lead to be effective in shielding out the radiation.

3. e. If you have a patient with concerns about radiation exposure, you should explain that you are using a lead apron and lead thyroid shield, you are using the long cone paralleling technique, and you take radiographs only when a need is indicated by clinical examination and not based on an arbitrary time schedule.

4. e. Aluminum filters are used in the PID to filter out the long waves. Only the short waves are useful in making an image on a film. Therefore, the filter removes the long waves and the patient receives less radiation.

5. b. The X-ray photons produced in the tube head have many different wave lengths.

6. b. The recommended collimation or restriction of the size of the X-ray beam at the patient's face is 2.75 inches.

7. a. As Low As Reasonably Achievable is the concept for all radiographers to keep in mind by controlling the amount of radiation the patient receives. Using fast film, at least 60 kV, the aluminum filter, lead collimator, long cone PID, and utilizing the paralleling technique, proper processing, and minimal retakes are all ways to adhere to the ALARA concept.

8. e. Film badges, pocket dosimeters, and film rings are all examples of personnel monitoring devices that measure the dose of radiation received by the members of the dental team.

9. d. The energy of the X-ray beam is transferred to the material through which it passes. This transfer of energy is called absorption.

10. b. Collimation means that a lead disc is used for the elimination of the peripheral portion of the X-ray beam. The lead disc is called the collimator. It restricts the size of the X-ray beam at the patient's face.

11. e. When a living organism is struck by photons, the molecules are broken into smaller pieces, they form new bonds within themselves and with other molecules, and some molecular bonds are disrupted.

12. b. +10 degrees vertical angulation is the correct vertical angulation for taking bitewing radiographs to produce minimal geometric distortion and open the contacts between the teeth.

13. d. In the bisecting the angle technique, the vertical angle of the beam is directed perpendicular to the line that bisects the angle made by the film and the long axis of the tooth being radiographed.

14. a. A full-mouth X-ray series always has periapical and bitewing films.

15. d. In dental radiography, the Snap-A-Ray film holders and XCP film holders are sterilized, and the treatment room is disinfected. No antiseptic agents are used.

16. b. Standing behind the lead barrier is the safest place for the operator while exposing intraoral films.

17. b. Exposed film packets should never be immersed in a disinfecting solution. Immersing them in any liquid will destroy the image. However, it is acceptable to wipe the exposed films with a dry paper towel to remove any saliva or blood.

18. d. Covering the exposure button with a plastic barrier is part of the infection control protocol for exposing X-rays.

19. b. Thermionic emission, which is when the electrons are boiled off of the tungsten filament, takes place in the cathode at the tungsten filament.

20. c. The periapical intraoral film records the most accurate image of crowns, roots, and supporting structures.

21. b. Proper film placement for the bicuspid/premolar bitewing radiograph must include the distal half of the mandibular cuspid. This way the bicuspids will appear in the center of the radiograph.

22. e. The primary diagnostic use of a bitewing radiograph is to check for interproximal decay and examine the crestal bone levels.

23. a. In a 20-film mount full-mouth set of X-rays, the central incisors, lateral incisors, and cuspids are radiographed using a size-1 film.

24. c. If the operator places the film backwards, the resulting image is one with low density and a herringbone pattern on the film.

25. c. The size of the silver halide crystals determines the speed of the film. The fastest film speed available is F speed.

26. a. For manual processing in the darkroom with the developing tanks, the proper sequence for immersion of the films is develop, rinse, fix, and wash.

27. c. Ammonium thiosulfate is the chemical found in fixer solution that clears the unexposed silver halide crystals.

28. d. Metol or hydroquinone is the chemical found in the developer that is responsible for building the black and gray tones.

29. d. Density is the degree of darkness or blackness on the film.

30. c. When the same film is exposed twice, a superimposed image will be the result. This operator error is called a double exposure. To prevent this error, the operator should align the unexposed films on a clean paper barrier. Once the film is exposed, it should be placed into a disposable cup.

31. c. Ionization is the term used to describe a substance losing electrons. Ionization is one of the many results of molecular change caused by radiation.

32. c. Lead is the most resistant material to the penetration of ionizing radiation. This is why the patient is draped with a lead-lined apron and thyroid collar.

33. a. Ninety-nine percent of the energy produced by the collision between electrons from the cathode and the anode is actually converted to heat. Only 1% of the energy produced is converted to X-ray photons.

34. d. On an edentulous patient, the maxillary tuberosity and the outer corner of the eye would serve as the landmarks of the maxillary molar radiograph.

35. b. If developer splashes on a film prior to processing, the result will be a black spot. Splashes of fixer would cause white spots.

36. c. Soft substances such as the dental pulp will appear dark on an X-ray film and are therefore radiolucent.

37. e. Underexposure, underdevelopment, and low mA and kV will all cause a light film.

38. b. A radiolucent structure appears dark on a radiograph.

39. d. Gold and amalgam appear radiopaque on an X-ray film. Both gold and amalgam are solid metal substances. Composite is a form of plastic called resin, which can be filled or unfilled. The filled composite shows radiopaque, just not as bright white as gold or amalgam.

40. d. A full-mouth X-ray survey appears in an upward curve similar to a smile. This curve is called the curve of Spee.

41. a. The resultant image of the operator using too much vertical angulation is foreshortening. The X-ray image is shorter than the actual size of the tooth in the mouth.

42. c. The occlusal radiograph is designed to show the complete arch of teeth, either maxillary or mandibular. Foreign bodies such as tumors or cysts are more readily identified in an occlusal radiograph.

43. b. Intensifying screens contain phosphors that emit blue or green light and are used only in extraoral films. Therefore, extraoral films require less radiation since the intensifying screens are present.

44. b. If the patient does not place his or her tongue on the hard palate, a dark image will appear above the apices of the maxillary anterior teeth.

45. c. A periapical abscess is the result of the death of the dental pulp. This occurs after eruption of the tooth into the mouth and therefore is not a developmental abnormality.

46. e. A charged coupling device (CCD) is made of silicon. This is used in the sensors of digital radiology.

47. d. An exaggerated curve of Spee will be the resultant image on a panoramic X-ray if the patient's chin is too low. Therefore, the operator must make sure that the patient's Frankfort plane is always parallel to the floor.

48. c. Prior to placing a dental implant, the operator needs to examine the bone quality and bone quantity, and locate anatomical structures. The panoramic radiograph is best for this purpose. A patient may be sent to the hospital for medical clearance and an MRI prior to implant placement.

49. A   X-ray Tube
   B   Tungsten Target
   C   Metal Housing of X-ray Tube Head
   D   Anode
   E   Insulating Oil
   F   Unleaded Glass Window of X-ray Tube
   G   Lead Collimator
   H   Position Indicating Device
   I   Aluminum Filter
   J   Tube Head Seal
   K   Tungsten Filament
   L   Cathode

50. k. Andibular left bicuspid periapical

51. c. Maxillary left bicuspid periapical

52. l. Mandibular left molar periapical

53. e. Right molar bitewing

54. d. Maxillary left molar periapical

9 ▶ Dental Office Procedures

CHAPTER OVERVIEW

Dentistry is a healthcare profession that has two main roles. One is to provide quality dental care to the patient and the other role is to profit as a business. The dental team provides oral healthcare that follows the standards set up by the dental profession itself and by federal and state agencies. While providing quality healthcare, the dental practice must run efficiently, safely, be productive, and be a profitable business.

IN ORDER FOR the dental practice to run efficiently, be productive, and make a profit, the dental assistant must understand dental practice management. Dentists are trained in dental school to diagnose dental diseases and problems, and to treat the patient. Dentists do not have as much training in practice management, which is why the business assistant or office manager becomes a vital member of the dental team. It is essential to maintain patient records, process business transactions, and communicate with the patients, staff, dentist, and the community.

One of the main reasons for good communication is patient retention. Patients seldom have cause to leave one dental practice for another because of unskilled or incompetent dentistry; however, they do leave if there was miscommunication with the dentist or the staff over errors on their statement or insurance submission, or if they feel that the dental staff did not clearly explain their treatment plan. This is why leadership and communication is essential in dental practice management.

KEY TERMS

accounts payable	clinical abbreviations	maximum allowable amount
accounts receivable	clinical record	non-expendable supplies
adjustment	consent form	non-participating dentist
advanced appointment system	credit balance	packing slip
aged accounts	debit balance	petty cash
American Dental Association (ADA)	deductible	predetermination
	dependent	prime time
appointment book matrix	direct reimbursement plan	productivity
assignment of benefits	dovetailing	purchase order
back ordered supply	dual insurance	recall/continuing care system
benefit plan summary	expendable supplies	shelf life
birthday rule	Fair Debt Collection	statement
bookkeeping	Practices Act	subscriber
broken appointment	fee schedule	usual, customary, and rea-
buffer period	financial record	sonable (UCR)
capital supplies	inventory system	vital record
carrier	invoice	
charting symbols	limitations	

► Concepts and Skills

In this chapter, the questions will be based on the many characteristics, functions, and tasks of the dental practice business assistant. Dental office procedures consist of eight main topics:

- Effective Leadership Skills
- Working with Dental Office Documents
- Appointment Management
- Continuing Care/Recall Management
- Accounts Receivable Management
- Accounts Payable Management
- Dental Insurance Management
- Supplies/Inventory

Effective Leadership Skills

To be an effective leader one must be enthusiastic, be a team member, accept culturally diverse people, recognize others' needs, be an effective listener and communicator, have self-confidence, be respectful, be organized and have time management skills, and be a genuine person.

Communication Skills

Communication is the process of understanding and being understood. There are many barriers to good communication, such as hearing but not listening, prejudging a person, and being preoccupied with your own ideas and thoughts so that you do not listen to the other person's words.

Dental assistants must develop their communication skills to know how to handle unusual requests. For example, if a new patient calls asking the price to restore his or her complete mouth, the business assistant should ask the patient to come in for an exam and consultation. There are too many variables and unknowns, such as tooth surfaces involved, extent of decay, and periodontal conditions, to give out such information over the phone.

Part of communicating is ensuring that everyone is on the same page, which is why it is essential that every dental office have a personnel manual outlining office staff policies and benefits, along with the rules of the office for employees. All new employees should be given a copy of the company manual and should study it very carefully.

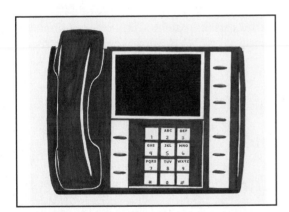

Figure 9.1 Multi-Line Telephone System

Telephone Skills

Ninety percent of all patients are introduced to a dental practice beginning with a telephone call to the office. Therefore, it is vital that the business assistant be knowledgeable in all aspects of dentistry, have excellent verbal skills, be enthusiastic, make the patient feel welcome to the office, and make the patient want to return.

Some telephone features in the dental practice include PC-linked phone systems, cellular phones, hands-free telephone systems, voicemail, call holding, caller identification, conference calling, speed dialing, and music-on-hold.

Working with Dental Office Documents

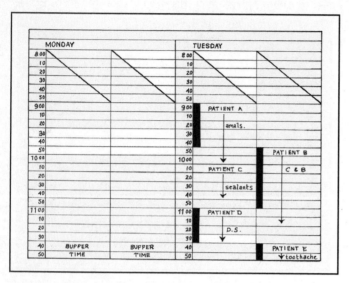

Figure 9.2 Paper Dental Files

The assistant must understand the importance of the Health Insurance Portability and Accountability Act (HIPAA). This is a federal act that requires the dental office to transmit certain patient health information electronically to protect the health information. This act also covers keeping the patient's personal and financial information private.

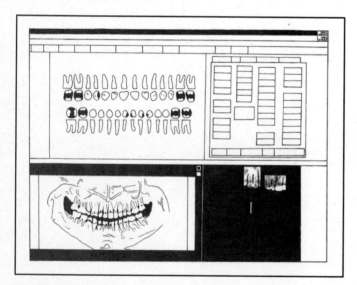

Figure 9.3 Electronic Dental Records

The patient's record consists of many documents. These records can be kept on paper, in electronic form, or both. The health history and registration form is completed on the patient's first visit to the office. The clinical chart is where the assistant and doctor note the findings of the examination and indicate all procedures completed. There are three different tooth numbering systems (see Chapter 7), and charting symbols are used along with clinical abbreviations to note information in the patient's clinical chart.

Parts of the patient's clinical record include:

Health History

The health history gives the doctor an overview of the patient's past and present medical conditions, medications, and allergies.

Registration Form

The registration form provides the patient's personal and financial information. This includes facts such as address, employer, birth date, insurance information, and so on.

Clinical Chart

The clinical chart identifies any of the patient's pre-existing conditions, and it is also here that the dentist outlines the treatment plan and services rendered.

Treatment Plans

Once the dentist has thoroughly examined the patient, he or she will prepare a written treatment plan that outlines the proposed treatment, an estimate of the costs, and any other options. Dental assistants must be familiar with all dental terminology to be able to understand and explain treatment plans. For example, if a plan shows an MOD restoration on tooth #3, that is a three-surface restoration on a maxillary molar. Then, if it calls for a PFM crown on tooth #30, the assistant should know that is a porcelain-to-metal crown on a mandibular molar. Similarly, treatment for tooth #19 in the Universal Numbering System refers to the mandibular left first molar. An assistant can explain how pit and fissure sealants prevent decay on the developmental faults on both primary and permanent teeth.

Prescriptions

Dentists write prescriptions for medications as needed, and a copy is usually made and stored in the patient's dental chart.

Lab Requisitions

The dentist must create a written requisition for each appliance to be fabricated in the dental laboratory. This includes partials, dentures, crowns, bridges, surgical stents, athletic mouth guards, and bleaching trays.

Radiographs

Radiographs are usually taken on new patients and periodically on returning patients at their recall appointments. Radiographs may be taken digitally or with film. There are two types of radiographs: intraoral or extraoral.

Intraoral Pictures

The dental office may utilize an intraoral camera to document the patient's intraoral condition. These pictures are either printed or stored electronically in the patient's chart.

Referrals/Correspondence from Other Doctors

The office may receive letters or radiographs from specialists or referring doctors that may become part of the patient's chart.

Consent Forms and Other Non-Clinical Documents

Once details of the dental treatment plan have been explained, the patient must then sign an informed consent form. Minors must have a parent or guardian sign the consent form. No work can be done without a signed consent form. For example, if a 14-year-old arrived at the dental office for a scheduled treatment without the forms signed by a parent or guardian, the dental assistant would have to reschedule the patient.

The ledger, which shows the financial record of the patient's dental care, is part of the patient's record; however, it is not part of the clinical record.

Filing systems are used to store records. There are different types of filing systems used in a dental office. These include: alphabetical, numerical, chronological, subject, and geographical. The alphabetical system places charts or documents in alphabetical order by the last name, then first name. Chronological filing would be by the date (1–31), and is used when storing insurance claims. Subject filing is also done alphabetically by the name of the subject. Geographical filing is done by a division of territory (state, city, or street).

Recall cards are filed in a chronological file system, patient records are filed in an alphabetical file system or a numerical filing system, and the contents inside the patient's record are filed in chronological order with the most current contents at the top.

A tickler file is a chronological file used to remind the assistant of daily, weekly, or monthly tasks to be completed.

Appointment Management

The dental office's success pivots on the appointment scheduling. This task may be assigned to one individual in the practice who then can implement the practice's scheduling policies.

The usual sequence of an appointment is:

1. Initial examination appointment
2. Diagnosis and formulation of treatment plan
3. Consultation with patient regarding treatment plan
4. Treatment appointment scheduled

Figure 9.4 Dental Filing System

Appointment books are either traditional paper books or computerized. There are many advantages in using the computerized book. These advantages include neatness and legibility, ability to access the patient's record and treatment plan, and various screen viewing modes. Additionally, operators or treatment rooms can be color coded, daily and monthly production can be monitored and scheduled, procedures can be posted to several different records from only one entry, and searching for appointment openings can be made easier. The one advantage a paper book has over a computerized book is if the power goes out or the computer crashes, there is still a way to see who is scheduled to come in. Some dental practices still use paper appointment books as a backup to the electronic system, while others perform a daily electronic backup.

Dental assistants must be familiar with logistics to ensure proper timing of appointments and managing time slots accordingly. For example, bridge work is generally done in two stages. The dental assistant must know how long the lab needs to prepare and then return the denture to the dental office in order to book the cementation appointment for an appropriate date. It is frustrating for everyone if the patient turns up for an appointment but there is no denture to be placed. Therefore, a crown cementation appointment is usually scheduled two weeks after the preparation appointment to allow the lab sufficient time.

It is best to schedule young children in the early morning so as not to interfere with their nap times. Older patients often like appointments in the late mornings or early afternoons to avoid rush hour traffic, and sometimes find it difficult to move quickly in the early morning. Late afternoon and evening appointments are good for working adults. Patients with special needs should be accommodated. For example, diabetic patients should be given early morning appointments. That way, patients can have their medication and eat a normal breakfast so that their sugar level is not compromised. If the surgery is completed at 8:30, the patient will be able to have lunch and keep glucose levels stable.

Emergency patients are asked specific questions on the phone when they call, such as:

"How long have you been in discomfort?"
"Which area of the mouth are you experiencing discomfort?"
"Is the discomfort a sharp pain or dull ache?"
"Is the tooth sensitive to hot, cold, or pressure?"

Emergency patients should be reassured that the dentist will see them as soon as possible to help relieve their discomfort.

The appointment book has a matrix, which is the framework or outline of the schedule. Holidays, lunch hours, starting times, ending times, vacations, continuing education seminars and meetings, and buffer times are all elements of the matrix.

A unit is an increment of time used when determining the length of the particular appointment. Most dental appointment books are made up of ten- or 15-minute units.

A buffer period is a short period of time in the day that is left open for scheduling emergency patients or used as catch-up time for the dentist and chairside assistant in a busy schedule. When a patient does not

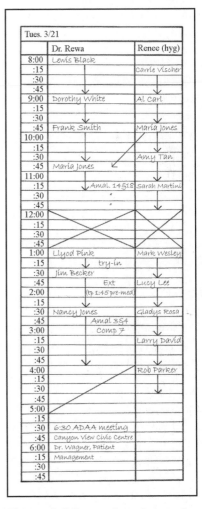

Figure 9.5 Paper Appointment Book

show up and does not call to cancel, this is known as a broken appointment. Skilled assistants are able to juggle these open time slots so that the dentist and staff are never idle. The assistant and dentist can use any extra time in the open schedule to write up charts, pour models, return patient phone calls, or make lab pick-up arrangements.

Prime time is the time most requested by patients. This is usually the first and last appointments of the day. Many working patients or parents prefer early morning or late afternoon appointments. This way, they can stop at the dental office before work or school, or leave straight from their dental appointment and go home in the afternoon.

A treatment plan is a list of the dental procedures to be completed for the patient, and it is divided into appointment visits with specific time allotments for each visit. The appointments are made based on the treatment plan. They are listed from most urgent to least important or elective procedures.

Short appointments can be dovetailed, which means working a second patient into the schedule during another patient's long treatment appointment, either at the beginning or end of the long appointment. The second patient is booked so that the chairside assistant can remain with the first patient while the dentist examines the second patient.

Production goals should be considered when appointing patient treatment. The office usually sets a minimum figure of how many new patients, units of crown and bridge, and hygiene production are done on a daily basis. This minimum goal is what covers the office overhead.

Continuing Care/Recall Management

A continuing care or recall system notifies patients when they are due to return to the dental office for routine dental care. This system helps patients maintain good oral health for a lifetime.

A routine cleaning and examination is the most common reason for the patient's recall visit. However, the patient may need to return to the office for other reasons, such as a limited exam of the treatment site after surgery, a limited exam of an eruption of a particular tooth, exam of a full or partial, follow-up on an endodontic treatment, or follow-up on an implant.

There are three types of continuing care/recall systems:

- Advanced Appointment Recall System
- Telephone Recall System
- Mail Recall System

Advanced Appointment Recall System

The recall visit is scheduled before the patient leaves the office. A continuing care/recall postcard is mailed out as a notice or reminder of the patient's pre-scheduled appointment. The advantage is that no extra cost or time is involved for the business assistant, and it projects future production in the appointment book.

Telephone Recall System

The business assistant calls patients when they are due for their recall visit and schedules the appointment. The disadvantage is that this system is very time-consuming.

Mail Recall System

A recall postcard is mailed to patients notifying them that they are due for their recall appointment, and they call the office for an appointment. Recall/continuing care postcards are filed in a chronological file and mailed out two weeks prior to the appointment date. These should be issued according to HIPAA guidelines. The disadvantages of this system are that it is costly and time-consuming.

Accounts Receivable Management

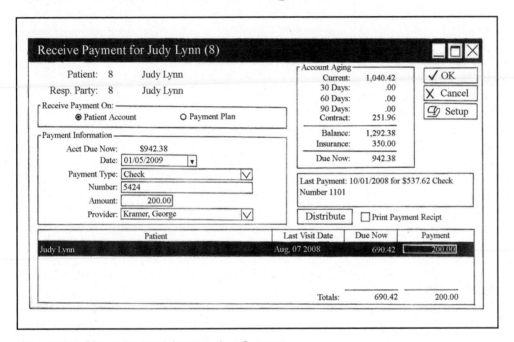

Figure 9.6 Computerized Accounting Systems

Accounts receivable is the total amount of money owed to the dentist for services rendered. The daily charges (fees for dental services) are posted onto the patient's ledger. The payments received are also posted to the patient's ledger. The total balance on all the patient's ledgers is the accounts receivable. The total accounts receivable is either owed to the doctor by the patient or the patient's dental insurance company.

There are times when patients cannot afford to pay for all services received, in which cases financial arrangements must be discussed with the patient. These arrangements often take the form of a payment schedule. These can be tailored based on the patient's ability to pay versus the dental office's need for income. As creditor or lender, the dental office is required to complete a Truth in Lending form, which is a federal document used when a treatment plan is extended to four or more monthly payments.

Bookkeeping is the process of recording financial transactions. Keeping accurate records is essential in account management. It is always best to take your time and double check the entries. For example, at the end of the day, all money, checks, and credit card slips must be deposited with a proper deposit slip. The total amount on that slip should agree with the payments column on the day sheet.

All daily charges are posted to the patient's account ledger. All payments made are also posted to the patient's ledger as they are collected. The total amount of the checks, cash, and credit card payments made must agree with the total of monies posted as payments in the computer that will be printed on a daily transaction sheet.

A debit balance is the amount owed to the dentist for services rendered. A credit balance is a total of what the dentist owes a patient. Credit balances usually stem from patients paying for services in advance (before the services are completed).

Statements or bills are mailed to the patients to show them their financial status and amount owed to the dentist. The statement indicates the charges, payments, and adjustments made to their account. Adjustments to the patient's accounts include professional adjustment, senior citizen discount, family discount, returned check fee, and, in some offices, service charges for balances that are over three months old.

The balance on the statement or ledger is the total amount of money owed to the dentist. The balance is aged into categories showing the patient how long the balance has been owed. The aging categories are current, 30–60 days, 60–90 days, and over 90 days.

An accounts receivable report is generated monthly so that the business assistant can follow up on the money owed by call or sending letters to the patient and/or the insurance company. Legal guidelines must be followed to avoid harassment of patients when collecting overdue amounts. When you have exhausted all other avenues trying to collect a patient's debt, the final step is to contact a collection agency. When working with accounts receivable, it is important to follow the Fair Debt Collection Practices Act, a federal act passed to protect the patient from unethical collection procedures.

Financial arrangements or payment plans can be arranged with the patient. Credit bureaus can be called for credit reports on patients that are setting up payment plans with the office if the business assistant has obtained the patient's consent.

Accounts Payable Management

Accounts payable refers to the amount of money owed by the dentist to others to run the dental practice. This is often referred to as overhead. The office overhead is much like running a household. The income is portioned out to cover monthly expenses. The following are some costs that dental businesses must consider.

Office Mortgage or Lease

The cost of the office space, whether it be leased (long term) or purchased through a mortgage, is an office expense. It is the most costly of all of the doctor's overhead expenses. Some dentists will share office space or building space with other medical/dental professionals in order to cut down on this overhead expense.

Utilities

The utilities are the same as your water and electric bill at home. The dentist must pay for the electricity, water, and sewage for the dental practice.

Dental Supplies

Dental supplies are an ongoing overhead expense. These are usually divided into two categories: expendables and capital expenses. Capital expenses include big ticket items such as equipment, computers, etc. Expendables are those consumable supplies that are used daily and must be replenished.

Staff Salaries/Payroll

Staff salaries are a major portion of accounts payable. To attract the best employees, you have to pay the best salaries. Employee benefits range from medical coverage to retirement plans, and this is often a large part of payroll expenses. A benefit plan summary is a description of the benefits that the employer offers to the employee.

Additional payroll expenses include preparing paychecks, making deductions, and completing the necessary forms, all of which are time-consuming. The Federal Insurance Contributions Act (FICA) is the federal law that requires employers to withhold taxes for Social Security and Medicare programs.

Payroll Taxes

A yearly wage and tax statement for each employee is made on the W-2 form, showing the income, taxes, and other deductions.

Insurance

The dentist may pay all or a portion of medical insurance premiums for the staff.

Petty Cash

A small amount of money is kept in the office for incidental expenses or making change for cash-paying patients.

Dental Insurance Management

Many patients have dental insurance and, as a courtesy, the dental office will often bill the insurance company directly for the dental services rendered using a claim form. A claim form is generated for every date of service. The claims are either printed on paper and faxed, or mailed to the insurance company, or created digitally and sent electronically to the insurance company using the computer. Electronic claims are either sent to a clearing house or directly to the insurance company. A clearing house pre-screens the dental insurance claim to ensure that all pertinent information is complete and correct.

Under the HIPAA, all healthcare providers, health plans, and healthcare clearing houses that transmit data electronically must use a universal language and a standard format. The universal language is the American Dental Association (ADA) *Current Dental Terminology* (CDT) *Code on Dental Procedures and Nomenclature*. Each specific dental procedure is identified by a code.

The codes start with a D, are followed by four numerals, and are categorized according to the type of procedure. The CDT has a complete list of the current dental procedure codes, along with a description of the procedure.

Dental insurance policies can be quite complex, and there is a wide variation in procedures covered from one insurance company to the next. Dental insurance plans outline payments based on a set fee allowance for each dental procedure, known as a fee schedule. Benefit plans often have certain restrictions or limitations that may include age limits for particular procedures, waiting periods, and frequency of certain services.

The percentage of the insurance claim the company will pay depends on the type of procedure and the insurance contract. Because of the complicated nature of insurance policies, it is difficult to predict which procedure and what percentage a particular policy will cover. That is why dentists submit treatment plans to the insurance companies before starting work to get an estimate of how much of the treatment will be covered. This is known as predetermination of benefits.

The highest total amount an insurance carrier will pay toward the cost of dental treatment in a given benefit period is known as the annual maximum allowable amount. Dental procedures must be properly categorized for insurance purposes. For example, adult prophylaxis and study models are considered preventative/diagnostic services.

If a patient has two insurance policies, this is termed dual insurance. The two insurance companies coordinate their benefits. The first company billed is the primary carrier and the other is the secondary carrier. When more than one carrier is involved, benefits are coordinated in two possible ways:

- Standard coordination of benefits
- Non-duplication of benefits

The subscriber is the person who owns the insurance policy, and a dependent is a spouse or child of the subscriber. The subscriber signs the assignment of benefits line on the dental insurance claim form. The assignment of benefits is the authorization by the subscriber for the dental carrier to issue benefits directly to the provider, who is the treating dentist. When the assignment of benefits line is signed by the patient, the payment on the claim is paid directly to the dental office.

The insured person must pay the deductible portion of the total dental treatment costs before the benefits go into effect.

Generally, dental insurance plans cover minor children, but adult children may be covered by the parent's policy if they are full-time students. When both parents have dental plans, the primary carrier is determined by the parents' birth dates. The one with the birthday closest to January is the primary carrier. This is known as the birthday rule. Children of divorced parents, each with a dental plan, are generally covered by the plan of the parent with whom the child lives. This is known as the primary carrier. The plan of the other parent is known as the secondary carrier.

There are many abbreviations used in dentistry and dental insurance. For example, UCR stands for usual, customary, reasonable. For more about commonly used abbreviations, consult the appendix at the back of this book. Every dental procedure has an ADA code that is required on each dental claim form for each procedure billed to the insurance carrier. Each procedure description and procedure code is listed on a single line on the claim form.

"Signature on file" is written on all claims instead of the subscriber's signature so that the claim forms can be billed electronically. A "signature on file" card is signed by the patient on the first visit and kept inside the record.

The provider is the attending dentist who performs the dental treatment. The provider's name, address, license number, tax ID number, and phone number are all listed on every claim form.

Supplies/Inventory

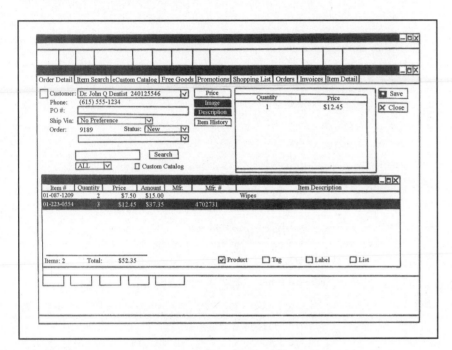

Figure 9.7 Computerized Inventory Control Systems

Dental supplies can be divided into three categories: expendable, non-expendable, and capital.

Expendable Supplies

Expendable supplies are single-use items that are disposable and thrown away after one use. Examples include cotton rolls, gauze, local anesthetic, stationery, plastic barriers, gloves, and headrest covers.

Non-Expendable Supplies

Non-expendable supplies are reusable items that are not a major expense. Examples include most dental instruments, curing lights, and hand pieces. These supplies are sterilized and then reused.

Capital Supplies

Capital supplies are the more costly items that are seldom replaced, for example, computers, sterilizers, dental chairs, and dental units.

An inventory system is a list of all supplies used in the dental office that includes capital, expendable, and non-expendable items. Capital items are usually tracked on a spreadsheet or individual cards. Expendable and non-expendable items are tracked using either a computerized inventory system, or a manual card or list inventory system. If a card system is used, an individual card represents each item.

Inventory system information is usually tracked according to the minimum order amount, maximum order amount, date ordered, amount ordered, unit price, and arrival date of the item, along with the product name, brand name, supplier name, and the supplier's address and phone number.

The amount ordered of each item is based upon the shelf life of the item, the rate of use, the amount of money available for purchase, the amount of storage space, the supplier's delivery time, and the special pricing of the item.

Purchase orders are used for large institutions and often include standardized order forms for the supplies. A packing slip is enclosed with the items when they arrive, and it specifies the contents of the package, the amount of items enclosed, and any items that are on back order. An invoice is a list of the cost of the contents in the package, and can also be a statement unless the supplier sends separate statements. The invoices must be compared to the statement that is received at the end of the month, and they must correspond.

If an item ordered is not in stock and will be shipped at a later date, a back order memo is issued and the supplier will ship the item when it becomes available.

If an item is returned to the supplier, a credit memo is issued for the amount of the item.

Any supply that contains hazardous material must come with a material safety data sheet (MSDS). This sheet is provided to the purchaser by the manufacturer, and it provides information about the hazardous material. The U.S. government requires that MSDS sheets be saved and filed for employee and Occupational Safety and Health Administration (OSHA) reference. All team members must know where to find the MSDS book in an office. Biohazard labels must be affixed accordingly to any items that are transferred to alternate containers.

▶ Practice Questions

1. What is the third barrier to good communication in addition to preoccupation and not listening?
   a. prejudging
   b. selective perception
   c. body language
   d. motivation
   e. none of the above

2. On the first visit, each patient must complete what form along with the registration form?
   a. a treatment plan
   b. an insurance claim form
   c. a health history form
   d. a prescription
   e. a dental lab slip

3. What is the dental specialty that deals with the movement of teeth and the correction of malocclusions?
   a. pediatric dentistry
   b. endodontics
   c. prosthodontics
   d. orthodontics
   e. periodontics

4. What is the dental specialty that deals with the gingival, surrounding tissue, and bone?
   a. pediatric dentistry
   b. endodontics
   c. prosthodontics
   d. orthodontics
   e. periodontics

5. What is the main concern of the dental public health?
   a. treatment of diseases of the pulp
   b. preventing and controlling dental diseases, and promoting dental health through organized community efforts
   c. the nature of the diseases affecting the teeth
   d. restoring severely decayed teeth in children
   e. preventing tooth loss in senior citizens

6. What is the best way to ensure that a patient will arrive for his or her dental appointment?
   a. confirm the patient's appointment
   b. educate the patient
   c. charge the patient a fee for missed appointments
   d. pick up the patient
   e. coordinate a ride for the patient

7. What is the regularly scheduled time for emergencies called?
   a. buffer period
   b. productivity
   c. units
   d. dovetail
   e. both a and d

8. What are the prime appointments in the scheduling day?
   a. during lunch
   b. any time of the day
   c. first and last appointments of the day
   d. immediately after lunch
   e. at 11:00 A.M.

9. If an appointment book has six time slots per hour, how much time does each unit represent?
   a. 5 minutes
   b. 10 minutes
   c. 15 minutes
   d. 20 minutes
   e. 30 minutes

10. Staff meetings, holidays, dentist and staff vacations, and starting and closing times are all components of what?
   a. office recall system
   b. calendar
   c. matrix
   d. units in the day
   e. both a and c

11. What is the correct sequence for a patient's appointments?
   a. initial exam, diagnosis and treatment plan, consultation, scheduling appointments
   b. consultation, initial exam, diagnosis and treatment plan, scheduling appointments
   c. diagnosis and treatment plan, scheduling appointments, consultation, initial exam
   d. scheduling appointments, diagnosis and treatment plan, consultation, initial exam

12. Take-home pay is the amount for which a check is written after all deductions (taxes) have been taken out. What is this called?
  a. gross pay
  b. net pay
  c. withholding payroll
  d. annual income
  e. month-to-date pay

13. How is FICA commonly described?
  a. federal income tax
  b. state withholding tax
  c. state disability
  d. social security
  e. local taxes

14. Which of the following records is considered a vital record?
  a. bank reconciliation
  b. recall card
  c. cancelled checks
  d. petty cash voucher
  e. patient's clinical chart

15. Which tooth numbering system uses a 1–32 numeric system for the permanent dentition and an A–Z letter system for the primary teeth?
  a. Palmer Notation System
  b. Bracket System
  c. Universal System
  d. ADA System
  e. CDA System

16. How many teeth are present in the primary dentition?
  a. 18
  b. 20
  c. 30
  d. 32
  e. 36

17. The crown cementation appointment is usually scheduled how long after the crown preparation appointment?
   a. one week
   b. two weeks
   c. four weeks
   d. two days
   e. none of the above

18. What is the system in which all of the dental practice costs are organized, verified, categorized, and paid?
   a. accounts receivable
   b. accounts payable
   c. accounts billing
   d. pre-treatment estimate
   e. both b and c

19. If a new patient calls and asks the price to restore his or her complete mouth, what should the business assistant do?
   a. estimate the price on the phone
   b. refer the patient elsewhere
   c. put the dentist on the phone to discuss treatment and quote prices
   d. ask the patient to come in for an exam and consultation
   e. ask the patient to call back at another time

20. If a treatment plan shows an MOD restoration on tooth #3, which procedure needs to be performed?
   a. two-surface restoration on a maxillary bicuspid
   b. three-surface restoration on a maxillary molar
   c. three-surface restoration on a mandibular molar
   d. three-surface restoration on a mandibular bicuspid
   e. three-surface restoration on a maxillary right second molar

21. If a treatment plan shows a PFM crown on tooth #30, which procedure needs to be performed?
   a. a full gold crown on a maxillary molar
   b. a porcelain-to-metal crown on a maxillary molar
   c. a full gold crown on a mandibular molar
   d. a porcelain-to-metal crown on a mandibular molar
   e. both c and d

22. When completing a deposit slip, the total amount on the slip should agree with which column on the day sheet?
    a. accounts receivable
    b. charges
    c. production
    d. payments
    e. both a and d

23. What are the total charges for dental treatment rendered on a given day called?
    a. accounts payable
    b. accounts receivable
    c. production
    d. patient balances
    e. both b and c

24. If a treatment plan total is $2,000, and the patient makes an $800 down payment on the first visit and then three equal monthly payments on the remainder of the balance, what is the monthly payment?
    a. $300
    b. $400
    c. $500
    d. $600
    e. $1,000

25. If a 15-year-old patient shows up for his or her appointment for sealants on all four permanent first molars, and a treatment plan and consent form have not been signed by one of the parents, what must be done?
    a. The treatment should be performed; it is only sealants.
    b. The patient must sign a consent form for the treatment.
    c. You should contact the parents and try to obtain consent for treatment over the telephone.
    d. You should reschedule the patient to return after written consent is received.
    e. both c and d

26. How long after a three-unit bridge preparation appointment should the cementation appointment be made?
    a. one month
    b. after the patient has paid for it, or the patient portion
    c. when the insurance claim has been filed
    d. when the lab schedule allows for it to be returned to the dentist
    e. after the insurance carrier has paid for it

27. What appointment time is best for oral surgery on a diabetic patient?
    a. 8:30 A.M.
    b. 11:00 A.M.
    c. 2:00 P.M.
    d. 3:30 P.M.
    e. 4:30 P.M.

28. Which of the following documents is recommended for a new staff employee in the office?
    a. office policy
    b. daily schedule
    c. recall report
    d. personnel manual
    e. accounts receivable report

29. In the Universal Tooth Numbering System, which is tooth #19?
    a. mandibular left first molar
    b. mandibular left second molar
    c. mandibular right third molar
    d. mandibular right first molar
    e. mandibular left second bicuspid

30. Why are pit and fissure sealants recommended?
    a. to restore dental caries on the occlusal surfaces
    b. to correct discoloration from extrinsic stains
    c. to prevent decay on the developmental faults on both primary and permanent teeth
    d. to prevent decay on teeth with existing composite restorations
    e. both c and d

31. What is the final step in collections?
    a. a severe letter
    b. a nasty telephone call
    c. another nasty phone call
    d. collection agency
    e. both b and d

32. A yearly wage and tax statement is on which of the following forms?
    a. W-4 form
    b. 940 form
    c. 941 form
    d. W-2 form
    e. 1040 form

33. On a dental insurance claim form, who signs the assignment of benefits line?
   a. dentist
   b. subscriber
   c. assistant
   d. carrier
   e. dependent

34. When the patient is not available to sign a claim form, what is the acceptable procedure?
   a. Submit the claim for predetermination.
   b. Type in "signature not available."
   c. Type in "signature on file."
   d. Leave the signature boxes blank.
   e. all of the above choices would be acceptable.

35. On an insurance claim, the percentage of payment will vary depending on:
   a. the type of procedure.
   b. the insurance contract.
   c. where the patient seeks dental treatment.
   d. both a and b
   e. all of the above

36. What does the term *insurance carrier* refer to in insurance management?
   a. insurance company
   b. employer
   c. dependent
   d. dentist
   e. insurance benefits

37. Where are insurance codes and procedures for dental treatment located?
   a. office procedures manual
   b. Centers for Disease Control (CDC) publication
   c. CDT, published by the American Dental Association (ADA)
   d. OSHA regulations
   e. ADA journal

38. The dentist submits the treatment plan to the carrier before treatment begins to get an estimate of how much of the treatment will be covered. What is this called?
   a. predetermination of benefits
   b. coordination of benefits
   c. eligibility
   d. financial arrangements
   e. pre-existing conditions

39. How would you arrange the following names in alphabetical filing order?
   a. John T. Hamilton Jr., Steven Hanley, John T. Hamilton Sr.
   b. Steven Hanley, John T. Hamilton Jr., John T. Hamilton Sr.
   c. John T. Hamilton Sr., John T. Hamilton Jr., Steven Hanley
   d. John T. Hamilton Jr., John T. Hamilton Sr., Steven Hanley
   e. Steven Hanley, John T. Hamilton Sr., John T. Hamilton Jr.

40. When the assignment of benefits is signed by the patient on an insurance claim form, who receives the money?
   a. patient
   b. carrier
   c. employee
   d. provider
   e. dependent

41. What is the stipulated sum called that an insured person must pay toward the cost of dental treatment before the benefits go into effect?
   a. maximum
   b. coinsurance
   c. deductible
   d. exclusion
   e. co-payment

42. Why would dental insurance still cover a 19-year-old?
   a. patient is paying for his or her own insurance
   b. patient is working and is a part-time student
   c. patient is a full-time student
   d. patient is living at home
   e. none of the above

43. What does UCR stand for in dental insurance?
   a. unusual, customary, reasonable
   b. usual, carrier, reasonable
   c. usual, customary, reasonable
   d. usual, coverage, reasonable
   e. usual, customary, receivable

44. What are adult prophylaxis and study models considered when categorizing procedures for insurance?
   a. major services
   b. basic services
   c. routine services
   d. preventative/diagnostic services
   e. specialty services

45. When the child's parents are divorced, and there are two dental plans, how are the primary and secondary carrier generally determined?
  a. the parents' birth dates
  b. the father is always primary
  c. the mother is always primary
  d. the parent with whom the child resides
  e. the parent who brings the child to the dental office

46. When the child's parents are married and there are two dental plans, how are the primary and secondary carrier generally determined?
  a. the parents' birth dates
  b. the child's birth dates
  c. the mother is always primary
  d. the father is always primary
  e. none of the above

47. Where should all continuing care/recall postcards be kept?
  a. in the patient's chart
  b. in an alphabetical file under the patient's last name
  c. in an alphabetical file under the patient's first name
  d. in a chronological file according to the patient's recall appointment
  e. in a chronological file according to the patient's date of birth

48. What is the petty cash fund used to purchase?
  a. office equipment
  b. dental supplies
  c. small incidental purchases
  d. staff lunches
  e. none of the above

49. When should dental supply invoices be checked by the business assistant?
  a. as the shipment is being unpacked
  b. against the packing slip
  c. weekly
  d. monthly
  e. both a and b

50. Which dental supply when purchased is supplied with a material safety and data sheet (MSDS)?
  a. X-ray film
  b. glutaraldehyde solution
  c. ZOE cement
  d. orange solvent
  e. all of the above

▶ Practice Answers and Explanations

1. a. Prejudging, preoccupation, and non-listening are the three barriers to good communication.

2. c. The health history is completed along with the patient registration form on the patient's first visit.

3. d. Orthodontics is the dental specialty that deals with the correction of malocclusions and the movement of teeth.

4. e. Periodontics is the dental specialty that deals with diseases of the gingival tissue and surrounding tissue and bone.

5. b. Preventing and controlling dental diseases and promoting dental health through organized community efforts is the main concern of dental public health.

6. a. Confirmation of a patient's appointment is usually done two days prior to the appointment and is the best way to ensure that patients will arrive for their dental appointment.

7. a. A buffer period is a short amount of time set aside for emergencies.

8. c. The prime appointments of the day are the appointment times most frequently requested and are first thing in the morning and last thing in the afternoon.

9. b. If there are six time slots or units in an hour, then each unit is worth ten minutes.

10. c. The appointment book matrix consists of components such as starting and closing times, lunch hours, staff meetings, vacations, and holidays. The matrix is the framework on which appointments can be scheduled.

11. a. The correct sequence for a patient's appointment is initial exam, diagnosis and treatment plan, consultation, and scheduling of treatment appointments.

12. b. The net pay is the total gross pay less the deductions such as taxes and social security benefits.

13. d. FICA represents the social security benefits withdrawn from an employee's check.

14. e. The patient's clinical chart is a vital record that cannot be replaced. All documentation and charting is completed in the patient's clinical chart.

15. c. The Universal System is the tooth numbering system that uses number 1–32 to identify the permanent dentition, and the letters A–T to identify the primary dentition.

16. b. There are 20 teeth present in the primary dentition. There are 32 teeth present in the permanent dentition.

17. b. The crown cementation or crown seat appointment is usually scheduled two weeks after the crown preparation appointment, depending upon the request of the lab.

18. b. Accounts payable is the system in which all of the dental practice costs are organized, verified, categorized, and paid. These costs include dental supplies, staff salaries, lab fees, rent, and insurance.

19. d. If a patient calls and requests a price or cost for a particular procedure other than an exam or cleaning, the assistant should ask the patient to schedule an exam and consultation so that a cost can be given to the patient after the doctor examines the patient's oral cavity.

20. b. #3-MOD. The restoration is a three-surface restoration on the maxillary right first molar.

21. d. #30-PFM. The crown is a porcelain fused-to-metal crown on the mandibular right first molar.

22. d. The total of the payments column of the day sheet should always agree with the total amount on the deposit slip when preparing a deposit.

23. c. Production is the total charges or dental treatment rendered on a given day.

24. b. The total is $2000 less the $800 down payment, leaving a $1,200 balance. $1,200 divided by three monthly payments is $400 per month for three months.

25. d. Dental treatment on minors must have a consent form signed by the parent. A 15-year-old is a minor.

26. d. The dental laboratory schedule determines the delivery date for the new cast restoration.

27. a. The best time for an oral surgery appointment for diabetic patients is 8:30 A.M. This way, the patients can have their medication and eat a normal breakfast so that their sugar level is not compromised. If the surgery is completed at 8:30, the patient will be able to have lunch.

28. d. The personnel manual lists the office staff policies and benefits, along with the rules of the office for employees.

29. a. The mandibular left first molar is denoted as #19 in the Universal System.

30. c. Pit and fissure sealants are recommended to prevent decay on the developmental faults on both primary and permanent teeth.

31. d. The final step in collections after collection calls and letters are made is referring the account to a collection agency.

32. d. The W-2 form is the yearly wage and tax statement that every employer issues to each employee.

33. b. The subscriber signs the assignment of benefits line on a dental insurance claim to allow the insurance carrier to pay the provider directly for the dental services rendered.

34. c. The words "signature on file" are printed on the subscriber signature line when the computer generates the dental claim form. This is in lieu of the subscriber's signature. The patient/subscriber signs a "signature on file" form on the first visit.

35. d. The percentage of payment that the insurance carrier pays depends upon the type of procedure, the insurance contract, and where the patient seeks the dental treatment.

36. a. The term *insurance carrier* refers to the insurance company.

37. c. The *CDT*, published by the American Dental Association, contains the individual codes and descriptions for every procedure to be printed on the dental claim form.

38. a. The pre-determination of benefits is an estimate of how much the insurance carrier will pay on a given treatment plan.

39. d. The names are filed in alphabetical order based on the last name, then first name, then middle name and Jr. or Sr. Therefore, the correct order is John T. Hamilton Jr., John T. Hamilton Sr., Steven Hanley.

40. d. When the assignment of benefits line is signed by the patient or "signature on file" is printed on this line, the payment on the claim is paid directly to the provider.

41. c. The deductible is a stipulated sum that an insured person must pay toward the cost of the dental treatment before the benefits go into effect.

42. c. Most dental insurances terminate when children turn 19 unless they are full-time students. If the patient is over 18 years of age, is a dependent, and is a full-time student, the name and address of the school that the patient is attending must be listed on the claim form.

43. c. UCR stands for usual, customary, and reasonable. UCR describes the fees used on a dental insurance claim form.

44. d. All procedures performed are coded with a procedure code, and the many procedures are grouped into several categories. Study models and an adult prophylaxis are in the preventative/diagnostic services category.

45. d. When there is dual coverage for a child dependent, both parents have coverage for the dependent, and the parents are divorced, determination of primary and secondary coverage is based upon with whom the child resides. The parent with whom the child resides the most is the primary carrier.

46. a. When there is dual coverage for a child dependent, both parents have coverage for the dependent, and the parents are married, determination of primary and secondary coverage is based upon the month of birth of the parents. The parent with the birthday month closest to January is the primary carrier.

47. d. All continuing care/recall cards should be filed in a chronological file based on the patient's next recall visit. The cards are mailed to the patient approximately two weeks prior to the appointment.

48. c. The petty cash fund is used to purchase small incidental items for the office.

49. e. When a dental supply shipment is received, the business assistant should check the invoice and compare it to the packing slip when the shipment is being unpacked.

50. e. The United States government requires manufacturers to supply a materials and safety data sheet (MSDS) for all supplies that are hazardous.

10 ▶ Law and Ethics

CHAPTER OVERVIEW

Law and ethics are integral parts of dental assisting and dentistry as a whole. Ethical decision making can often be difficult, but a dental professional must always think first of the patient's welfare and safety. It is important for dental assistants to fully understand the laws of the state in which they work. Each state has its own Dental Practice Act, and it is the assistant's responsibility to understand that legislation and to keep updated on the regulations and regulatory changes.

THIS CHAPTER IS divided into two parts. The first part deals with dental ethics and the second part deals with dental law. Generally, ethical standards are higher than legal ones. Something can be legal but unethical—for example, the slavery laws in the nineteenth century.

KEY TERMS

abandonment	child abuse	defamation of character
assignment of duties	code of ethics	Dental Practice Act
autonomy	confidentiality	direct supervision
board of dentistry	consent	due care

KEY TERMS

elder abuse	implied consent	negligence
ethics	informed consent	nonmaleficence
fact witness	invasion of privacy	patient of record
felony	justice	standard of care
fraud	malpractice	veracity
general supervision	mandated reports	

▶ Concepts and Skills

Dental healthcare professionals are expected to adhere to ethical standards when dealing with patients and the general public. This chapter is divided into nine topics:

- Sources of Ethics
- Basic Ethical Principles
- Professional Code of Ethics
- Ethical Principles and Dilemmas
- State Dental Practices Act
- Dental Board
- Supervision of Duties
- Dental Team–Patient Relationship
- Reporting of Abuse and Neglect

Sources of Ethics

From an early age, we learn how to deal with and treat others. There are many ways we learn about personal ethics. These sources include parents, basic instincts, teachers, moral codes, and examples of others.

Parents

Parents are our first influences. They teach us about moral and ethical decision making. Ethical choices and decisions are made starting at very young ages, and parents are the guides.

Basic Instincts

Most of us have some level of intuition or "feeling" about whether something is right or wrong. It is important to pay attention to those feelings and always put the patient's best interests first.

Teachers

School is one of the first places where individuals encounter moral and/or ethical decisions. Teachers are the facilitators in this area of learning. They help to instill a sense of right and wrong in children.

Moral Codes

Some individuals have a set of moral codes or religious beliefs that are followed to aid them in making ethical choices and decisions. Every religion has a moral code that members should abide by and use as guidelines when making moral and ethical decisions.

Examples of Others

Role models of those making ethical decisions or living their lives with positive morals and values are invaluable. Individuals can be influenced by watching the good choices made by someone else.

Basic Ethical Principles

Healthcare providers are always guided by ethical principles. There are six basic principles of ethical dental care. They are: veracity, justice, autonomy, nonmaleficence, beneficence, and confidentiality.

Veracity

This is the act of being truthful. A dental professional should always be truthful with patients. An example of this in the dental setting is letting patients know the condition of their teeth and diagnosis.

Justice

This is being fair and honest. Justice is an ethical principle on which this country was founded, and it continues to be an important value. Patients should expect justice from their dental healthcare providers.

Autonomy

Most dentists operate their own business, and as such, determine how best to protect patient privacy and provide patients with appropriate treatment. Dentists must do this within the limits of practiced treatment.

Nonmaleficence

This is known as the principle of "do no harm." The dental professional has an obligation not to harm the patient. Therefore, the professional should not knowingly perform any procedure that will hurt the patient.

Beneficence

This is known as "doing good." The dental professional has an obligation to promote good dental health for every patient.

Confidentiality

Patients have the right to expect that their treatment will not be discussed with other patients or shared with anyone outside the dental office without their expressed consent. The obvious exception is if the patient is a minor; in this case, the dental team will want to discuss treatment with parents or guardians. Patients have the right to keep their child's dental history and treatment private. The dental professional must respect this. With the adoption of the Health Insurance Portability and Accountability Act (HIPAA), more dental professionals are ensuring their practices adhere to confidentiality and patient privacy standards.

Professional Code of Ethics

Each professional organization (e.g., ADA, ADAA) formulates a professional code of ethics. This is a higher standard or ideal that is set voluntarily by the members of the organization. These standards are not laws, but serve as a way for the profession to self-regulate.

Standard of Care

This is the cornerstone of the code of ethics for dentistry. This guideline demands that each dental professional provide care at the same level as their peers in similar treatment situations.

Informed Ethical Decisions

Dental healthcare professionals are faced with ethical decisions daily. Being informed about the situation will help the professional make better choices. One way to avoid malpractice lawsuits is for the dentist to inform the patient about any risks with any dental procedure, and have the patient sign the consent form, particularly if the treatment plan will take longer than one year to complete. Parents or guardians must sign consent forms for minors.

Professional Standards

Dental healthcare professionals are held to a code of conduct of professionalism and education. This should allow them to make sound judgments.

Ethical Principles and Dilemmas

Each day, dental healthcare professionals are faced with many ethical dilemmas. One must adhere to one's own personal ethical principles and those of the profession to reach a sound ethical decision.

Dental law, unlike a professional code of ethics, is established statutes that serve as a minimum standard of care for the profession of dentistry.

State Dental Practice Act

Each state has its own Dental Practice Act. This act dictates what that state has decided will be law regarding dental duties, including which dental healthcare professional can perform which particular task(s).

Dental Board

The dental board is a group of individuals (dentists, assistants, hygienists, and laypeople) appointed by the state's governor to serve the public by interpreting and enforcing the laws set forth in the state Dental Practice Act.

Supervision of Duties

Some states have levels of supervision; for example, general and direct supervisions. General supervision allows for certain duties to be performed while the dentist is away from the office, but has left expressed consent and direction that this service be completed in his or her absence. Direct supervision refers to the performance of a dental task with the dentist present somewhere in the dental office. Refer to your state Dental Practice Act to determine if levels of supervision are listed.

Dental Team–Patient Relationship

To better understand the dental team–patient relationship, it is best to understand the following definitions and how they relate to each situation.

Standard of Care

This is the level of skill, knowledge, and care that is the same for other dental professionals treating patients under similar conditions. For example, it is not acceptable for a dentist to refuse treatment to a patient with HIV.

Due Care

Due care is the legal term for the care that a reasonable person would exercise in similar circumstances. It is the absence of negligence.

Abandonment

This is the termination of the dentist–patient relationship by the dentist without a reasonable notice to the patient. For example, it is abandonment when the dentist moves to another state without informing his or her patients, or otherwise arranging for their care. In fact, if a dentist takes a vacation or closes the office for more than a day or two without emergency coverage, this is considered abandonment.

Negligence

Negligence is the failure of the dental professional to exercise due care that a reasonable person would in similar circumstances. Negligence implies carelessness or inattention to one's duties. For example, failure to correctly diagnose a condition could be considered negligence, but failure to provide a treatment plan is not.

Malpractice

Malpractice is professional wrongdoing resulting in injury or loss to the patient. Failure to meet a standard of conduct that is recognized by a profession becomes malpractice when a patient is injured because of error. That injury is the result of negligence, carelessness, or lack of skill of the professional healthcare worker. In a malpractice suit, dental records are legally admissible as evidence, although the dentist legally owns the clinical records and radiographs. In fact, dental assistants can be called as fact witnesses, which is someone who was present when the act was committed and tells what she or he witnessed.

Lawsuits require proof of pain and suffering (damages), negligence (lack of standard of care), cause (the negligence caused the damages), and a doctor-patient status (the individual must be a patient of record).

Informed Consent

This is the consent given by the patient for a specific treatment once he or she has been informed of the procedure, possible complications, side-effects, and possible outcomes.

Implied Consent

This is consent that is indicated by the patient's actions. For example, the patient sits in the dental chair.

Patient Referrals

Dental professionals record the problem, the reason for referring the patient, and the name and type of practitioner the patient should seek for a professional opinion about treatment. Documentation of all referrals safeguards against legal action of malpractice claims.

Patient Negligence

Contributory negligence is documentation of the patient's failure to keep, make, or follow up with appointments as recommended by the dentist. Failure to seek the attention of a specialist may also contribute to the patient's decline in dental health.

Fraud

This is the submission of information in a deceitful manner in order to gain something unlawfully. Insurance fraud is a felony and there are consequences for dental professionals filing claims that are incorrect.

Invasion of Privacy

This is the sharing of personal or private patient information with those who are not directly involved in the care of the patient. For example, posting the day's Treatment Schedule in an area(s) where patients can view the other patients' names is not permitted. Additionally, the selling of patient private contact information is not allowed.

Chart Documentation

In chart documentation, it is not acceptable to have a group chart for family members. Each chart entry must be made in ink, dated, and signed by both the dentist and assistant. Any errors are corrected by drawing a straight line through the mistake and beginning the entry on the next line.

For example, patients' financial ledgers are not part of their clinical record and must be kept separate.

Defamation of Character

This is the written or spoken words that cause injury to the patient's character, name, or reputation. This is covered under tort law. Libel is false and malicious written comments, while slander is spoken false or malicious words.

HIPAA

This is known as the Health Insurance Portability and Accountability Act of 1996. This act is a federal regulation that ensures the privacy of the patient's personal healthcare information.

Reporting of Abuse and Neglect

Dental healthcare providers might examine patients who have injuries to the head and neck area that stem from abuse or neglect. All dental professionals have a legal responsibility by law to report suspected cases to the authorities.

Child/Elder Abuse

Some states legally mandate healthcare professionals to report suspected cases of abuse. Abuse is defined as any act that leads to the impairment or endangerment of another or omits normal care and treatment. Dental assistants must report suspected abuse to the proper authorities.

Dental Neglect

Dental professionals are required by law to report any types of abuse that are suspected or witnessed. Dental neglect is a form of abuse. This is a very serious matter and should be brought to the dentist's attention. The dentist will make the decision and place the call to report the abuse.

▶ Practice Questions

1. Which of the following determines which duties the dental assistant can perform?
  a. federal law
  b. state law
  c. the contracting group
  d. the dentist
  e. both b and d

2. To what does the standard of moral principles and professional standards of conduct refer?
  a. code of ethics
  b. litigation
  c. state dental practice act
  d. dental jurisprudence
  e. code of dental morals

3. Which of the following is NOT a negligent act?
  a. failure to diagnose
  b. failure to refer
  c. failure to sterilize
  d. failure to give a treatment plan
  e. both b and d

4. What must the dentist do if a dental procedure has any risk of failure?
  a. refer the case to a specialist
  b. inform the patient
  c. get an expert witness
  d. make sure all charting is accurate
  e. stop treatment

5. All dentists have a duty to conform to a standard of care. If a case of negligence arises, the dentist would be judged by the standard of care of all dentists in what geographic area or organization?
  a. the United States
  b. the state in which he or she is practicing
  c. the county in which he or she is practicing
  d. the local dental society
  e. the immediate area in which he or she is practicing

6. Which of the following describes: an act that a reasonable and careful person under similar circumstances would NOT do; or, the failure to perform an act that a reasonable and careful person would do under similar circumstances?
   a. negligence
   b. defamation of character
   c. fraud
   d. dental jurisprudence
   e. both a and c

7. An insurance company requests verification of a patient's birth date and complete name. A copy of the patient's entire record, including the health history that indicates evidence of HIV, is sent to the insurance company. What is this action considered?
   a. fraud
   b. assault and battery
   c. invasion of privacy
   d. defamation of character
   e. both c and d

8. A patient asks the dentist or other dental professional to change the date of treatment on a dental claim to insure more benefits. What is this act called?
   a. abandonment
   b. breach of contract
   c. negligence
   d. fraud
   e. defamation of character

9. Which of the following cannot sign a consent form?
   a. parent
   b. adult patient
   c. minor patient
   d. legal guardian
   e. none of the above

10. A dentist moves to another state without informing his or her patients and fails to arrange for care for patients still in need of treatment. What is this action known as?
    a. fraud
    b. abandonment
    c. negligence
    d. assault and battery
    e. none of the above

11. You are summoned to provide firsthand knowledge as testimony in a lawsuit against a dental practice. What would you be in this case?

    a. defendant

    b. plaintiff

    c. fact witness

    d. expert witness

    e. both a and c

12. Which of the following terms is defined as the severance of a professional relationship with a patient who is still in need of dental care and attention without giving adequate notice to the patient?

    a. withdrawal

    b. abandonment

    c. malpractice

    d. neglect

    e. fraud

13. In a malpractice court case, what happens to dental records?

    a. they are not admissible as evidence

    b. they should be written in pencil

    c. they are legally admissible as evidence

    d. they are sent to the patient for review first

    e. they are sent to the witness for review first

14. In each state, what contains the legal restrictions and controls on the dentist, dental professionals, and the practice of dentistry?

    a. ADAA Code of Ethics

    b. state board of dentistry

    c. state Dental Practice Act

    d. both b and c

    e. both a and b

15. Which of the following is NOT included in the informed consent form?

    a. benefits of treatment

    b. risks of treatment

    c. nature of proposed treatment

    d. payment plan for treatment

    e. both b and d

16. What professional term means "do no harm"?
   a. nonmaleficence
   b. justice
   c. beneficence
   d. autonomy
   e. ethics

17. What does HIPAA stand for?
   a. Health Insurance Portability and Accountability Act
   b. Health Insurance Privacy and Accountability Act
   c. Health Institute of Public and Accessibility Act
   d. Hospital Infection Procedures and Asepsis Measures
   e. Hospital Internal Protocol and Accountability Processes

18. What does confidentiality mean?
   a. The patient has a right to privacy.
   b. The dental office does not reveal any personal information about the patient.
   c. The patient has autonomy.
   d. The office can share information with another health care provider.
   e. both a and b

19. Who owns the clinical record and dental radiographs?
   a. the dentist
   b. the patient
   c. the state
   d. the insurance company
   e. the board of dentistry

20. If a mistake is made during chart documentation, what is the proper way of correcting the error?
   a. using white correction fluid to cover the mistake and start over
   b. drawing a straight line through the mistake and beginning on the next line
   c. erasing it
   d. scribbling it out so it is completely darkened and cannot be read
   e. using a pencil and writing corrections as close to the mistake as possible

21. A group chart is acceptable when all family members are patients.
   a. True
   b. False

22. A patient's financial ledger is part of her or his clinical record.
   a. True
   b. False

23. All dental professionals are required to report abuse.
   a. True
   b. False

24. It is acceptable for a dentist to refuse treatment to a patient with HIV.
   a. True
   b. False

25. Each chart entry must be made in ink, dated, and signed by both the dentist and the assistant.
   a. True
   b. False

26. If a patient's treatment plan will take longer than one year to complete, a written informed consent form must be discussed with and signed by the patient.
   a. True
   b. False

27. It is not a criminal act for a dental assistant to perform an illegal function as long as the dentist has asked him or her to do so.
   a. True
   b. False

28. When patients enter a dental office, they are giving implied consent for a dental exam.
   a. True
   b. False

29. Broken appointments should only be noted in the patient's chart when a fee is being applied for the broken appointment.
   a. True
   b. False

30. When presenting a treatment plan, the patient should be told of the benefits, risks, and treatment alternatives.
   a. True
   b. False

▶ Practice Answers and Explanations

1. b. State law determines which duties the dental assistant can perform. These regulations are found in the state Dental Practice Act. Each state is different.

2. a. The code of ethics is a voluntary set of standards a profession establishes.

3. d. A dental professional is obligated to diagnose, to refer the patient to a needed specialist, and to sterilize all instrumentation. Failure to give a treatment plan is not a negligent act.

4. b. The dentist must explain to the patient the risks, benefits, and options prior to beginning any treatment. If the dentist feels that the treatment may not be completely successful, he or she must disclose this to the patient.

5. b. In any litigation, a dentist is judged by his or her peers in the state in which he or she works.

6. a. Negligence is what a reasonable and careful person under similar circumstances would NOT do. It is also the failure to perform an act that a reasonable and careful person would do under similar circumstances.

7. c. Invasion of privacy is the act of disclosing a patient's personal information without his or her consent. In this case, the dental office supplied the insurance company with more information than was requested.

8. d. Changing the date on an insurance claim form may lead the insurance company to pay the dentist or employee added monetary benefits. This is fraudulent.

9. c. By law, minors are not allowed to enter into a contract. Therefore, a consent form must be signed by a parent or legal guardian.

10. b. Abandonment is the refusal of a dentist to care for an existing patient who has a pending treatment plan without giving the patient reasonable notice.

11. c. A fact witness is one who was present at the time of the alleged wrongful act. This witness is usually summoned to provide testimony about what he or she witnessed.

12. b. If a dentist no longer wishes to provide treatment to a patient with an existing treatment plan, he or she must follow the proper patient dismissal protocol. If he or she does not, this is considered abandonment.

13. c. Dental records are legal documents and are admissible as evidence in all litigations.

14. c. Each state defines the legal scope of dental practice and the requirements necessary to practice dentistry. This is outlined in the state Dental Practice Act.

15. d. The informed consent form describes the benefits of the treatment, the risks involved, and the nature of the proposed treatment. The payment plan is never included in this consent form.

16. a. Nonmaleficence is described as causing or doing no harm to the patient.

17. a. HIPAA stands for the Health Insurance Portability and Accountability Act.

18. e. Every patient has a right to privacy, and the dental office should never reveal any personal information about the patient. This is known as confidentiality.

19. a. Even though the patient pays for the radiographs, the radiographs and clinical record are owned by the dentist. Patients can have radiographs and clinical records copied or transferred to another dentist if they request this in writing and pay a transfer fee.

20. b. The proper way of correcting a charting error is to draw a straight line through the mistaken entry and to begin anew on the next line. Charting should never be completed in pencil or erasable ink, and correction fluid should never be used.

21. b. Every patient must have his or her own chart.

22. b. The patient's clinical record includes radiographs, periodontal charting, tooth charting, referrals to other dentists, prescriptions, and lab requests. Financial documents are not part of the clinical chart.

23. a. Dental professionals are mandated to report any suspected child, elder, or spousal abuse. Reporting such abuse can help the patient to receive assistance.

24. b. When a dentist refuses to treat a patient based on the patient's medical history, this is considered to be discrimination.

25. a. All chart entries should be made in non-erasable ink, dated, and signed by both the dental assistant and the dentist performing the treatment (except in those cases where the dentist works alone).

26. a. An informed consent form must be discussed with and signed by the patient if the treatment plan extends longer than one year.

27. b. Even if the dentist authorizes the dental assistant to perform an illegal function, it is still a criminal act. Punishment may include a fine or other penalty.

28. a. When a patient enters a dental office for an examination, it is considered implied consent.

29. b. All broken or cancelled appointments must be noted in the patient's chart, regardless of whether there is a charge for the appointment.

30. a. The presentation of a treatment plan includes the explanation of the benefits, risks, and alternatives of treatment.

Dental Assisting
Practice Exam I

CHAPTER OVERVIEW

This practice exam is the first of two 100-question practice tests based on actual dental assisting exams commonly used in the field today. Use this exam to find out how much you already know and how much you still need to learn.

THE PRACTICE EXAM in this chapter is modeled on real dental assisting exams set by the national certification board, Dental Assisting National Board (DANB), and the state dental assisting association, where offered. The former credential is the Certified Dental Assistant (CDA) and the latter is the Registered Dental Assistant (RDA).

The CDA Exam consists of 300 questions in three parts: general chairside (GC), radiation health and safety (RHS), and infection control (ICE). The RDA Exam consists of two parts: the written exam and the practical. Note that the practical aspects of the exam are not covered here. This test is a hybrid that covers material common to both exams.

Before taking this exam, study Chapter 3, the LearningExpress Test Preparation System, to help you develop skills to succeed in the dental assisting exams and any future tests you make take.

Take the first 100-question exam, allowing yourself enough time to complete it. Generally, the CDA exam will have 300 multiple-choice questions to be answered over four hours, so allow yourself 75 minutes to complete these questions. When you take the official exam, you will not be allowed to bring anything into the testing centers. Treat this exam similarly.

Please use the answer sheet on page 205. Once you are finished, go to the Practice Answers and Explanations on page 227, and count the number of questions you answered correctly.

1.	ⓐ	ⓑ	ⓒ	ⓓ	ⓔ
2.	ⓐ	ⓑ	ⓒ	ⓓ	ⓔ
3.	ⓐ	ⓑ	ⓒ	ⓓ	ⓔ
4.	ⓐ	ⓑ	ⓒ	ⓓ	ⓔ
5.	ⓐ	ⓑ	ⓒ	ⓓ	ⓔ
6.	ⓐ	ⓑ	ⓒ	ⓓ	ⓔ
7.	ⓐ	ⓑ	ⓒ	ⓓ	ⓔ
8.	ⓐ	ⓑ	ⓒ	ⓓ	ⓔ
9.	ⓐ	ⓑ	ⓒ	ⓓ	ⓔ
10.	ⓐ	ⓑ	ⓒ	ⓓ	ⓔ
11.	ⓐ	ⓑ	ⓒ	ⓓ	ⓔ
12.	ⓐ	ⓑ	ⓒ	ⓓ	ⓔ
13.	ⓐ	ⓑ	ⓒ	ⓓ	ⓔ
14.	ⓐ	ⓑ	ⓒ	ⓓ	ⓔ
15.	ⓐ	ⓑ	ⓒ	ⓓ	ⓔ
16.	ⓐ	ⓑ	ⓒ	ⓓ	ⓔ
17.	ⓐ	ⓑ	ⓒ	ⓓ	ⓔ
18.	ⓐ	ⓑ	ⓒ	ⓓ	ⓔ
19.	ⓐ	ⓑ	ⓒ	ⓓ	ⓔ
20.	ⓐ	ⓑ	ⓒ	ⓓ	ⓔ
21.	ⓐ	ⓑ	ⓒ	ⓓ	ⓔ
22.	ⓐ	ⓑ	ⓒ	ⓓ	ⓔ
23.	ⓐ	ⓑ	ⓒ	ⓓ	ⓔ
24.	ⓐ	ⓑ	ⓒ	ⓓ	ⓔ
25.	ⓐ	ⓑ	ⓒ	ⓓ	ⓔ
26.	ⓐ	ⓑ	ⓒ	ⓓ	ⓔ
27.	ⓐ	ⓑ	ⓒ	ⓓ	ⓔ
28.	ⓐ	ⓑ	ⓒ	ⓓ	ⓔ
29.	ⓐ	ⓑ	ⓒ	ⓓ	ⓔ
30.	ⓐ	ⓑ	ⓒ	ⓓ	ⓔ
31.	ⓐ	ⓑ	ⓒ	ⓓ	ⓔ
32.	ⓐ	ⓑ	ⓒ	ⓓ	ⓔ
33.	ⓐ	ⓑ	ⓒ	ⓓ	ⓔ

34.	ⓐ	ⓑ	ⓒ	ⓓ	ⓔ
35.	ⓐ	ⓑ	ⓒ	ⓓ	ⓔ
36.	ⓐ	ⓑ	ⓒ	ⓓ	ⓔ
37.	ⓐ	ⓑ	ⓒ	ⓓ	ⓔ
38.	ⓐ	ⓑ	ⓒ	ⓓ	ⓔ
39.	ⓐ	ⓑ	ⓒ	ⓓ	ⓔ
40.	ⓐ	ⓑ	ⓒ	ⓓ	ⓔ
41.	ⓐ	ⓑ	ⓒ	ⓓ	ⓔ
42.	ⓐ	ⓑ	ⓒ	ⓓ	ⓔ
43.	ⓐ	ⓑ	ⓒ	ⓓ	ⓔ
44.	ⓐ	ⓑ	ⓒ	ⓓ	ⓔ
45.	ⓐ	ⓑ	ⓒ	ⓓ	ⓔ
46.	ⓐ	ⓑ	ⓒ	ⓓ	ⓔ
47.	ⓐ	ⓑ	ⓒ	ⓓ	ⓔ
48.	ⓐ	ⓑ	ⓒ	ⓓ	ⓔ
49.	ⓐ	ⓑ	ⓒ	ⓓ	ⓔ
50.	ⓐ	ⓑ	ⓒ	ⓓ	ⓔ
51.	ⓐ	ⓑ	ⓒ	ⓓ	ⓔ
52.	ⓐ	ⓑ	ⓒ	ⓓ	ⓔ
53.	ⓐ	ⓑ	ⓒ	ⓓ	ⓔ
54.	ⓐ	ⓑ	ⓒ	ⓓ	ⓔ
55.	ⓐ	ⓑ	ⓒ	ⓓ	ⓔ
56.	ⓐ	ⓑ	ⓒ	ⓓ	ⓔ
57.	ⓐ	ⓑ	ⓒ	ⓓ	ⓔ
58.	ⓐ	ⓑ	ⓒ	ⓓ	ⓔ
59.	ⓐ	ⓑ	ⓒ	ⓓ	ⓔ
60.	ⓐ	ⓑ	ⓒ	ⓓ	ⓔ
61.	ⓐ	ⓑ	ⓒ	ⓓ	ⓔ
62.	ⓐ	ⓑ	ⓒ	ⓓ	ⓔ
63.	ⓐ	ⓑ	ⓒ	ⓓ	ⓔ
64.	ⓐ	ⓑ	ⓒ	ⓓ	ⓔ
65.	ⓐ	ⓑ	ⓒ	ⓓ	ⓔ
66.	ⓐ	ⓑ	ⓒ	ⓓ	ⓔ

67.	ⓐ	ⓑ	ⓒ	ⓓ	ⓔ
68.	ⓐ	ⓑ	ⓒ	ⓓ	ⓔ
69.	ⓐ	ⓑ	ⓒ	ⓓ	ⓔ
70.	ⓐ	ⓑ	ⓒ	ⓓ	ⓔ
71.	ⓐ	ⓑ	ⓒ	ⓓ	ⓔ
72.	ⓐ	ⓑ	ⓒ	ⓓ	ⓔ
73.	ⓐ	ⓑ	ⓒ	ⓓ	ⓔ
74.	ⓐ	ⓑ	ⓒ	ⓓ	ⓔ
75.	ⓐ	ⓑ	ⓒ	ⓓ	ⓔ
76.	ⓐ	ⓑ	ⓒ	ⓓ	ⓔ
77.	ⓐ	ⓑ	ⓒ	ⓓ	ⓔ
78.	ⓐ	ⓑ	ⓒ	ⓓ	ⓔ
79.	ⓐ	ⓑ	ⓒ	ⓓ	ⓔ
80.	ⓐ	ⓑ	ⓒ	ⓓ	ⓔ
81.	ⓐ	ⓑ	ⓒ	ⓓ	ⓔ
82.	ⓐ	ⓑ	ⓒ	ⓓ	ⓔ
83.	ⓐ	ⓑ	ⓒ	ⓓ	ⓔ
84.	ⓐ	ⓑ	ⓒ	ⓓ	ⓔ
85.	ⓐ	ⓑ	ⓒ	ⓓ	ⓔ
86.	ⓐ	ⓑ	ⓒ	ⓓ	ⓔ
87.	ⓐ	ⓑ	ⓒ	ⓓ	ⓔ
88.	ⓐ	ⓑ	ⓒ	ⓓ	ⓔ
89.	ⓐ	ⓑ	ⓒ	ⓓ	ⓔ
90.	ⓐ	ⓑ	ⓒ	ⓓ	ⓔ
91.	ⓐ	ⓑ	ⓒ	ⓓ	ⓔ
92.	ⓐ	ⓑ	ⓒ	ⓓ	ⓔ
93.	ⓐ	ⓑ	ⓒ	ⓓ	ⓔ
94.	ⓐ	ⓑ	ⓒ	ⓓ	ⓔ
96.	ⓐ	ⓑ	ⓒ	ⓓ	ⓔ
96.	ⓐ	ⓑ	ⓒ	ⓓ	ⓔ
97.	ⓐ	ⓑ	ⓒ	ⓓ	ⓔ
98.	ⓐ	ⓑ	ⓒ	ⓓ	ⓔ
98.	ⓐ	ⓑ	ⓒ	ⓓ	ⓔ
100.	ⓐ	ⓑ	ⓒ	ⓓ	ⓔ

Practice Exam I: _____ of 100 questions right

One of the main reasons you are taking this practice exam, aside from getting practice in answering the kinds of questions found on the dental assisting exams, is to identify your strengths and weaknesses. Make a note of the types of questions you miss and the topics on which you need to concentrate your study time. Don't neglect any subject unless you have a nearly perfect score. Develop a study plan, and after studying your textbook, start reviewing the individual topics in Chapters 4 to 10.

You can also take this exam online by using the scratch-off card at the back of this book. Sign in at www.learningexpressfreeoffer.com to take the test and have your answers scored instantly.

▶ **Practice Questions**

1. What is the source of the greatest dose of radiation to structures in the patient's jaw when exposing dental radiographs?
   a. secondary radiation
   b. leakage from the X-ray tube
   c. the primary beam
   d. scatter from the PID
   e. scatter from the patient's face

2. Which of the following is the fastest film speed?
   a. AA speed
   b. C speed
   c. D speed
   d. E speed
   e. F speed

3. What does MPD stand for?
   a. maximum penetration dosage
   b. minimum penetration dosage
   c. maximum permissible dose
   d. minimum permissible dose
   e. most permissible detector

4. Which of the following statements is false?
   a. Duplicating film is not exposed to X-rays.
   b. Duplicating film is used in a darkroom.
   c. Duplicating film is used to make copies of radiographs.
   d. Duplicating film has an emulsion on one side.
   e. Duplicating film may be used intraorally.

5. Which of the following items are addressed by the Consumer-Patient Radiation Health and Safety Act of 1981?
   a. accreditation of personnel training programs
   b. mandatory certification of all operators of ionizing radiation equipment
   c. quality and maintenance of X-ray equipment
   d. both a and d
   e. all of the above

6. What human tissue is most sensitive to radiation?
   a. reproductive cells
   b. thyroid gland
   c. connective tissue
   d. retina of the eye
   e. both a and d

7. A full-mouth survey
   a. always has periapicals and bitewings.
   b. has a minimum of 20 films.
   c. is always taken on a comprehensive examination appointment.
   d. varies in need and number of films according to selection criteria and mouth size.
   e. can be replaced with a Panorex film.

8. Which term describes the time period between exposure to radiation and the signs and symptoms of biological damage?
   a. chronic period
   b. acute period
   c. latent period
   d. cumulative period
   e. absorption period

9. What precautions are necessary when taking a full-mouth survey of a patient with a negative medical history?
   a. gloves and eyewear
   b. gloves
   c. gloves, eyewear, and a mask
   d. remove eyeglasses
   e. double gloves

10. The kilovoltage (kV) of a dental X-ray machine
   a. affects the quantity of X-rays.
   b. measures the electrical output.
   c. affects the penetrating power.
   d. affects the quality of X-rays.
   e. none of the above

11. Which radiographic technique displays the most accurate image of crowns, roots, and supporting structures of a specific area in the oral cavity?
   a. bitewing film
   b. extraoral film
   c. periapical film
   d. occlusal film
   e. panorex film

12. What is the optimum developing temperature and time for manual processing?

    a. 68° F for ten minutes

    b. 68° F for four and a half to five minutes

    c. 85° F for 90 seconds

    d. 95° F for 20 to 30 seconds

    e. 68° F for two minutes

13. What chemical is present in the developer that builds the black and gray tones of the image?

    a. sodium carbonate

    b. ammonium thiosulfate

    c. ammonium gluteraldehyde

    d. metol or hydroquinone

    e. potassium thiosulfate

14. What affects the density of an image on a radiographic film?

    a. milliamperage

    b. kilovoltage

    c. source-to-tube distance

    d. proper processing

    e. all of the above

15. A charged coupling device (CCD) is primarily made of which of the following substances?

    a. calcium tungsten

    b. phosphor

    c. silicon

    d. lead

    e. aluminum

16. For which of the following is the panoramic radiograph NOT used diagnostically?

    a. a general survey

    b. confirmation of fractures of the mandible

    c. detection of impacted third molars

    d. location of third molars

    e. detection of caries

17. Pre-surgical implant radiographs are taken to

    a. determine bone quality.

    b. determine bone quantity.

    c. determine crestal bone levels.

    d. locate anatomical structures.

    e. locate the cementoenamel junctions.

18. Which of the following would a patient be allowed to wear when having a panoramic radiograph taken?
   a. earrings
   b. hearing aid
   c. wristwatch
   d. necklace
   e. partial denture

19. Which of the following describes a cephalometric (extraoral film) radiograph?
   a. It is often used to measure changes and predict growth patterns.
   b. It is commonly used by orthodontists.
   c. It contains a soft-tissue outline.
   d. both a and b
   e. all of the above

20. What dental specialty deals with the diseases of the pulp?
   a. orthodontics
   b. periodontics
   c. endodontics
   d. oral surgery
   e. prosthodontics

21. What dental specialty focuses on replacing missing teeth?
   a. orthodontics
   b. periodontics
   c. endodontics
   d. oral surgery
   e. prosthodontics

22. What dental specialty deals with the preventive and restorative care of children's teeth from birth to adolescence?
   a. periodontics
   b. prosthodontics
   c. dental public health
   d. orthodontics
   e. none of the above

23. What term do you use to describe gestures and body movements made by a person that indicate a feeling in a given situation?
   a. body mechanics
   b. non-verbal cues
   c. body language
   d. patient rights
   e. both b and c

24. Which organization prohibits discriminatory hiring based on race, religion, color, sex, national origin, disability, or age?

a. HIPAA

b. EEOC

c. OSHA

d. EPA

e. none of the above

25. Which of the following is NOT an example of external marketing in a dental practice?

a. dental practice Yellow Pages directory

b. dental practice Web site

c. open houses for non-patients

d. follow-up calls

e. dental practice building sign

26. What is the written communication that identifies the dentist's philosophy and policies, and defines the responsibilities of the patients and dental staff?

a. the hierarchy of needs

b. the office policy

c. external marketing

d. the health history form

e. the privacy policy

27. Which of the following is NOT a component of a clinical record?

a. health history

b. dental lab prescription

c. radiographs

d. recall cards

e. prescription for a medicine

28. Which of the following records is considered a vital record?

a. bank reconciliation

b. petty cash voucher

c. patient clinical chart

d. recall card

e. cancelled check

29. If an assistant chooses to transmit a transaction about a patient electronically, under which act does this task fall?

a. ADA

b. HIPAA

c. HHS

d. OSHA

e. ADAA

30. What symptoms are associated with an acute myocardial infarction?
- **a.** nausea
- **b.** weakness
- **c.** pain radiating down arm, jaw, face
- **d.** shortness of breath
- **e.** all of the above

31. What should a conscious diabetic patient who is not feeling well be offered?
- **a.** orange juice
- **b.** soda
- **c.** milk
- **d.** an alcoholic beverage
- **e.** candy

32. What is considered to be a proper course of action when assisting a patient who has had a fainting spell?
- **a.** place the patient's feet level with his or her head
- **b.** place the patient's feet above his or her head
- **c.** administer oxygen only
- **d.** none of the above
- **e.** both a and c

33. What does it indicate when a patient presents itching and hives?
- **a.** heart attack
- **b.** allergic reaction
- **c.** syncope
- **d.** postural hypotension
- **e.** both b and d

34. What is postural hypotension?
- **a.** high blood pressure
- **b.** low blood pressure
- **c.** dizziness caused by too quickly assuming the upright position
- **d.** loss of consciousness
- **e.** none of the above

35. When a patient is suffering from an angina attack, what is administered and how?
- **a.** nicotine, by a patch
- **b.** epinephrine, by injection
- **c.** orange juice, by liquid
- **d.** nitroglycerin, sublingually
- **e.** none of the above

36. What organ does not function properly in a diabetic patient?
   a. heart
   b. lung
   c. liver
   d. pancreas
   e. kidneys

37. What causes hyperventilation?
   a. increased respiration
   b. decreased respiration
   c. too much carbon dioxide and not enough oxygen
   d. too much oxygen and not enough carbon dioxide
   e. none of the above

38. In a malpractice court case, which of the following statements about dental records is correct?
   a. not admissible as evidence
   b. better to be written in pencil
   c. sent to the patient first
   d. better to be written in red pen
   e. legally admissible as evidence

39. Which of the following terms is defined as the severance of a professional relationship with a patient who is still in need of dental care and attention without giving adequate notice to the patient?
   a. negligence
   b. fraud
   c. withdrawal
   d. abandonment
   e. malpractice

40. Who controls the functions that may be performed by a registered dental assistant?
   a. his or her employer
   b. American Dental Assistants Association
   c. American Dental Association
   d. state Dental Practice Act
   e. the county dental society

41. Which organization grants the CDA licensure?
   a. American Dental Association
   b. state dental association
   c. American Dental Assistants Association
   d. Dental Assisting National Board
   e. an accredited dental assisting school

Answer questions 42–46 using the following figure.

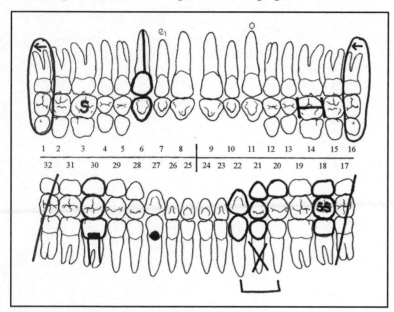

Figure 11.1 Clinical Charting

42. Which tooth has had endodontic treatment with a build up and a crown?

 a. #30
 b. #6
 c. #11
 d. #18
 e. #3

43. Which tooth has had an occlusal sealant placed?

 a. #27
 b. #18
 c. #19
 d. #3
 e. both b and d

44. Which tooth has Class V facial decay?

 a. #8
 b. #14
 c. #18
 d. #27
 e. none of the above

45. Which tooth is impacted mesially?

    a. #1

    b. #16

    c. #17

    d. #21

    e. #32

46. Which tooth is replaced with a bridge?

    a. #21

    b. #17

    c. #22

    d. #3

    e. #20

Answer questions 47–50 using the following figure.

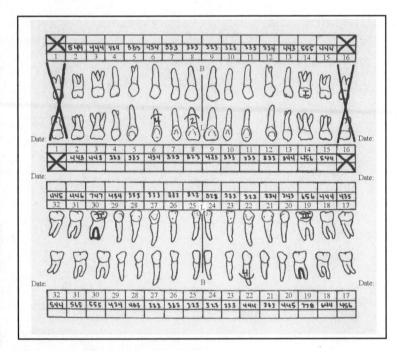

Figure 11.2 Periodontal Charting

47. Which tooth has a Class II furcation?

    a. #3

    b. #4

    c. #19

    d. #30

    e. #31

48. Which tooth has the largest periodontal pocket depth on a lingual reading?
    a. #19
    b. #18
    c. #30
    d. #31
    e. #32

49. Which tooth has a recession of 4 mm on the facial surface?
    a. #22
    b. #6
    c. #19
    d. #30
    e. #31

50. Which tooth has Class III mobility?
    a. #30
    b. #22
    c. #19
    d. #14
    e. #31

51. When using the clock concept, to what do team positions relate?
    a. dental chair
    b. X-ray unit
    c. computer during charting
    d. sterilization center
    e. both a and b

52. What does HVE stand for?
    a. high voltage electricity
    b. high volume excavation
    c. high velocity evacuation
    d. high volume evacuation
    e. both c and d

53. Which term refers to using the mouth mirror for vision of the working field?
    a. retraction
    b. illumination
    c. transillumination
    d. direct vision
    e. indirect vision

54. When administering a local anesthetic injection, what will the operator do to the anesthetic syringe to check if the needle is in the middle of a blood vessel?
   a. irrigate
   b. aspirate
   c. non-aspirate
   d. infiltrate
   e. disengage

55. What is the name of the opening of the anesthetic needle through which the solution flows while administering anesthetic?
   a. barrel
   b. threaded tip
   c. gauge
   d. lumen
   e. hub

56. What is the name of the end of the piston rod/plunger on the anesthetic syringe that has a sharp point?
   a. window
   b. harpoon
   c. barrel
   d. hub
   e. lumen

57. Where does the dental assistant sit in relation to the operator?
   a. four to six inches lower than the operator
   b. four to six inches higher than the operator
   c. four to six inches higher than the patient's mouth
   d. wherever it is comfortable for the operator
   e. closer to the patient

58. What does the hub end of the needle attach to on the anesthetic syringe?
   a. threaded tip
   b. harpoon
   c. piston rod/plunger
   d. thumb ring
   e. protective cap

59. When placing a rubber dam, when is single tooth isolation typically used?
   a. restorative procedures
   b. Class III composite restorations
   c. crown and bridge procedures
   d. sealant procedures
   e. endodontic procedures

60. What does "ligate the clamp" mean when discussing a rubber dam?
    a. tying a piece of floss around the rubber dam frame
    b. placing floss on the rubber dam napkin to prevent leakage
    c. tying a piece of floss around the bow of the clamp as a safety measure
    d. flossing the septum interproximally
    e. inverting the rubber dam, especially around the clamped tooth

61. How many holes does a rubber dam punch have on the punch plate?
    a. seven
    b. five
    c. four
    d. ten
    e. eight

62. What is another term for the clamped tooth?
    a. anchor tooth
    b. stabilizing tooth
    c. prepped tooth
    d. ligated tooth
    e. isolated tooth

Answer questions 63–65 using the following figure.

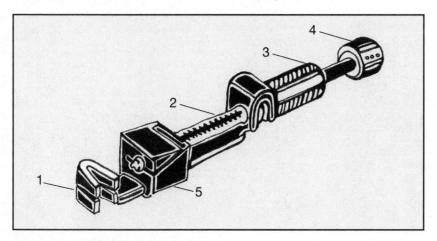

Figure 11.3 Tofflemire Matrix Retainer

63. Identify #1.
    a. guide channels
    b. outer nut
    c. spindle
    d. diagonal slot vise
    e. inner nut

64. Identify #2.

    a. guide channels

    b. outer nut

    c. spindle

    d. diagonal slot vise

    e. inner nut

65. Identify #5.

    a. guide channels

    b. outer nut

    c. spindle

    d. diagonal slot vise

    e. inner nut

66. What does the inner nut of the Tofflemire matrix do?

    a. adjusts the size of the matrix band

    b. holds the matrix band in the diagonal slot vise

    c. guides the matrix band to the right or left side

    d. tightens the matrix band so it does not slip

    e. none of the above

67. If a Tofflemire matrix is placed on tooth #13 DO, where should the wedge be placed?

    a. #12 and #13; buccal

    b. #12 and #13; lingual

    c. #13 and #14; buccal

    d. #13 and #14; lingual

    e. #14 and #15; buccal

68. Which of the following is NOT a hand-cutting instrument?

    a. gingival margin trimmer

    b. biangle chisel

    c. discoid-cleoid

    d. hatchet

    e. hoe

69. Which of the following is NOT a burnisher?

    a. fishtail/t-ball

    b. football

    c. acorn

    d. shepherd's hook

    e. beavertail

70. Which of these instruments would NOT be found on an amalgam tray?
   a. condenser
   b. half hollenback
   c. discoid-cleoid
   d. mylar strip
   e. articulating paper

71. Which of these items would NOT be found on a composite tray?
   a. mylar strip
   b. shade guide
   c. woodsen instrument
   d. cord packer
   e. curing light

72. What instrument is used for final enlargement of the canal?
   a. barbed broach
   b. K-type file
   c. lentulo spiral
   d. spreader
   e. none of the above

73. What instrument is used for excising or incising gingival tissue during periodontal surgery?
   a. orban knife
   b. lab knife
   c. periosteal elevator
   d. Kirkland knife
   e. both a and d

74. Which forcep is a universal forcep for the maxillary arch during oral surgery?
   a. 150
   b. 151
   c. 10S
   d. 88R
   e. 15

75. Which type of crowns are used as permanent restorations on primary teeth in pediatric dentistry?
   a. PFM
   b. full gold
   c. stainless steel
   d. aluminum shell
   e. custom acrylic

76. Which of the following instruments is used for placing orthodontic brackets in their final position?
   a. orthodontic scaler
   b. band seater
   c. ligature director
   d. howe plier
   e. contouring plier

77. What is an intrinsic stain?
   a. occurs on the outside surface of the tooth and can be removed by polishing
   b. occurs on the inside surface of the tooth and cannot be removed by polishing
   c. originates within the tooth prior to eruption
   d. can be caused by red wine or coffee
   e. occurs after eruption on the outside of the tooth

78. When holding the slow-speed hand piece during coronal polishing, which hand grasp is used?
   a. modified pen
   b. thumb-to-nose
   c. palm/thumb
   d. palm
   e. both a and c

79. Which of the following is a contraindication for placing pit and fissure sealants?
   a. tooth is newly erupted
   b. tooth is not sufficiently erupted
   c. no present decay on the tooth
   d. patient has good oral hygiene
   e. patient has regular recall visits to the dentist

80. Which of the following is NOT a final impression material?
   a. polyvinyl siloxane
   b. polyether
   c. polysulfide
   d. alginate
   e. none of the above

81. The alloy used in an amalgam restoration contains many different metals. What is the main material of the alloy?
   a. silver
   b. platinum
   c. zinc
   d. palladium
   e. copper

82. How can the amalgam material be retained in the tooth preparation?
  a. retention
  b. stickiness
  c. bonding
  d. curing
  e. both a and c

83. Which order should be followed for the bonding process for a composite restoration?
  a. etch, primer, adhesive
  b. etch, adhesive, primer
  c. primer, etch, adhesive
  d. adhesive, primer, etch
  e. both a and b

84. What does the term "flash" mean regarding composites?
  a. a stuck piece of floss
  b. excess composite material
  c. taking a picture when the procedure is completed
  d. the composite was over-cured
  e. no etch was used

85. Which of the following permanent cements uses a glass slab for mixing?
  a. polycarboxylate
  b. zinc oxide and eugenol (ZOE)
  c. glass ionomer (GI)
  d. zinc phosphate cement (ZPC)
  e. temp bond

86. What does the term "anti-cariogenic" mean?
  a. resists caries formation
  b. encourages caries formation
  c. uses fluoride to strengthen the tooth structure
  d. removes the smear layer
  e. both a and c

87. Which of the following restorations is a Class II restoration?
  a. #14 O
  b. #19 MO
  c. #9 MID
  d. #24 DI
  e. #18 L

88. Which of the following restorations is a Class IV restoration?
   a. #14 DO
   b. #8 MI
   c. #9 ML
   d. #24 DL
   e. #6 M

89. What must the dentist do if a dental procedure has any risk of failure?
   a. refer the case to a specialist
   b. inform the patient
   c. get an expert witness
   d. make sure all charting is accurate
   e. stop treatment

90. What would a dentist or business manager be committing if he or she agreed to a patient's requests to change the date of treatment on the dental claim to insure more benefits?
   a. abandonment
   b. breach of contract
   c. negligence
   d. fraud
   e. defamation of character

91. Who does NOT need to sign a consent form?
   a. parent
   b. adult patient
   c. minor patient
   d. legal guardian
   e. none of the above

92. Which duct is connected to the parotid salivary gland?
   a. Stensen's duct
   b. Bartholin's duct
   c. Lingual duct
   d. Wharton's duct
   e. both c and d

93. What is inflammation of and changes to the tongue called?
   a. black hairy tongue
   b. fissured tongue
   c. geographic tongue
   d. glossitis
   e. cellulites

94. Which bacteria require oxygen to grow?
   a. aerobes
   b. anaerobes
   c. facultative anaerobes
   d. algae
   e. protozoa

95. Which term refers to the portion of the mandible directly posterior to the last molar?
   a. ramus
   b. angle of the mandible
   c. mandibular notch
   d. retromolar area
   e. oblique ridge

96. What does OSHA stand for?
   a. Occupational Safety and Health Administration
   b. Occasional Safety and Hazard Association
   c. Occupational Supply and Analgesic Association
   d. Organizational Supplies and Anesthetic Administration
   e. none of the above

97. What type of cleaner is used to disinfect dental office treatment rooms or operatories?
   a. gluteraldehyde
   b. iodophor
   c. synthetic phenol compound
   d. bleach solution
   e. none of the above

98. Within how many days of starting work must the Hepatitis B vaccine (HBV) be offered to new employees in a dental office?
   a. 30 days
   b. 60 days
   c. 10 days
   d. 15 days
   e. 120 days

99. What does the sterilization process do?
   a. kills most microorganisms, but not spores
   b. kills some microorganisms, including spores
   c. kills all microorganisms, but not spores
   d. kills all microorganisms, including spores
   e. none of the above

100. When clinical charting, what do blue symbols indicate? What do red symbols indicate?

    a. needs to be done; is already completed

    b. is a present or existing condition; needs to be done

    c. is already completed; is a present or existing condition

    d. both a and c

    e. none of the above

▶ Practice Answers and Explanations

1. c. When patients are exposed to dental radiographs, they receive a dose of radiation from the primary beam and secondary radiation. The greatest dose of radiation is from the primary beam.

2. e. F speed film is the fastest speed film available. The arrangement of the silver halide crystals on the film emulsion of F speed film uses less radiation to produce an image than other speed film available. Therefore, a patient will be exposed to a lower dose of radiation by using F speed film.

3. c. MPD stands for maximum permissible dose. This limit has been established for occupationally exposed workers. The current MPD limit for whole-body exposure per year is 5.0 Rem or 0.05 Sv.

4. e. Duplicating film is used in a darkroom to make copies of radiographs. It has an emulsion only on one side and is not exposed to X-rays. It is not placed in the patient's mouth.

5. e. The Consumer-Patient Radiation Health and Safety Act of 1981 addresses accreditation of personnel training programs, mandatory certification of all operators of ionizing radiation equipment, quality and maintenance of X-ray equipment, and inspection of equipment.

6. a. Reproductive cells are the human tissue most sensitive to radiation. Nerve and muscle cells are the human tissues with the least sensitivity to radiation.

7. e. Selection criteria allows for X-rays to be prescribed for a specific reason rather than as a matter of routine. A full-mouth survey varies in need and number of films according to selection criteria and mouth size.

8. c. The latent period is the time period between exposure to radiation and the first signs and symptoms of biological damage.

9. c. Gloves, eyewear, and a mask should always be worn when exposing X-rays on patients.

10. d. Kilovoltage (kV) controls the anode in the X-ray tube head. It is the property that controls the electrical output, penetrating power, and the quality of the X-rays produced.

11. c. The periapical film displays the most accurate image of the crowns, roots, and the supporting structures of a specific area in the oral cavity.

12. b. The optimum developing temperature and time for manual processing is 68° F for four-and-a-half to five minutes.

13. d. Metol or hydroquinone is the chemical present in the developer that builds the black and gray tones of the image.

14. e. Milliamperage, kilovoltage, proper processing, and source-to-tube distance all affect the density or degree of darkness on an image.

15. c. A CCD is an X-ray sensor made up primarily of silicon and used for taking digital radiographs.

16. e. The panoramic radiograph has much less detail than a bitewing or periapical film and is therefore not a diagnostic for the detection of caries.

17. c. A pre-surgical implant radiograph is taken to determine bone quality and bone quantity, and to locate anatomical structures.

18. c. When taking a panoramic radiograph, the patient is instructed to remove any removable appliances in the mouth, as well as earrings, hearing aides, and necklaces so that their image will not be superimposed onto the oral structures. A wristwatch will not appear in the radiograph.

19. e. A cephalometric (extraoral film) radiograph is commonly used by orthodontists to measure changes and to predict growth patterns in the mouth. It contains a soft tissue outline.

20. c. Endodontics deals with the diseases of the pulp of the tooth.

21. e. Prosthodontics deals with the replacement of missing teeth with implant restorations, crowns and bridges, and removable full and partial dentures.

22. e. Pedodontics deals with the preventive and restorative care of children's teeth from birth through adolescence.

23. e. Non-verbal cues and body language are the gestures and body movements a person makes in a given situation that indicate their feelings.

24. b. The Equal Employment Opportunity Commission (EEOC) prohibits discriminatory hiring based on race, religion, color, sex, national origin, disability, or age.

25. d. Follow-up calls are placed to patients of record to communicate with them regarding their dental care. External marketing is designed to attract new perspective patients.

26. b. The office policy is the written communication that identifies the dentist's philosophy and policies, and defines the responsibilities of the patients and the dental staff. This policy is sometimes posted in the reception area, and a copy is given to every new patient.

27. d. The recall card is a reminder that is mailed to patients to urge them to either call for an appointment or remind them of an existing appointment. It is not part of the patient's clinical record. The clinical record contains all documentation regarding the clinical treatment, including the patient's health history, clinical charting, treatment plans, radiographs, prescriptions, letters to and from other doctors, and lab prescriptions.

28. c. The patient chart is considered a vital record and is legally admissible as evidence in court.

29. b. The Health Insurance Portability and Accountability Act (HIPAA) controls the patient's privacy when transmitting information about a patient electronically and when managing the patient's dental record.

30. e. Nausea; weakness; pain radiating down the arm, jaw, and face; and shortness of breath are all symptoms of an acute myocardial infarction.

31. a. A diabetic patient who is conscious and not feeling well should be offered orange juice, as his or her blood sugar level may be low. A citrus liquid is best for the conscious patient to improve the sugar level quickly.

32. b. Proper protocol in assisting patients who faint is to place their feet above their head. This can be done by placing the patient in the subsupine chair position. This will help return the oxygenated blood flow to the brain.

33. b. Itching and hives can sometimes be signs of an allergic reaction. This can quickly progress to breathing problems. Staff should pay special attention to a patient with these types of symptoms.

34. c. Postural hypotension is dizziness caused by a patient assuming the upright position too quickly. The patient's equilibrium is placed off-balance, causing the dizziness to occur.

35. d. Nitroglycerin is administered sublingually (under the tongue) when a patient is suffering from an angina attack. Nitroglycerin is available in pill or spray form, and is found in most dental office emergency kits.

36. d. The pancreas does not function properly in a diabetic patient. It can malfunction by producing too much insulin, not enough insulin, or no insulin at all.

37. d. Hyperventilation is caused by two factors: too much oxygen and not enough carbon dioxide in the blood. The patient should breathe into a paper bag or into his or her own cupped hands to return carbon dioxide flow, instead of oxygen flow, to the lungs.

38. e. Dental records are legally admissible as evidence in a malpractice court case.

39. d. Abandonment is the severance of a professional relationship with a patient who is still in need of dental care and attention without giving adequate notice to the patient.

40. d. The role and level of responsibility that a registered dental assistant will have while working are governed by each state's Dental Practice Act.

41. d. The Dental Assisting National Board (DANB) is the national organization that grants a certified dental assistant license to candidates upon passing completion of a written test.

42. a. Tooth #30 is charted as endodontic treatment (root canal), with a build-up and a crown.

43. d. Tooth #3 is charted as having an occlusal sealant placed. The tooth has a single "S" placed on the occlusal surface.

44. d. Tooth #27 is charted as having Class V facial decay.

45. b. Tooth #16 is charted as being mesially impacted. The tooth is circled to denote impaction and the arrow points toward the midline.

46. a. Tooth #21 is charted as missing and is replaced with a three-unit bridge from #20 to #22. The "X" over the root denotes that the tooth is missing.

47. d. Tooth #30 has a Class II furcation on the lingual side, which is denoted with a triangle at the furcation of the root.

48. c. Tooth #30 has a lingual periodontal pocket depth reading of 7-4-7.

49. a. Tooth #22 has a recession of 4mm on the facial surface.

50. c. Tooth #19 has a Class III mobility, denoted with the roman numeral III on the crown portion of #19.

51. a. The clock concept refers to the positions of team members at the dental chair. There is a clock concept for both right- and left-handed operators.

52. e. HVE stands for high volume or velocity evacuation. The dental assistant uses an HVE while the operator prepares the tooth structure with the hand piece.

53. e. Indirect vision is the process of looking into the mouth mirror to see the working field. Indirect vision allows the operator and team members to work in an ergonomically friendly manner. Some areas of the mouth are best seen using the indirect vision method.

54. b. In dentistry, an aspirating syringe is the anesthetic syringe of choice. The operator will aspirate while injecting anesthetic to verify that the needle is not too close to or injected into a blood vessel.

55. d. The lumen is the hollow cylinder in the anesthetic needle that allows the anesthetic solution to flow through into the injection site.

56. b. The harpoon is attached to the end of the piston rod/plunger. The harpoon is engaged into the rubber stopper of the anesthetic carpule, giving the dentist the ability to aspirate.

57. b. The dental assistant sits four to six inches higher than the operator. This allows the dental assistant to see better and to more easily transfer dental instruments.

58. a. The threaded tip is located at the very top of the anesthetic syringe. It is designed to have the needle attached to it. It is threaded to make sure the needle is firmly in place.

59. e. In endodontic procedures, single tooth isolation is used. Only the tooth being worked on is exposed through the rubber dam and clamped.

60. c. It is highly recommended that an 18-inch piece of floss be tied around the bow of the rubber dam clamp prior to placing it in the patient's mouth. The floss can be used as a retrieval source if the clamp is dislodged or falls to the back of the patient's throat.

61. b. A rubber dam punch has five holes in the punch plate. Each hole is designated for a specific purpose and tooth.

62. a. The clamped tooth is also known as the anchor tooth. This tooth is usually not the tooth being worked on, except in the case of single tooth isolation, and is one to two teeth distal to the tooth being worked on. The anchor tooth is the stabilizing force of the rubber dam placement.

63. b. The outer nut is #4, and it tightens the spindle.

64. c. The spindle is #2. The spindle holds the matrix band in place and can be tightened or loosened as needed.

65. d. The diagonal slot vise is #5. The diagonal slot vise holds the ends of the matrix band and is tightened by the spindle, which enters through the middle of the box-like diagonal slot vise.

66. a. The inner nut of the Tofflemire matrix adjusts the size of the matrix band to make the band larger or smaller, in order to tighten or loosen the band around the tooth.

67. d. The tooth being worked on is #13 on the distal occlusal surface. Therefore, the wedge should be placed where the interproximal surface is being restored. The wedge would be inserted between #13 and #14. The rule of thumb is that wedges are placed from the lingual surface to act as a contact point.

68. c. The discoid-cleoid is a carver used in amalgam restorations procedures. The discoid-cleoid carves the occlusal surface of freshly placed amalgam. It does not cut tooth structure.

69. d. The shepherd's hook is a type of explorer. Explorers are used to detect decay and check existing restorations for competence. They do not smooth a freshly placed amalgam restoration. That is the function of a burnisher.

70. d. A mylar strip is a type of matrix used when placing composite restorations. Mylar strips allow the ultraviolet light of the curing unit to penetrate the resin material, allowing the material to cure, or set, properly. There is no need for a mylar strip on an amalgam tray set-up since there is nothing to cure.

71. d. A cord packer would not be found on a composite tray. It is an instrument used to pack retraction cord into the sulcus surrounding a prepped tooth. It would be found on a crown and bridge tray.

72. e. The final enlargement of a root canal is completed with a reamer. In order to achieve obturation more smoothly, enlargement of the canal is done with a reamer.

73. e. Both the Orban knife and the Kirkland knife are used during periodontal surgery to make incisions or excise tissues. The knife chosen is the operator's preference.

74. a. A 150 forcep is used to remove any tooth on the maxillary arch. Since the forcep can remove any tooth on the maxillary arch, it is referred to as a universal forcep.

75. c. Stainless steel crowns are used by pediatric dentists to restore primary teeth that have been severely destroyed by caries. The stainless steel crowns act as permanent restorations until the primary teeth fall out. Stainless steel crowns are not esthetically pleasing, but do act as a competent restorative measure until exfoliation.

76. a. The orthodontic scaler has a variety of uses, one of which is placing orthodontic brackets in their final position. It can also remove excess cement and check appliances at following visits.

77. b. An intrinsic stain occurs within the tooth structure itself, and shows through the enamel. Intrinsic stains cannot be removed by polishing methods. Intrinsic stains can be exogenous (stains that occur after eruption) or endogenous (stains that occur prior to eruption). Endogenous stains are always intrinsic.

78. a. The modified pen grasp is used for coronal polishing. This allows the operator to establish a firm fulcrum while maintaining control over a spinning hand piece in the patient's mouth.

79. b. If a tooth is not fully erupted, it is a contraindication to placement of a pit and fissure sealant. It will be harder to control salivary flow over this area. Moisture control is of the utmost importance during pit and fissure sealant placement.

80. d. Alginate is not a final impression material. More modern final impression materials are typically rubber based. Alginate is not a rubber-based material and cannot duplicate the detailed information needed in a final impression. Alginate is from the hydrocolloid family of impression materials.

81. a. An amalgam restoration is commonly called a silver filling due to its silver appearance. It appears silver because the largest metal content in the alloy is silver.

82. e. Amalgams traditionally were held in place by retention. Today, a more modern approach to amalgam placement is to bond the amalgam to the existing tooth structure. Both methods of amalgam placement are accepted and used in modern dentistry.

83. a. Etch, primer, and adhesive is the proper order for the bonding process prior to the placement of composite or another resin-based restorative material. The operator may combine these into one- or two-step methods.

84. b. Flash refers to excess composite material found after final curing of the resin-based restorative material. Flash is often found during the final polish and adjusts the steps of the procedure. The operator will try to find it, but it can be difficult as the material is similar to the color of the teeth. One trick is to run an explorer over the area where the new resin-based restoration was placed. This will often locate flash if any is present.

85. d. A glass slab is used for mixing ZPC permanent cement. ZPC is an exothermic (gives off heat) material. Therefore, mixing the material on a cool glass slab inhibits the exothermic reaction and delays the set time of the material.

86. e. Anti-cariogenic refers to a material's ability to use a time-released fluoride to strengthen the underlying tooth structure, thereby making it resistant to caries formation.

87. b. An example of a Class II restoration is #19 MO. A Class II restoration is posterior interproximal decay.

88. b. An example of a Class IV restoration is #8 MI. A Class IV restoration is anterior interproximal decay involving the incisal edge.

89. b. The dentist must always inform the patient of the benefits, risks, and alternatives to treatment of any type in the dental office. This includes the possibility of the procedure failing.

90. d. It is a fraudulent act to change the date of treatment on a patient's insurance information to allow for more benefits coverage. The patient should be told that this is against the law and the office does not commit acts of fraud.

91. c. Minors are not allowed by law to enter into an agreement that binds them to a financial obligation. Therefore, they are not permitted to sign an informed consent form.

92. a. Stensen's duct is the duct that leads from the parotid salivary glands in both cheeks and empties out on the buccal surfaces of the maxillary first molars. It delivers saliva from the gland into the oral cavity.

93. d. The term *glossitis* refers to an inflammation of the tongue. Glossitis can worsen into other conditions of the tongue.

94. a. Aerobes are microorganisms that require oxygen to grow.

95. d. The retromolar area is also known as the retromolar pad. This area is located on the mandible just distal to the last tooth in each quadrant. It is covered by gingiva and other supportive tissues of the mouth.

96. a. OSHA stands for the Occupational Safety and Health Administration. OSHA is concerned with the safety and health of the dental office employee. It is the dentist's responsibility to make sure employees are safe and protected at all times.

97. b. Iodophor is the disinfectant used to disinfect the dental office treatment room or operatory. Iodophor is capable of killing many levels of microorganisms and does not have a strong smell.

98. c. Within ten days of employment, a new employee must be offered the HBV. If the employee has already been vaccinated, the employee must submit proof for his or her confidential employee medical record. The employee is free to refuse receiving the vaccine as well, but should then fill out a declination form.

99. d. Sterilization is the end of all life. All microorganisms, including spores, are destroyed through this process.

100. b. Blue symbols on clinical charts indicate present dental restorations or existing conditions that do not need to be repaired or referred. Red symbols on clinical charts indicate dental work that needs to be done or completed as part of the treatment plan.

12 ▶ Dental Assisting Practice Exam II

CHAPTER OVERVIEW

This practice exam is the second 100-question practice exam. This exam should be used as a final method of preparation to make sure that you have reviewed all the material. It should also be used to make sure that you have been successful with your study plan that you created after writing the first practice exam. Use this exam to find out how much you still need to review.

THIS PRACTICE EXAM, like the one in Chapter 11, is modeled on actual dental assisting exams set by the national and state certification boards for the Certified Dental Assistant (CDA) and the Registered Dental Assistant (RDA) credentials. Like the first exam, this test is a hybrid that covers material common to both the national and state exams.

Once again, don't forget to review Chapter 3, the LearningExpress Test Preparation System, to help you to fine-tune your skills to succeed in the dental assisting tests.

As you take this 100-question exam, time yourself. Allow 75 minutes to complete the exam.

Please use the Answer Sheet on page 235. Once you are finished, go to the Practice Answers and Explanations on page 257, and count the number of questions you answered correctly.

1. ⓐ ⓑ ⓒ ⓓ ⓔ
2. ⓐ ⓑ ⓒ ⓓ ⓔ
3. ⓐ ⓑ ⓒ ⓓ ⓔ
4. ⓐ ⓑ ⓒ ⓓ ⓔ
5. ⓐ ⓑ ⓒ ⓓ ⓔ
6. ⓐ ⓑ ⓒ ⓓ ⓔ
7. ⓐ ⓑ ⓒ ⓓ ⓔ
8. ⓐ ⓑ ⓒ ⓓ ⓔ
9. ⓐ ⓑ ⓒ ⓓ ⓔ
10. ⓐ ⓑ ⓒ ⓓ ⓔ
11. ⓐ ⓑ ⓒ ⓓ ⓔ
12. ⓐ ⓑ ⓒ ⓓ ⓔ
13. ⓐ ⓑ ⓒ ⓓ ⓔ
14. ⓐ ⓑ ⓒ ⓓ ⓔ
15. ⓐ ⓑ ⓒ ⓓ ⓔ
16. ⓐ ⓑ ⓒ ⓓ ⓔ
17. ⓐ ⓑ ⓒ ⓓ ⓔ
18. ⓐ ⓑ ⓒ ⓓ ⓔ
19. ⓐ ⓑ ⓒ ⓓ ⓔ
20. ⓐ ⓑ ⓒ ⓓ ⓔ
21. ⓐ ⓑ ⓒ ⓓ ⓔ
22. ⓐ ⓑ ⓒ ⓓ ⓔ
23. ⓐ ⓑ ⓒ ⓓ ⓔ
24. ⓐ ⓑ ⓒ ⓓ ⓔ
25. ⓐ ⓑ ⓒ ⓓ ⓔ
26. ⓐ ⓑ ⓒ ⓓ ⓔ
27. ⓐ ⓑ ⓒ ⓓ ⓔ
28. ⓐ ⓑ ⓒ ⓓ ⓔ
29. ⓐ ⓑ ⓒ ⓓ ⓔ
30. ⓐ ⓑ ⓒ ⓓ ⓔ
31. ⓐ ⓑ ⓒ ⓓ ⓔ
32. ⓐ ⓑ ⓒ ⓓ ⓔ
33. ⓐ ⓑ ⓒ ⓓ ⓔ

34. ⓐ ⓑ ⓒ ⓓ ⓔ
35. ⓐ ⓑ ⓒ ⓓ ⓔ
36. ⓐ ⓑ ⓒ ⓓ ⓔ
37. ⓐ ⓑ ⓒ ⓓ ⓔ
38. ⓐ ⓑ ⓒ ⓓ ⓔ
39. ⓐ ⓑ ⓒ ⓓ ⓔ
40. ⓐ ⓑ ⓒ ⓓ ⓔ
41. ⓐ ⓑ ⓒ ⓓ ⓔ
42. ⓐ ⓑ ⓒ ⓓ ⓔ
43. ⓐ ⓑ ⓒ ⓓ ⓔ
44. ⓐ ⓑ ⓒ ⓓ ⓔ
45. ⓐ ⓑ ⓒ ⓓ ⓔ
46. ⓐ ⓑ ⓒ ⓓ ⓔ
47. ⓐ ⓑ ⓒ ⓓ ⓔ
48. ⓐ ⓑ ⓒ ⓓ ⓔ
49. ⓐ ⓑ ⓒ ⓓ ⓔ
50. ⓐ ⓑ ⓒ ⓓ ⓔ
51. ⓐ ⓑ ⓒ ⓓ ⓔ
52. ⓐ ⓑ ⓒ ⓓ ⓔ
53. ⓐ ⓑ ⓒ ⓓ ⓔ
54. ⓐ ⓑ ⓒ ⓓ ⓔ
55. ⓐ ⓑ ⓒ ⓓ ⓔ
56. ⓐ ⓑ ⓒ ⓓ ⓔ
57. ⓐ ⓑ ⓒ ⓓ ⓔ
58. ⓐ ⓑ ⓒ ⓓ ⓔ
59. ⓐ ⓑ ⓒ ⓓ ⓔ
60. ⓐ ⓑ ⓒ ⓓ ⓔ
61. ⓐ ⓑ ⓒ ⓓ ⓔ
62. ⓐ ⓑ ⓒ ⓓ ⓔ
63. ⓐ ⓑ ⓒ ⓓ ⓔ
64. ⓐ ⓑ ⓒ ⓓ ⓔ
65. ⓐ ⓑ ⓒ ⓓ ⓔ
66. ⓐ ⓑ ⓒ ⓓ ⓔ

67. ⓐ ⓑ ⓒ ⓓ ⓔ
68. ⓐ ⓑ ⓒ ⓓ ⓔ
69. ⓐ ⓑ ⓒ ⓓ ⓔ
70. ⓐ ⓑ ⓒ ⓓ ⓔ
71. ⓐ ⓑ ⓒ ⓓ ⓔ
72. ⓐ ⓑ ⓒ ⓓ ⓔ
73. ⓐ ⓑ ⓒ ⓓ ⓔ
74. ⓐ ⓑ ⓒ ⓓ ⓔ
75. ⓐ ⓑ ⓒ ⓓ ⓔ
76. ⓐ ⓑ ⓒ ⓓ ⓔ
77. ⓐ ⓑ ⓒ ⓓ ⓔ
78. ⓐ ⓑ ⓒ ⓓ ⓔ
79. ⓐ ⓑ ⓒ ⓓ ⓔ
80. ⓐ ⓑ ⓒ ⓓ ⓔ
81. ⓐ ⓑ ⓒ ⓓ ⓔ
82. ⓐ ⓑ ⓒ ⓓ ⓔ
83. ⓐ ⓑ ⓒ ⓓ ⓔ
84. ⓐ ⓑ ⓒ ⓓ ⓔ
85. ⓐ ⓑ ⓒ ⓓ ⓔ
86. ⓐ ⓑ ⓒ ⓓ ⓔ
87. ⓐ ⓑ ⓒ ⓓ ⓔ
88. ⓐ ⓑ ⓒ ⓓ ⓔ
89. ⓐ ⓑ ⓒ ⓓ ⓔ
90. ⓐ ⓑ ⓒ ⓓ ⓔ
91. ⓐ ⓑ ⓒ ⓓ ⓔ
92. ⓐ ⓑ ⓒ ⓓ ⓔ
93. ⓐ ⓑ ⓒ ⓓ ⓔ
94. ⓐ ⓑ ⓒ ⓓ ⓔ
96. ⓐ ⓑ ⓒ ⓓ ⓔ
96. ⓐ ⓑ ⓒ ⓓ ⓔ
97. ⓐ ⓑ ⓒ ⓓ ⓔ
98. ⓐ ⓑ ⓒ ⓓ ⓔ
98. ⓐ ⓑ ⓒ ⓓ ⓔ
100. ⓐ ⓑ ⓒ ⓓ ⓔ

Practice Exam II: _____ of 100 questions right

One of the main reasons to take this practice exam is to see how you improved over the first practice exam, which you took before you established your study plan. Reviewing the material (and taking the practice tests) in Chapters 4 to 10 should have improved your score significantly. What percentage of the answers did you get correct this time? What areas still need work? Make a note of what you need to review and allot your remaining study time accordingly.

Success is the result of good planning and hard work.

▶ Practice Questions

1. What sort of agency is the Centers for Disease Control and Prevention (CDC)?
   a. advisory
   b. regulatory
   c. authoritative
   d. informational
   e. none of the above

2. What sort of agency is the Occupational Safety and Health Administration (OSHA)?
   a. advisory
   b. regulatory
   c. authoritative
   d. informational
   e. none of the above

Answer questions 3–7 using the following figure.

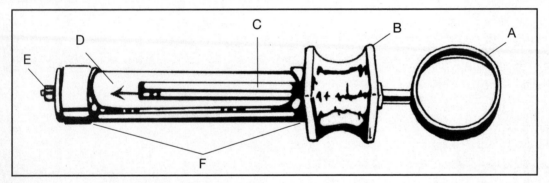

Figure 12.1 Local Anesthetic Syringe

3. Identify A.
   a. harpoon
   b. piston rod/plunger
   c. threaded tip/hub end of the syringe
   d. barrel of the syringe
   e. thumb ring

4. Identify E.
   a. harpoon
   b. piston rod/plunger
   c. threaded tip/hub end of the syringe
   d. barrel of the syringe
   e. thumb ring

5. Identify F.
   a. piston rod/plunger
   b. threaded tip/hub end of the syringe
   c. barrel of the syringe
   d. thumb ring
   e. harpoon

6. Identify D.
   a. harpoon
   b. piston rod/plunger
   c. threaded tip/hub end of the syringe
   d. barrel of the syringe
   e. thumb ring

7. Identify C.
   a. harpoon
   b. piston rod/plunger
   c. threaded tip/hub end of the syringe
   d. barrel of the syringe
   e. thumb ring

8. How quickly must a filled sharps container, considered hazardous waste, be properly removed from the dental office?
   a. 10 days
   b. 30 days
   c. 60 days
   d. 90 days
   e. 180 days

9. Which of the following statements is true of infectious waste?
   a. It can be disposed of in regular garbage.
   b. It can transmit a contagious disease.
   c. It can cause serious harm to the environment.
   d. It causes no harm to handlers.
   e. none of the above

10. How should you treat a patient suffering from an asthma attack?
   a. Position the patient in the upright position and call 911.
   b. Position the patient in the supine position, administer oxygen, and call 911.
   c. Position the patient in the upright position, give the patient his or her bronchodilator, allow him or her to self-treat, and watch to see if the asthma symptoms are relieved.
   d. Position the patient in the supine position, give the patient his or her bronchodilator, allow him or her to self-treat, and watch to see if the asthma symptoms are relieved.
   e. Call 911, then make the patient comfortable while waiting.

11. What dental material stimulates secondary dentin growth?
   a. liner
   b. base
   c. final impression material
   d. alginate
   e. plaster or stone

12. Which of the following dental materials would be used as a base?
   a. PVS impression material
   b. alginate impression material
   c. ZOE
   d. ZPC
   e. dycal

13. What is placed in an autoclave or statim prior to the sterilization process?
   a. paper towels
   b. a hand towel wrapped with sterilization tape
   c. sterilization pouches
   d. an instrument holder
   e. none of the above

14. How many minutes does a normal autoclave cycle run?
   a. 60 minutes
   b. 45 minutes
   c. 30 minutes
   d. 15 minutes
   e. none of the above

15. When should a patient be told to wrap his or her lips tightly around the saliva ejector to expel fluids from his or her mouth?
   a. sometimes
   b. always
   c. never
   d. all of the above
   e. none of the above

16. What can be used to make a custom tray?
   a. triad tray material
   b. acrylics
   c. alginate
   d. both a and b
   e. none of the above

17. What medicament is used to irrigate the root canals during root canal therapy?
   a. water
   b. rubbing alcohol
   c. sodium hypochlorite
   d. glutaraldehyde
   e. none of the above

18. What type of flooring is recommended in the dental treatment rooms or operatories?
   a. carpet
   b. hardwood floors
   c. linoleum
   d. laminate flooring
   e. none of the above

19. Why would you use the ultrasonic cleaner?
   a. to remove debris from instruments
   b. to sterilize instruments
   c. to disinfect instruments
   d. to pre-clean instruments prior to sterilization
   e. both a and d

20. Which of the following statements about gut sutures is/are accurate?
   a. They are dissolvable within five to seven days.
   b. They are non-dissolvable and need to be removed in five to seven days.
   c. They are made from animal gut.
   d. both a and c
   e. none of the above

21. What is another name for biological monitoring?
   a. process indicators
   b. process integrators
   c. spore testing
   d. chemical monitoring
   e. none of the above

22. When is biological monitoring done? When is chemical monitoring done?
   a. daily; weekly
   b. weekly; daily
   c. monthly; weekly
   d. weekly; monthly
   e. none of the above

23. What is the responsibility of a regulatory agency? What is the responsibility of an advisory agency?
   a. enforcing rules; making educated suggestions
   b. making educated suggestions; enforcing rules
   c. infection control; equipment safety
   d. equipment safety; infection control
   e. none of the above

24. Which bandage often covers periodontal surgical sites?
   a. Ward's Wonder Pack
   b. perio pak
   c. polyether impression material
   d. sutures
   e. none of the above

25. MSDS stands for
   a. Material Standards of Dentistry Safety.
   b. Modern Safety and Digital Sonar.
   c. Material Safety and Data Sheets.
   d. Modern Standards and Data Signatures.
   e. none of the above

26. What is the name of the foot pedal that controls the dental hand pieces?
   a. operator's pedal
   b. rheostat
   c. hand-piece switch
   d. foot control
   e. none of the above

27. Which hand should hold the HVE?
   a. right
   b. left
   c. closest hand to the transfer zone
   d. either hand; it does not matter
   e. none of the above

28. During what procedure is a bur used?
   a. prep tooth structure
   b. finish and polish a restoration
   c. remove decay
   d. sectioning crowns
   e. all of the above

29. How are burs identified?
   a. number and size
   b. number and shape
   c. cutting edges and length
   d. shank and neck
   e. all of the above

30. What should be used when recapping anesthetic needles?
   a. two hands
   b. one-handed scoop technique
   c. a needle recapping device/needle guard
   d. both b and c
   e. none of the above

31. What color are nitrous oxide tanks? What color are oxygen tanks?
   a. green; blue
   b. blue; green
   c. gray; black
   d. black; gray
   e. none of the above

32. What is Stage IV of anesthesia?
   a. analgesia
   b. excitement
   c. general anesthesia
   d. respiratory failure or cardiac arrest
   e. none of the above

33. During an amalgam procedure, what two instruments are exchanged the most during the filling stage?
   a. wooden and plastic instrument
   b. carrier and carver
   c. carrier and condenser
   d. condenser and burnisher
   e. none of the above

34. For how many years must the employer dentist store the medical records of his or her employees?
   a. 10 years
   b. 20 years
   c. 30 years
   d. 40 years
   e. 50 years

35. How many roots do maxillary molars have? How many roots do mandibular molars have?
   a. two; three
   b. one; two
   c. four; two
   d. three; two
   e. none of the above

36. Most teeth are composed of what material?
   a. pulpal tissues
   b. dentin
   c. cementum
   d. enamel
   e. periodontal ligaments

37. How many teeth are in a child's primary dentition?
   a. 10
   b. 15
   c. 20
   d. 25
   e. 30

38. What charting system is used to identify children's primary teeth?
 a. letters
 b. numbers
 c. numbers and letters
 d. descriptions
 e. none of the above

39. Where can the Cusp of Carabelli be found, and on what surface?
 a. mandibular second molars; buccal
 b. maxillary anteriors; lingual
 c. mandibular first bicuspids; occlusal
 d. maxillary first molars; lingual
 e. none of the above

40. Where do mamelons occur, and on what type of erupted teeth?
 a. first molars, second molars; partially
 b. first bicuspids, second bicuspids; newly
 c. centrals, laterals; newly
 d. first bicuspids, second bicuspids; partially
 e. none of the above

41. What part of the tooth is the height of contour?
 a. smallest
 b. cervical
 c. widest
 d. longest
 e. none of the above

42. How are the mandible bone and maxilla bone described?
 a. dense; porous
 b. porous; dense
 c. thin; thick
 d. bulky; wide
 e. none of the above

43. What comprises the periodontium?
 a. gingiva, cementum, tooth structure
 b. cementum, alveolar bone, periodontal ligaments
 c. bone, pulpal tissue, cementum
 d. the apical foramen, bone, periodontal ligaments
 e. none of the above

44. What teeth are children missing from their primary dentitions that are found in the permanent dentition?

   a. second molars
   b. cuspids
   c. bicuspids/premolars
   d. first molars
   e. none of the above

45. What do the ameloblast body cells form?

   a. enamel
   b. dentin
   c. cementum
   d. pulpal tissues
   e. none of the above

46. When a baby is born, how many teeth are in development?

   a. 32
   b. 40
   c. 44
   d. 52
   e. none of the above

47. How many bones does the human body have?

   a. 152
   b. 180
   c. 200
   d. 206
   e. none of the above

48. When coronal polishing, what adds to the rate of abrasion?

   a. speed of the polishing cup
   b. grit of the prophy paste
   c. pressure applied by the operator
   d. a, b, and c
   e. none of the above

49. What must the dentist not lose when transferring instruments?

   a. line of sight
   b. grasp on the instrument
   c. fulcrum
   d. indirect vision
   e. none of the above

50. At what RPM do high-speed and low-speed hand pieces rotate?
  a. 25,000 and 450,000
  b. 500,000 and 45,000
  c. 450,000 and 25,000
  d. 45,000 and 500,000
  e. none of the above

51. Which form of radiation ionizes atoms?
  a. radar
  b. microwaves
  c. gamma rays
  d. radio waves
  e. visible light

52. What do you call the transfer of energy as it passes through matter?
  a. cumulative
  b. reproduction
  c. mutation
  d. absorption
  e. penetration

53. Which human tissue is least sensitive to radiation?
  a. bone marrow
  b. reproductive cells
  c. nerve and muscle
  d. small lymphocyte
  e. both b and c

54. What is the maximum permissible dose of radiation for a healthcare worker?
  a. 0.10 Sv/year
  b. 0.05 Sv/year
  c. 0.005 Sv/year
  d. 0.001 Sv/year
  e. 0.002 Sv/year

55. Which of the following does NOT reduce the exposure of radiation to the patient?
  a. using a rectangular PID
  b. using the fastest speed film
  c. using the fastest digital image receptor
  d. using the paralleling technique
  e. using an eight-inch cylinder on the X-ray machine

56. What is the most accurate technique used to measure the amount of radiation an operator receives?
   a. Multiply the number of films an operator exposes by .02 Rem.
   b. Check the operator's hands for erythemia.
   c. Count the number of full-mouth X-rays taken in one week.
   d. Have the operator wear a film badge.
   e. both a and d

57. What is the recommended collimation of the X-ray beam at the surface of the patient's skin?
   a. 2.75 inches
   b. 2.00 inches
   c. 3.75 inches
   d. 5.00 cm
   e. 2.75 cm

58. Which term refers to a radiopaque outline of the root of a tooth that is no longer present in the mouth?
   a. taurodont
   b. root canal shadow
   c. dilacerated roots
   d. root amputation
   e. lamina dura at the extraction site

59. Which item appears as a circular radiopaque area in the center of a pulp?
   a. pulp stone
   b. taurodont
   c. lingual tori
   d. palatal tori
   e. none of the above

60. Using too much vertical angulation when exposing an X-ray causes what effect?
   a. an extra wide image
   b. an elongated image
   c. a foreshortened image
   d. collimator cut off
   e. a blurry film

61. What is the operator error if an image shows two different images superimposed?
   a. The operator pushed the exposure button twice.
   b. The same film was exposed twice (double exposure).
   c. The X-ray tube head drifted.
   d. The film was exposed to light.
   e. The film was not exposed.

62. Which of the following appears radiopaque on an X-ray?
   a. air space
   b. occlusal amalgam restoration
   c. periodontal abscess
   d. caries
   e. incisive foramen

63. One percent of the energy generated by the collision of the electrons in the X-ray tube head is converted to:
   a. heat.
   b. liquid.
   c. X-rays.
   d. visible light.
   e. both a and c

64. At what part of film processing is the film emulsion softened and the exposed silver halide crystals removed from the film base?
   a. developing cycle
   b. wash cycle
   c. fixing cycle
   d. rinse cycle
   e. latent period

65. What size of film should be used when taking a maxillary occlusal film on a child with primary anterior teeth, and how should it be placed facing the maxillary teeth?
   a. size 0 and vertically
   b. size 0 and horizontally
   c. size 1 and vertically
   d. size 2 and horizontally
   e. size 2 and vertically

66. When taking a mandibular occlusal film, the film should be facing the mandibular teeth. Where should the patient's occlusal plane face?
   a. facing parallel with the floor
   b. facing down at a 45° angle
   c. facing up at a 45° angle
   d. both a and c
   e. it does not matter for occlusal films

67. How does the incisive foramen appear in an X-ray, and where is it located?
- **a.** radiolucent, below the apices of #24 and #25
- **b.** radiolucent, near the mandibular bicuspids
- **c.** radiolucent, between the roots of #8 and #9
- **d.** radiopaque, between the roots of #8 and #9
- **e.** radiolucent, inside the genial tubercles

68. Which patient positioning error causes an exaggerated curve of Spee on a panoramic extraoral film?
- **a.** patient's chin is too low
- **b.** patient's chin is too high
- **c.** patient's tongue was not contacting the palate
- **d.** patient's head was tilted to the right
- **e.** patient's head was tilted to the left

69. What are the advantages to using digital imaging compared to film-based imaging?
- **a.** image density can be adjusted
- **b.** image contrast can be adjusted
- **c.** image brightness can be adjusted
- **d.** image can be inverted
- **e.** all of the above

70. Which dental specialty deals with the diseases of the supporting structures, gingiva, and alveolar bone of the oral cavity?
- **a.** pedodontics
- **b.** prosthodontics
- **c.** periodontics
- **d.** dental public health
- **e.** endodontics

71. Which dental specialty performs the removal of oral lesions and facial reconstruction?
- **a.** prosthodontics
- **b.** oral and maxillofacial surgery
- **c.** periodontics
- **d.** endodontics
- **e.** none of the above

72. What is the most common filing system for arranging patient dental charts?
- **a.** numerical filing system
- **b.** alphabetical filing system
- **c.** geographical filing system
- **d.** subject filing system
- **e.** tickler filing system

73. When transferring a patient's dental record from one dental office to another, the assistant must do all except which of the following?
    a. copy the radiographs and retain the originals
    b. transfer the entire record
    c. retain the original record in the office
    d. obtain consent from the patient or legal representative
    e. charge the patient a small fee for the record transfer

74. Which tooth numbering system assigns each of the four quadrants a bracket to designate the quadrant of the mouth, and each tooth in any quadrant is assigned a number from one to eight beginning at the midline?
    a. Universal
    b. Palmer Notation
    c. ISO
    d. FDI
    e. both c and d

75. When the mesio-buccal cusp of the maxillary first molar occludes mesial to the mesial-buccal groove of the mandibular first molar, how is the occlusion described according to Angle's Classifications of Malocclusion?
    a. Class I
    b. Class II, Division 1
    c. Class II, Division 2
    d. Class III
    e. both b and c

76. Which factor helps determine the amount of a dental supply to order at one time?
    a. rate of use of the item
    b. expiration date or shelf life of the item
    c. amount of money available to spend
    d. amount of storage in the office for the item
    e. all of the above

77. What time of day is considered most appropriate to treat young children?
    a. just prior to nap time
    b. immediately following nap time
    c. early morning
    d. late in the day
    e. after lunch

78. What are the three types of recall systems used in a dental office?
   a. telephone, advanced mail, and fax
   b. telephone, mail, and e-mail
   c. advanced appointment, mail, and telephone
   d. advanced appointment, e-mail, and electronic recall
   e. postcard, telephone, and fax

79. What is an advanced appointment recall/continuing care system?
   a. Patients book their next visit while at the office.
   b. Patients receive a card asking them to call the office to book their next appointment.
   c. Patients are called approximately a month before they are due for another appointment.
   d. Patients receive recall cards approximately two weeks before their next appointment, confirming the date and time of their next appointment.
   e. both a and d

80. What are accounts receivable?
   a. all money that the dentist owes to creditors
   b. all money owed to the dentist by insurance carriers only
   c. all money owed to the dentist for completed treatment
   d. all money that the dentist owes to the lab
   e. both a and d

81. What is a ledger card?
   a. a record that shows the patient's lab expenses
   b. a record that shows the patient's financial information
   c. a record that shows the accounts receivable
   d. a record that shows the accounts payable
   e. a record that shows the patient's insurance benefit information

82. Which of the following data is not required on an insurance claim form?
   a. patient's relationship to the subscriber
   b. subscriber's name
   c. dentist's tax ID number
   d. patient's date of birth
   e. dentist's date of birth

83. What determines the percentage of payment that the insurance carrier will pay?
   a. the type of procedure
   b. the insurance contract
   c. where the patient seeks dental treatment
   d. both a and b
   e. all of the above

84. What does UCR stand for in dental insurance?

    a. unusual, coverage, regular

    b. usual, carrier, reasonable

    c. usual, customary, reasonable

    d. usual, coverage, reasonable

    e. usual, customary, receivable

85. What must a dentist do if a procedure has any risk of failure?

    a. get an expert witness

    b. refer the case to a specialist

    c. stop treatment

    d. inform the patient of the risk

    e. refer the patient to another dentist

86. What word(s) describes disease transmission, abandonment, and failure to diagnose?

    a. negligence

    b. fraud

    c. withdrawal

    d. malpractice

    e. both b and d

Answer questions 87–91 using the following figure.

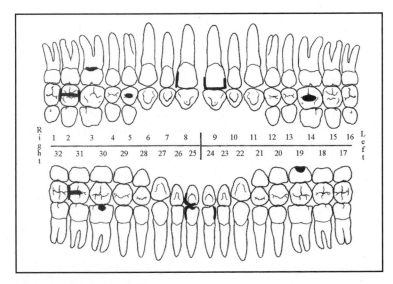

Figure 12.2 Clinical Charting

87. Which two teeth show Class IV decay?

    a. #3, #9

    b. #8, #24

    c. #9, #25

    d. #3, #19

    e. #25, #24

88. Which two teeth show Class I decay?
   a. #2, #31
   b. #14, #30
   c. #5, #14
   d. #5, #30
   e. #3, #19

89. Which two teeth show Class II decay?
   a. #9, #25
   b. #5, #14
   c. #8, #24
   d. #2, #31
   e. #3, #19

90. Which two teeth show Class V decay?
   a. #24, #8
   b. #5, #14
   c. #19, #30
   d. #19, #3
   e. #3, #30

91. Which two teeth show Class III decay?
   a. #24, #8
   b. #24, #25
   c. #9, #25
   d. #19, #3
   e. #14, #5

92. What is the correct order for the three steps included in the bonding process for a composite restoration?
   a. etch, primer, adhesive
   b. etch, isolate, primer
   c. primer, etch, adhesive
   d. adhesive, primer, etch
   e. etch, adhesive, primer

93. What does the term *flash* mean when discussing composites?
   a. stuck piece of floss
   b. excess composite material
   c. a picture when the procedure is complete
   d. excess bonding agent
   e. over-curing the material

94. A matrix band that fits tooth #3 also fits which other tooth?
   a. #14
   b. #30
   c. #19
   d. #31
   e. #15

95. Which type of bur shank fits in the contra-angle attachment?
   a. straight shank
   b. latch-type shank
   c. friction-grip shank
   d. both a and b
   e. both b and c

96. Which instrument is not used to carve an amalgam restoration?
   a. discoid-cleoid
   b. acorn burnisher
   c. gingival margin trimmer
   d. Hollenbeck
   e. football burnisher

97. What part of the rubber dam is ligated with a piece of floss?
   a. clamp, around the bow
   b. clamp, around the jaws
   c. frame
   d. punch
   e. forceps

98. Which oral habit is characterized by involuntary grinding and clenching of the teeth?
   a. tongue thrusting
   b. chewing tobacco
   c. cheek biting
   d. bruxism
   e. mouth breathing

99. What dental term describes abnormally small teeth?
   a. macrodontia
   b. dens in dente
   c. microdontia
   d. ankylosis
   e. anodontia

100. Which permanent tooth replaces tooth L?

    a. #27

    b. #19

    c. #18

    d. #17

    e. #21

► Practice Answers and Explanations

1. a. The CDC is an advisory agency. The center conducts scientific research and then issues recommendations based on the research conclusions. Other regulatory agencies often take the CDC's recommendations and turn them into regulations, or rules, that must be adhered to.

2. b. The OSHA is a regulatory agency. Any rules or regulations issued by the OSHA must be adhered to, as OSHA has the power to enforce them. The OSHA can fine a dental office for not complying with the regulations specific to federal or state regulations. Check with your own state to understand the OSHA regulations in that state.

3. e. The thumb ring is used by the operator for purposes of aspiration.

4. c. The threaded tip allows the hub end of the anesthetic needle to be attached securely to administer anesthetic to the patient.

5. d. The barrel of the syringe is where the carpule is held in place.

6. a. The harpoon engages into the rubber stop in the anesthetic carpule to allow for aspiration to check needle placement.

7. b. The piston rod/plunger pushes the rubber stop in the anesthetic carpule up, forcing the anesthetic through the needle.

8. e. According to the OSHA, after the hazardous waste container reaches its capacity, it must be removed from the dental office within 180 days.

9. b. Infectious waste is capable of transmitting a contagious disease through inappropriate handling or while not wearing effective PPE.

10. c. Patients who are having difficulty breathing should always be placed in an upright position. Sitting up allows the lungs to expand. The patients' bronchodilator should be within reach and given to them immediately so they can treat themselves. Their symptoms should begin to get better within 30–60 seconds.

11. a. Liner is the material that stimulates secondary dentin growth. Some liners also include a time-released fluoride, which has an anticariogenic quality and also prevents future decay while protecting the pulp.

12. c. ZOE (zinc oxide and eugenol) is used as a base. A base insulates the pulp from hot and cold temperatures. ZOE is mixed to a thick doughy consistency and rolled into a ball for placement on the floor of the preparation.

13. c. Sterilization pouches are used for instrument packaging prior to placement into the autoclave for sterilization.

14. c. An average autoclave cycle runs 30 minutes. This is for wrapped instruments or cassettes.

15. c. Patients should never be told to wrap their lips around a saliva ejector. Patients could experience "suck back," where the fluid from the last patient is forced back up the hose. This is very rare, but is a possibility.

16. d. A custom tray can be fabricated using an acrylic material or triad tray material, and a study model of the patient's arch. This can be done by the lab or by the chairside assistant in the lab in the dental office.

17. c. Sodium hypochlorite is used to irrigate canals during a root canal therapy. It is a mixture of bleach and water inserted into the canals with an irrigating syringe, to help kill any bacteria in the canals during the cleaning process.

18. c. Linoleum is the recommended flooring for dental treatment rooms. This type of flooring makes cleaning any possible spills or messes easy and hygienic.

19. e. The ultrasonic cleaner removes debris from instruments as a method of pre-cleaning prior to sterilization. The ultrasonic cleaner takes the place of hand scrubbing, which is no longer allowed by many OSHA state regulations.

20. d. Gut sutures are made from animal gut (typically cat or sheep are the most popular in dentistry) and are dissolved within five to seven days. These types of sutures are a popular choice because they dissolve as the patient heals.

21. c. Biological monitoring is commonly referred to as spore testing. These tests monitor the sterilization capabilities of each sterilizer being used in the dental office. The tests are a safeguard for the office to ensure that the instruments are being properly sterilized.

22. b. Biological monitoring is completed weekly and the results are mailed to the lab for testing under the microscope. Chemical monitoring is completed daily, with every run of the sterilizer, using either process indicators or process integrators.

23. a. A regulatory agency has the power of enforcement of laws behind it. An advisory agency bases its suggestions on scientific research and data, but has no enforcement capabilities.

24. b. A perio pak is the bandage placed over the surgical site following periodontal surgery. This bandage is used to protect the site from bacteria and foods that enter the oral cavity while the tissues are healing.

25. c. MSDS stands for material safety and data sheets. Each dental product manufactured in the United States is shipped with an MSDS. Every dental office needs to have an MSDS binder next to the OSHA binder. An MSDS binder is required as part of OSHA compliance and is useful in the event of an emergency or spill with certain dental products.

26. b. The rheostat is the proper name for the foot pedal that controls the dental hand pieces. The rheostat should always be positioned so the operator can successfully reach it with ease.

27. a. The HVE is always held in the chairside assistant's right hand while the left hand is either transferring an instrument or utilizing the air/water syringe.

28. e. A dental bur is used to prepare tooth structure, finish and polish a restoration, remove decay, and section crowns.

29. b. Burs are identified by number and shape. Carbide burs are identified by numbers, and diamond burs are identified by their shapes.

30. d. Anesthetic needles should be recapped using either the one-handed scoop technique or a needle guard recapping device. The dental team should never use a two-handed recapping procedure. The dental assistant should never receive an uncapped needle from a dentist following an injection. A greater chance of sticking oneself with a contaminated needle occurs when not adhering to recommended needle recapping procedures.

31. b. Nitrous oxide tanks are color-coded blue, while oxygen tanks are color-coded green.

32. d. Stage IV of anesthesia is respiratory failure or cardiac arrest. By knowing the patient's health history and baseline vital signs, and by updating vital signs through the procedure, this can be prevented.

33. c. The amalgam carrier and the condenser are exchanged the most during the filling portion of the procedure. These two instruments accomplish the placement phase of the restoration.

34. c. Employee confidential medical records must be stored for 30 years by the dentist.

35. d. Maxillary molars have three roots, and mandibular molars have two roots. There are instances when a maxillary tooth can have four roots, but it is not common.

36. b. Dentin makes up most of the tooth. The enamel acts as a protective covering for the underlying layers. Dentin can regenerate itself and therefore adds to itself continually.

37. c. A child's primary dentition has 20 teeth present, ten on the maxillary and ten on the mandibular.

38. a. Children's teeth are charted using letters from the alphabet to indicate that primary dentition is being recorded. When children start to lose, or exfoliate, the primary teeth, they can have a mix of primary and permanent teeth in the mouth. This is called a mixed dentition. A mixed dentition is noted with letters for primary teeth and numbers for permanent teeth.

39. d. The cusp of Carabelli is an extra cusp found only on the maxillary first molars on the lingual surface. There are only two present in the mouth.

40. c. Mamelons are rounded areas of enamel that have not quite finished fusing together. They are found on the central and lateral incisors of newly erupted teeth. The mamelons usually wear away over time with the patient's bite; however, they can be buffed or smoothed down by the dentist if needed.

41. c. The height of contour is the widest part of the tooth. The widest part of the tooth is the middle of the buccal and lingual surfaces, and then it tapers down into the cervical third of the tooth.

42. a. The mandible is a dense, strong bone not fond of expansion. The maxilla is a more porous bone, which allows for expansion.

43. b. The periodontium consists of three parts. The alveolar bone, the cementum, and the periodontal ligaments all make up the periodontium, or supporting structures of the teeth and mouth.

44. c. Children do not have bicuspids or premolars in their primary dentitions. They have central incisors, lateral incisors, cuspids, first molars, and second molars. Bicuspids or premolars will erupt with the permanent teeth at approximately ages ten to twelve.

45. a. Ameloblasts are the body cells that form enamel. There are various forms of blasts that create dentin, cementum, and bone. Alternatively, there are clasts, which are body cells that resorb, or break down, enamel, dentin, cementum, or bone.

46. c. When a baby is born, there are 44 teeth in development. Most of the primary teeth are close to completion and the permanent teeth are growing and moving into position.

47. d. There are 206 bones in the human body. These bones compose the skeletal system and may also be included as parts of other body systems.

48. d. Abrasion is the act of taking away, or wearing away, too much enamel during the coronal polishing procedure. Many factors contribute to this occurring. The speed of the polishing cup is important, as too much speed will heat up the tooth and wear away tooth structure. The coarser the grit of the prophy paste, the more likely abrasion will occur. Finally, too much pressure being applied by the operator can influence the wear on the tooth structure as well.

49. c. Dentists are focused on the tooth or teeth they are working on, and rely on chairside dental assistants to provide what they need. Dentists should never lose their fulcrum by having to reach for an instrument. The instrument should be placed into the dentist's working hand while the assistant retrieves the previous instrument. This will move the procedure along more quickly and efficiently.

50. c. The high-speed hand piece rotates at a speed of 450,000 RPMs. Since it spins at such a high rate of speed, it also sprays out water to prevent overheating the tooth being worked on. The high speed is used for cutting tooth structure very quickly. The slow-speed hand piece rotates at a speed of 25,000 RPMs. The slow speed is utilized for polishing, finishing, and removal of decay.

51. c. Gamma rays are short wavelength radiation that can cause ionization in matter.

52. d. The transfer of energy as it passes through matter is called absorption. When this energy is absorbed, it causes molecular changes in matter.

53. c. Muscle and nerve tissue are the least sensitive to radiation. The reproductive cells are the most sensitive.

54. b. The maximum permissible dose for an occupational healthcare worker is 0.05 Sv/year, which is equivalent to 5.0 Rem/year.

55. e. Using an eight-inch cylinder does not lessen the amount of radiation that the patient receives. Using a 16-inch rectangular cylinder would lessen the amount of radiation that the patient receives since it is longer and there will be less divergence of the beam.

56. d. Film badges worn by personnel at all times while working, and then sent to a company for measurement services, is the best technique in measuring the amount of radiation received.

57. a. The X-ray beam should always be collimated so that it is no more than 2.75 inches at the patient's face.

58. e. The lamina dura at the extraction site shows a shadow of the roots of a tooth that has been extracted. It usually disappears within a few months.

59. a. A pulp stone, which is a calcification of the pulp, shows up radiopaque inside the radiolucent pulp.

60. c. Too much vertical angulation causes the resulting image to be foreshortened.

61. b. If the same film is exposed twice, or double exposed, the resulting image is two different images superimposed.

62. b. An occlusal amalgam restoration appears radiopaque on an X-ray. It is hard, and the X-rays do not penetrate it as much as other structures such as dentin, pulp, or enamel. The harder the substance or structure, the more radiopaque it will be.

63. c. Only one percent of the energy generated by the collision of the electrons in the X-ray tube head is converted to X-rays. The other 99% of the energy is converted to heat.

64. a. During the developing cycle of film processing, the exposed silver halide crystals are removed from the film base and the dark tones are produced on the film.

65. d. Size 2 X-ray film is used for taking occlusal films on children. It is placed horizontally when the primary anterior teeth are present.

66. c. The patient's occlusal plane should be facing up at a 45° angle when exposing a mandibular occlusal film. The angle helps the operator use the bisecting angle technique for occlusal films.

67. c. The incisive foramen appears radiolucent in an X-ray and is located between the roots of #8 and #9.

68. a. When patients are positioned in the panorex machine with their chin too low, the resulting image will show an exaggerated curve of Spee. If the patient's chin is too high, the resulting image will show a reverse curve of Spee or frown.

69. e. Advantages to using digital imaging compared to film-based imaging include the ability to adjust the density, contrast, and brightness of the image, and to invert the image.

70. c. Periodontics is the dental specialty that deals with diagnosis and treatment of diseases of the supporting structures of the teeth.

71. b. Oral and maxillofacial surgery is the dental specialty that deals with the diagnosis and surgical treatment of diseases, defects, and injuries to the hard and soft tissues of the head and neck.

72. b. Patient dental charts are most commonly arranged in an alphabetical filing system so that they are easily accessible.

73. b. When transferring a patient's dental record from one dental office to another, the assistant can copy the radiographs and retain the originals, obtain a written consent form from the patient or legal representative to transfer the record, and charge the patient a small fee for the record transfer. The entire record should never be transferred since it is a legal document and should always be retained in the office.

74. b. The Palmer Notation system of tooth numbering uses an L-shaped bracket that denotes one of the four quadrants of the oral cavity, and numbers from one to eight to represent the eight teeth in each of the four quadrants in the mouth.

75. d. According to Angle's classifications of malocclusion, Class III is defined as when the mesio-buccal cusp of the maxillary first molar occludes mesial to the mesial-buccal groove of the mandibular first molar.

76. e. When determining the amount of a dental supply to be ordered, the assistant must be aware of the rate of use of the item, the shelf life or expiration date, the amount of money in the budget to spend, and the amount of storage space available in the office.

77. c. Early morning is best when scheduling a young child for dental treatment as it does not interfere with naps or regularly scheduled activities.

78. c. Advanced appointment, mail, and telephone are the three types of recall/continuing care systems used in the dental office.

79. e. The advanced appointment system is the most common and efficient recall/continuing care system used in the dental office today. Patients book their next visit while they are at the office for an exam or a treatment. They then receive a postcard approximately two weeks before their next appointment, as a reminder and confirmation of the date and time of their next appointment.

80. c. All money owed to the dentist for completed dental treatment is accounts receivable. This money can be owed by patients or insurance carriers.

81. b. A ledger card is a record that shows the patient's financial information. It has a running balance of how much the patient owes the dentist, along with all charges, payments, and adjustments.

82. e. The dentist's name, address, telephone, tax ID number, and state license number are required on all dental claim forms. However, the dentist's date of birth is not required.

83. e. The percentage of payment that the dental insurance carrier will pay will vary depending upon the type of procedure, the insurance contract, and the office in which the patient seeks the dental treatment.

84. c. UCR stands for usual, customary, and reasonable fees on which a dental benefits program bases payments.

85. d. The dentist must inform the patient of any risks involved if the dental treatment has any risk of failure.

86. a. Disease transmission, abandonment, and failure to diagnose are all acts of negligence.

87. c. Class IV decay is shown on teeth #9 and #25, which is decay located on the interproximal surfaces (mesial and distal) of anterior teeth involving the incisal angle.

88. c. Class I decay is shown on teeth #5 and #14, which is decay located on the pits and fissures of occlusal surfaces of posterior teeth.

89. d. Class II decay is shown on teeth #2 and #31, which is decay located on the interproximal surfaces (mesial and distal) of posterior teeth.

90. d. Class V decay is shown on teeth #19 and #3, which is decay located on the gingival third of the facial, lingual, or buccal surfaces of both anterior and posterior teeth.

91. a. Class III decay is shown on teeth #24 and #8, which is decay located on the interproximal surfaces (mesial and distal) of anterior teeth.

92. a. The correct order for the three steps included in the bonding process for a composite restoration is etch, primer, and adhesive.

93. b. The term *flash* refers to an excess piece of composite material on the restoration.

94. c. A matrix band that fits tooth #3 will also fit tooth #19.

95. b. The latch-type bur shank is the only shank that will fit into the contra-angle attachment for the slow-speed hand piece.

96. c. The gingival margin trimmer is an instrument used for cavity preparation and is not used for carving amalgam.

97. a. A piece of dental floss is used to ligate the rubber dam clamp and is tied around the bow of the clamp to avoid having the patient swallow the clamp.

98. d. Bruxism is characterized by involuntary grinding and clenching of the teeth.

99. c. Microdontia is the term used to describe abnormally small teeth. When it affects the entire dentition, it is sometimes associated with Down syndrome or congenital heart disease.

100. e. Tooth #21, the mandibular left permanent first bicuspid, replaces L, the mandibular left primary first molar. The permanent first and second bicuspids replace the primary first and second molars.

Appendix I:
Dental Acronyms ▶

Below is a list of common dental acronyms. Acronyms are used frequently in dentistry and knowledge of them will prove useful.

AADC American Association of Dental Consultants

AADE American Association of Dental Examiners

AADGP American Academy of Dental Group Practice

AADPA American Academy of Dental Practice Administration

AADR American Association for Dental Research

AAE American Association of Endodontists

AAFO American Association for Functional Orthodontics

AAHD American Association of Hospital Dentists

AAO American Association of Orthodontists

AAOM American Academy of Oral Medicine

AAOMP American Academy of Oral and Maxillofacial Pathology

AAOMR American Academy of Oral and Maxillofacial Radiology

AAOMS American Association of Oral and Maxillofacial Surgeons

AAP American Academy of Periodontology

AAPD American Academy of Pediatric Dentistry

AAPHD American Association of Public Health Dentistry

AARD American Academy of Restorative Dentistry

AAWD American Association of Women Dentists

ABDPH American Board of Dental Public Health

ABO American Board of Orthodontics

ABOMP American Board of Oral and Maxillofacial Pathology

ABOMS American Board of Oral and Maxillofacial Surgery

ABP American Board of Periodontology

ABPD American Board of Pediatric Dentistry

ACD American College of Dentists

ACOMS American College of Oral and Maxillofacial Surgeons

ACP American College of Prosthodontists

ADA American Dental Association

ADAA American Dental Assistants Association

ADEA American Dental Education Association

ADH Academy of Dentistry for the Handicapped

ADHA American Dental Hygienists Association

ADLTA American Dental Laboratory Technician Association

ADSA American Dental Society of Anesthesiology

ADTA American Dental Trade Association

AERA American Educational Research Association

AES American Endodontic Society

AES American Equilibration Society

AGD Academy of General Dentistry

AHA American Heart Association

AIT Academy for Implants and Transplants

ANSI American National Standards Institute

AOD Academy of Operative Dentistry

AOS American Orthodontic Society

APIC Association for Professionals in Infection Control

APS American Prosthodontic Society

ASAHP Association of Schools of Allied Health Professions

ASD Academy for Sports Dentistry

ASGD American Society for Geriatric Dentistry

ASFO American Society of Forensic Odontology

ASMS American Society of Maxillofacial Surgeons

ASTDD Association of State and Territorial Dental Directors

BHP Bureau of Health Professions

CDA Canadian Dental Association

CDA Certified Dental Assistant

CDABO College of Diplomates of the American Board of Orthodontics

CDC Centers for Disease Control and Prevention

CDEL Council on Dental Education and Licensure

CDPMA Certified Dental Practice Management Assistant

CDT Certified Dental Technician

CEREC Chairside Economical Restoration of Esthetical Ceramics

COA Certified Orthodontic Assistant

CODA Commission on Dental Accreditation

COMDA Committee on Dental Auxiliaries

COMSA Certified Oral Maxillofacial Surgery Assistant

CPR Cardiopulmonary Resuscitation Certification

DANB Dental Assisting National Board

DCA Department of Consumer Affairs

DDPA Delta Dental Plans Association

DDS Doctor of Dental Surgery

DEA Drug Enforcement Administration

DHMO Dental Health Maintenance Organization

DMD Doctor of Medical Dentistry

DVA Department of Veterans Affairs

EEOC Equal Employment Opportunity Commission

EFDA Expanded or Extended Function Dental Assistant

EPA Environmental Protection Agency

FADAA Fellowship of the American Dental Assistants Association

FCC Federal Communications Commission

FDA Food and Drug Administration

HAD Holistic Dental Association

HRSA Health Resources and Services Administration

IAOMT International Academy of Oral Medicine and Toxicology

IOM Institute of Medicine

MADAA Master of the American Dental Assistants Association

NADA National Association of Dental Assistants

NADL National Association of Dental Laboratories

NBC National Board for Certification in Dental Laboratory Technology

NCCA National Commission for Certifying Agencies

NCME National Council on Measurement in Education

NDA National Dental Association

NDAA National Dental Assistants Association

NIH National Institutes of Health

NIOSH National Institute for Occupational Safety and Health

NOCA National Organization for Competency Assurance

OSAP Occupational Safety and Asepsis Procedures

OSHA Occupational Safety and Health Administration

RDA Registered Dental Assistant

RDAEF Registered Dental Assistant in Extended Functions

RDH Registered Dental Hygienist

RHS Radiation Health and Safety

SCDA Special Care Dentistry Association

UAPD Union of American Physicians and Dentists

Appendix II: Dental Assisting Abbreviations

A	amp		**C**	centigrade or 100
@	at		**c**	with
aa	of each		**CA**	canceled appointment
abs	abscess		**ca**	carcinoma
a.c.	before meals		**C&B**	crown and bridge
a.d.	alternating days [to; up to]		**caps**	capsules
adj.	adjustment		**Carbo**	Carbocaine
amal	amalgam		**Carp**	carpule
anes	anesthetic		**cav**	cavity
ant	anterior		**CC**	chief complaint
aq	water		**CEJ**	cementoenamel junction
			cem	cement
B	buccal		**comp**	composite
BA	broken appointment		**consult**	consultation
BCC	basal cell carcinoma		**cur**	curettage
BF	bone fragment		**crn**	crown
BI	biological indicators			
bib	drink		**D**	distal
b.i.d.	twice a day		**d.d.**	Let it be given to
BP	blood pressure		**DEJ**	dentinoenamel junction
BS	blood sugar		**DO**	disto-occlusal
BWX	bitewing X-ray		**DOB**	date of birth
Bx	biopsy		**Dx**	diagnosis

endo	endodontics		**max**	maxillary
epi	epinephrine		**Med Alert**	Medical Alert
exam	examination		**mm**	millimeter
Ext	extraction		**MO**	mesio-occlusal
			MOD	mesio-occlusal-distal
F	facial		**MSDS**	material safety data sheets
ff	following			
FGC	full gold crown		**norm**	normal
FH	family history		**np**	new patient
FLD	full lower denture		**npo**	nothing by mouth
FLTR	fluoride treatment			
FMX	full mouth series (X-rays)		**O**	occlusal
frag	fragment		**occ**	occlusal
FUD	full upper denture		**o.d.**	every day
Fx	fracture		**odtp**	oral diagnosis and treatment plan
			OH	oral hygiene
ging	gingival		**OHI**	oral hygiene instruction
			o.m.	every morning
H	hour		**o.n.**	every night
h.d.	at hour of bedtime		**OSAP**	occupational safety and asepsis procedures
hr	hour			
h.s.	hour of sleep			
Hx	history		**Pa**	periapical
			pano	panorex (X-ray)
I	incisal		**PDL**	periodontal ligament
IA	inferior alveolar		**perio**	periodontal
imp	impression		**perm**	permanent
inc	incisal		**PFM**	porcelain fused to metal
			PLD	partial lower denture
L	lingual		**PO**	postoperative
la	local anesthetic		**post-op**	postoperative
lab	laboratory		**p.o.**	by mouth
lat	lateral		**PPE**	personal protective equipment
Lido	Lidocaine		**premed**	premedication
LL	lower left		**pre-op**	pre-operative
LPD	lower partial denture		**prep**	preparation
LR	lower right		**p.r.n.**	as required for
Lt	left		**prog**	prognosis
			prophy	prophylaxis
M	mesial		**pt**	patient
mand	mandibular		**PUD**	partial upper denture

Px	prophylaxis		stat	immediuately
			surg	surgery
Q	every		Sx	symptom
QC	quality control			
q.2h	every two hours		tab	tablet
q.4–6h	every four to six hours		temp	temporary
q.d.	every day		TFD	target to film distance
q.h.	every hour		t.i.d.	three times a day
q.i.d.	four times a day		TLC	tender loving care
quad	quadrant		TMJ	temporomandibular joint
			Tx	treatment
rad	radiation absorbed dose			
RBA	risks, benefits, and alternatives		UCR	usual, customary, and reasonable fee
RCT	root canal therapy/treatment		UL	upper left
Rem	radiation equipment man		UPD	upper partial denture
Resto	restoration		UR	upper right
Rp	root planing			
Rt	right		VA	vertical angle
Rx	prescription			
			Xylo	xylocaine
s	without			
sig	take thou (directions for use)		ZOE	zinc oxide eugenol
SRP	scaling, root planing			

Appendix III:
Dental Associations ▶

For further information, contact the following dental resources:

Academy for Implants and Transplants (AIT)
2250 Clarendon Blvd.
Arlington, SD 22201
www.ada.org/ada/organizations
P: 703-841-0300
F: 703-841-1570

Academy for Sports Dentistry (ASD)
118 Faye St.
Farmersville, IL 62533
www.sportsdentistry-asd.org
F: 310-536-0891

Academy of Dentistry for the Handicapped (ADH)
211 East Chicago Ave., Suite 1616
Chicago, IL 606111
P: 312-440-2660

Academy of General Dentistry (AGD)
211 East Chicago Ave., Suite 900
Chicago, IL 60611-1999
www.agd.org
P: 888-243-3368
F: 312-440-0559

Academy of Operative Dentistry (AOD)
P.O. Box 34425
Los Angeles, CA 90034
www.operativedentistry.com
P: 909-558-4640
F: 909-558-0253

American Academy of Dental Group Practice
  (AADGP)
2525 East Arizona Biltmore Circle, Suite 127
Phoenix, AZ 8501
www.aadgp.org
P: 602-381-1185
F: 602-381-1093

American Academy of Dental Practice
  Administration (AADPA)
1063 Whipporwill Lane
Palatine, IL 60067-7064
www.aadpa.org
P: 847-934-4404
F: 847-934-4410

American Academy of Esthetic Dentistry (AAED)
737 North Michigan Ave., Suite 2100
Chicago, IL 60611
www.estheticacademy.org
P: 312-981-6770
F: 312-981-6787

American Academy of Oral and Maxillofacial
   Pathology (AAOMP)
214 North Hale St.
Wheaton, IL 60187
www.aaomp.org
P: 630-510-4552 or 888-552-2667
F: 630-510-4501

American Academy of Oral and Maxillofacial
   Radiology (AAOMR)
P.O. Box 1010
Evans, GA 30809-1010
www.aaomr.org

American Academy of Oral Medicine (AAOM)
P.O. Box 2016
Edmonds, WA 98020-9516
www.aaom.com
P: 425-778-6162
F: 425-771-9588

American Academy of Pediatric Dentistry (AAPD)
211 East Chicago Ave., Suite 1700
Chicago, IL 60611-2663
www.aapd.org
P: 312-337-2169
F: 312-337-6329

American Academy of Periodontology (AAP)
737 North Michigan Ave., Suite 800
Chicago, IL 60611-6660
www.perio.org
P: 312-787-5518
F: 312-787-3670

American Academy of Restorative Dentistry (AARD)
P.P. Box 26385
Colorado Springs, CO 80936
www.restorativeacademy.com
P: 719-559-1945
F: 719-623-0387

American Association for Dental Research (AADR)
1619 Duke St.
Alexandria, VA 22314-3406
www.aadronline.org
P: 703-548-0066
F: 703-548-1863

American Association for Functional Orthodontics
   (AAFO)
106 South Kent St.
Winchester, VA 22601
www.aafo.org
P: 540-662-2200 or 800-441-3850
F: 540-665-8910

American Association of Dental Consultants (AADC)
10032 Wind Hill Dr.
Greenville, IN 47124
www.aadc.org
P: 800-896-0707
F: 812-923-2900

American Association of Dental Examiners (AADE)
211 East Chicago Ave., Suite 760
Chicago, IL 60611-2616
www.aadexam.org
P: 312-440-7464
F: 312-440-3525

American Association of Endodontists (AAE)
211 E. Chicago Ave., Suite 1100
Chicago, IL 60611-2691
www.aae.org
P: 800-872-3636 (North America) or 312-266-7255
   (International)
F: 866-451-9020 (North America) or 312-266-9867
   (International)

American Association of Hospital Dentists (AAHD)
401 North Michigan Ave., Suite 2200
Chicago, IL 60611
www.scdonline.org
P: 312-527-6764
F: 312-673-6663

American Association of Oral and Maxillofacial
   Surgeons (AAOMS)
9700 West Bryn Mawr Ave.
Rosemont, IL 60018
www.aaoms.org
P: 847-678-6200 or 800-822-6637
F: 847-678-6286

American Association of Orthodontists (AAO)
401 North Lindberg Blvd.
St. Louis, MO 63141-7816
www.aaortho.org
P: 314-993-1700
F: 314-997-1745

American Association of Public Health Dentistry
   (AAPHD)
3085 Stevenson Drive, Suite 200
Springfield, IL 62703
www.aaphd.org
P: 217-529-6941
F: 217-529-9120

American Association of Women Dentists (AAWD)
216 Jackson Blvd., Suite 625
Chicago, IL 60606
www.aawd.org
P: 800-920-2293
F: 312-750-1203

American Board of Dental Public Health (ABDPH)
827 Brookridge Drive NE
Atlanta, GA 30306
www.aaphd.org
P: 404-876-3530

American Board of Oral and Maxillofacial Pathology
   (ABOMP)
One Urban Center, Suite 690
4830 West Kennedy Blvd.
Tampa, FL 33609-2571
www.abomp.org
P: 813-286-2444 x 230
F: 813-289-5279

American Board of Oral and Maxillofacial Surgery
   (ABOMS)
625 North Michigan Ave., Suite 1820
Chicago, IL 60611
www.aboms.org
P: 312-642-0070
F: 312-642-8584

American Board of Orthodontics (ABO)
401 N. Lindberg Blvd.
St. Louis, MO 63141-7839
www.americanboardortho.com
P: 314-432-6130
F: 314-432-8170

American Board of Pediatric Dentistry (ABPD)
325 E. Washington St., Suite 208
Iowa City, IA 52240-3959
www.abpd.org
P: 319-341-8488 or 800-410-1250
F: 319-341-9499

American Board of Periodontology (ABP)
4157 Mountain Rd., PBN 249
Pasadena, MD 21122
www.abperio.org
P: 410-437-3749
F: 410-437-4021

American College of Dentists (ACD)
839J Quince Orchard Blvd.
Gaitherburg, MD 20878-1614
P: 301-977-3223
F: 301-977-3330

American College of Oral and Maxillofacial Surgeons
 (ACOMS)
2025 M. St. NW, Suite 800
Washington, DC 20036
www.acoms.org
P: 202-367-1182 or 800-522-6676
F: 202-367-2182

American College of Prosthodontists (ACP)
211 E. Chicago Ave., Suite 1000
Chicago, IL 60611
www.prosthodontics.org
P: 312-573-1260
F: 312-573-1257

American Dental Assistants Association (ADAA)
35 East Wacker Dr., Suite 1730
Chicago, IL 60601-2211
www.dentalassistant.org
P: 312.541.1550
F: 312.541.1496

American Dental Association (ADA)
211 East Chicago Ave.
Chicago, IL 60611-2678
www.ada.org
P: 312-440-2500

American Dental Education Association (ADEA)
1400 K. St. NW, Suite 1100
Washington, DC 20005
P: 202-289-7201
F: 202-289-7204

American Dental Hygienists' Association (ADHA)
444. N. Michigan Ave., Suite 3400
Chicago, IL 60611
www.adha.org
P: 312-440-8900

American Dental Society of Anesthesiology (ADSA)
211 E. Chicago Ave., Suite 780
Chicago, IL 60611
www.adsahome.org
P: 312-664-8270 or 800-255-3742
F: 312-224-8624

American Dental Trade Association (ADTA)
4222 King St.
Alexandria, VA 22302
P: 703-379-7755
F: 703-931-9429

American Educational Research Association (AERA)
1430 K. St. NW
Washington, DC 20005
www.aera.com
P: 202-238-3200
F: 202-238-3250

American Endodontic Society (AES)
265 North Main St.
Glen Ellyn, IL 60137
www.aesoc.com
P: 773-519-4879
F: 630-858-0525

American Equilibration Society (AES)
297 E. Ohio St., Suite 399
Chicago, IL 60611
www.aes-tmj.org
P: 847-965-2888
F: 856-579-7007

American Heart Association (AHA)
7272 Greenville Ave.
Dallas, TX 75231
www.americanheart.org
P: 800-242-8721

American National Standards Institute (ANSI)
1819 L. St. NW, 6th Floor
Washington, DC 20036
www.ansi.org
P: 202-293-6020
F: 202-293-9287

American Orthodontic Society (AOS)
11884 Greenville Ave., Suite 112
Dallas, TX 75243
www.orthodontics.com
P: 800-448-1601

American Prosthodontic Society (APS)
737 N. Michaigan Ave., Suite 2100
Chicago, IL 60611
www.prostho.org
P: 312-981-6780
F: 312-981-6787

American Society for Geriatric Dentistry (ASGD)
401 N. Michigan Ave., Suite 2200
Chicago, IL 60611
www.scdonline.org
P: 312-527-6764
F: 312-673-6663

American Society of Forensic Odontology (ASFO)
13048 N. Research Blvd., Suite B
Austin, TX 78750
www.newasfo.com
F: 250-426-2354

American Society of Maxillofacial Surgeons (ASMS)
444 E. Algonquin Rd.
Arlington Heights, IL 60005-4664
www.maxface.org
P: 800-849-4682
F: 847-981-5462

Association for Professionals in Infection Control
   (APIC)
1275 K. Ave., Suite 1000
Washington, DC 20005-4006
www.apic.org
P: 202-789-1890
F: 202-789-1899

Association of Schools of Allied Health Professions
   (ASAHP)
4400 Jenifer St. NW, Suite 333
Washington, DC 20015
www.asahp.org
P: 202-237-6481
F: 202-237-6485

Association of State and Territorial Dental Directors
   (ASTDD)
105 Westerly Rd.
New Bern, NC
www. astdd.org
P: 252-637-6333
F: 252-637-3343

Bureau of Health Professions (BHP)
www.bhpr.hrsa.gov
P: 877-464-4772

Canadian Dental Association (CDA)
2555 St. Laurent Blvd., Suite 203
Ottawa, ON, Canada K1G 4K3
www.cdaa.ca
P: 613-521-5495
F: 613-521-5572

Centers for Disease Control and Prevention (CDC)
National Center of Infectious Diseases
1600 Clifton Rd.
Atlanta, GA 30333
www.cdc.gov
P: 800-232-4636

College of Diplomates of the American Board of
  Orthodontics (CDABO)
3260 Upper Bottom Rd.
St. Charles, MO 63303
www.cdabo.org
P: 636-922-5551
F: 636-244-1650

Commission on Dental Accreditation
  (CODA of ADA)
211 East Chicago Ave.
Chicago, IL 60611-2678
www.ada.org/prof/ed/accred/commission/index.asp
P: 312-440-2500

Council on Dental Education and Licensure (CDEL)
211 East Chicago Ave.
Chicago, IL 60611-2678
www.ada.org/ada/contact/index.asp
P: 312-440-2500

Delta Dental Plans Association (DDPA)
1515 22nd St., Suite 1200
Oak Brook, IL 60523
www.deltadental.com
P: 630-574-6001
F: 630-574-6999

Dental Assisting National Board, Inc. (DANB)
444 North Michigan Ave., Suite 900
Chicago, IL 60611
www.danb.org
P: 1-800-367-3262 or 312-642-3368
F: 312-642-1475

Department of Veterans Affairs (VA)
810 Vermont Ave. NW
Washington, DC 20420
www.va.gov
P: 800-827-1000

Drug Enforcement Administration (DEA)
Mailstop: AES
8701 Morrissette Dr.
Springfield, VA 22152
www.usdoj.gov
P: 202-307-1000

Environmental Protection Agency (EPA)
Ariel Rios Building
1200 Pennsylvania Ave. N.W.
Washington, DC 20460
www.epa.gov
P: 202-272-0167
F: 202-272-0165

Federal Communications Commission (FCC)
445 12th St. NW
Washington, DC 20554
www.fcc.gov
P: 888-225-5322
F: 866-418-0232

Federation of Special Care Organizations and
  Dentistry
401 N. Michigan Ave., Suite 2200
Chicago, IL 60611
www.scdonline.org
P: 312-527-6764
F: 312-673-6663

Food and Drug Administration (FDA)
Office of Consumer Affairs
5600 Fishers Lane
Rockville, MD 20857
www.fda.gov
P: 800-463-6332

Health Resources and Services Administration
  (HRSA)
5600 Fishers Lane
Rockville, MD 20857
www.hrsa.gov
P: 301-443-2216

Holistic Dental Association (HAD)
PO Box 151444
San Diego, CA 92175
www.holisticdental.org
P: 619-923-3120
F: 619-615-2228

Indian Health Service (IHS)
The Reyes Building
801 Thompson Ave., Suite 400
Rockville, MD 20852-1627
www.ihs.gov
P: 301-443-1011

Institute of Medicine (IOM)
500 Fifth St. NW
Washington, DC 20001
www.iom.edu
P: 202-334-2352
F: 202-334-1412

International Academy of Oral Medicine and
  Toxicology (IAOMT)
8297 ChampionsGate Blvd., Suite 193
ChampionsGate, FL 33896
www.iaomt.org
P: 863-420-6373
F: 863-419-8136

National Association of Dental Assistants (NADA)
900 Washington St., Suite G-13
Falls Church, VA 22046
www.ndaonline.org/auxilary.asp
P: 703-237-8616

National Association of Dental Laboratories (NADL)
325 John Knox Rd., Suite L103
Tallahassee, FL 32303
www.nadl.org
P: 850-205-5626 or 800-950-1150
F: 850-222-0053

National Board for Certification in Dental Laboratory
  Technology (NBC)
325 John Knox Rd., Suite L103
Tallahassee, FL 32303
www.nbccert.org
P: 850-205-5626 or 800-950-1150
F: 850-222-0053

National Commission for Certifying Agencies
  (NCCA)
2025 M St. NW
Washington, DC 20036
www.noca.org/Resources/NCCAAccreditation/
tabid/82/Default.aspx
P: 202-367-1165
F: 202-367-2165

National Council on Measurement in Education
(NCME)
2810 Crossroads Dr., Suite 3800
Madison, WI 53718
www.ncme.org
P: 608-443-2487
F: 608-443-2474

National Dental Assistants Association (NDAA)
3517 16th St. NW
Washington, DC 20010
www.ndaonline.org/auxilary.asp
P: 202-588-1697
F: 202-588-1244

National Dental Association (NDA)
3517 16th St. NW
Washington, DC 20010
www.ndaonline.org
P: 202-588-1697
F: 202-588-1244

National Institute for Occupational Safety and Health
(NIOSH)
1600 Clifton Rd.
Atlanta, GA 30333
www.cdc.gov/niosh
P: 404-639-3311 or 800-CDC-INFO

National Institutes of Health (NIH)
900 Rockville Pike
Bethesda, MD 20892
www.nih.gov
P: 301-496-4000

National Organization for Competency Assurance
(NOCA)
2025 M St. NW
Washington, DC 20036
www.noca.org
P: 202-367-1165
F: 202-367-2165

Occupational Safety and Health Administration
(OSHA)
U.S. Department of Labor
200 Constitution Ave.
Washington, DC 20210
www.osha.gov
P: 800-321-6742

Office of Safety and Asepsis Procedures (OSAP)
Research Foundation
P.O. Box 6297
Annapolis, MD 21401
www.osap.org
P: 410-571-0003 or 800-298-6727
F: 410-571-0028

Special Care Dentistry Association (SCDA)
401 N. Michigan Ave., Suite 2200
Chicago, IL 60611
www.scdonline.org
P: 312-527-6764
F: 312-673-6663

Union of American Physicians and Dentists (UAPD)
180 Grand Ave., Suite 1380
Oakland, CA 94612
www.uapd.com
P: 510-839-0193 or 800-622-0909
F: 510-763-8756

Appendix IV: State Dental Assisting Organizations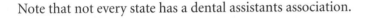

Note that not every state has a dental assistants association.

California Dental Assistants Association (CDAA)
1017 L St. #176
Sacramento, CA 95814-3502
P: 916-491-4116
www.cdaaweb.org

Colorado Dental Assistants Association (CDAA)
www.codaa.com

Florida Dental Assistants Association
7762 NW 58th Way
Parkland, FL 33067
P: 850-681-3629
F: 863-533-2185
www.floridadental.org

Illinois Dental Assisting Association (ILDAA)
www.ildaa.com

Iowa Dental Assistants Association
www.idaada.org

Louisiana Dental Assistants Association
www.ladaa.org

Massachusetts Dental Assistants Association
mdaa@massdentalassistants.org
www.massdentalassistants.org

Michigan Dental Assistants Association
P. O. Box 118
Lennon, MI 48449
www.midaa.org

Missouri Dental Assistants Association
www.modaa.org

Nebraska Dental Assistants Association
www.nebraskadentalassistants.org

New Jersey Dental Assistants Association
www.njdaa.org
P: 908-889-2417

New York Dental Assistants Association
www.nydaa.net
www.newyorkdentalassistantsassociation.com
nydaassoc@aol.com
P: 716-826-7324

North Carolina Dental Assistants Association
www.ncdentalassistant.org

North Dakota Dental Assistants Association
www.nddaa.org

Northeast PA Dental Assisting Society
nepadas@aol.com

Northern Kentucky Dental Assistants Association
www.nkdas.org
nkdas06@yahoo.com

Ohio Dental Assistants Association (ODAA)
home.fuse.net/kspradlin/ODAAmain.htm

Oregon Dental Assistants Association (ODAA)
www.oregondentalassistants.com

Pennsylvania Dental Assistants Association
www.padentalassistants.org
P: 312-541-1500

Rhode Island Dental Assistants Association
info@ridaa.com

South Carolina Dental Assistants Association
www.scdentalassistantsassociation.com

South Dakota Dental Assistants Association
www.sddha.org

Tennessee Dental Assistants Association
www.tndaa.org

Texas Dental Assistants Association
2113 Spur Court
Denton, TX 76210
www.tdaa.org

Glossary

abandonment no longer treating a patient with an existing treatment plan or not providing a referral to another provider

abscess localized area of exudate caused by an infection

absorb to take in to the body tissue

absorption photons in the X-ray beam that interact with matter

accounts payable system where all the dentist's financial obligations or expenses to operate the dental practice are paid for and kept track of; including expenses such as lab fees, dental supplies, staff payroll, rent, insurance, taxes, etc.

accounts receivable system where production, daily charges for services rendered, payments received, adjustments, and new balances are calculated

acid etch a phosphoric acid used in bonding procedures that encourages the enamel rods and dentinal tubules to open in order for the restorative material to bond

adjustment alteration of an account balance; for example, senior discount, professional allowance, non-sufficient funds check, bank fees, insurance payment, and personal payment

advanced appointment system a type of recall system in which a routine appointment is made before the patient leaves the office

aged accounts balances owed to the dental practice that are categorized based on how long the balance has been present; for example, current, 30–60 days, 60–90 days, and over 90 days

alginate irreversible hydrocolloid impression material used to take preliminary impressions

alloy a mixture of two or more metals

aluminum filter filter in the X-ray tube head that absorbs the longer wave-length, less penetrating radiation

alveolar process bone that supports the maxillary teeth

alveolitis inflammation and infection associated with the disturbance of a blood clot after extraction of an impacted tooth

amalgam an alloy combined with mercury as a restoration material

ameloblasts cells that form enamel

ameloclasts cells that absorb enamel

American Dental Association (ADA) codes and nomenclature codes used on claim forms to identify each procedure performed

ammonium thiosulfate chemical in fixer responsible for removing the unexposed silver halide crystals and producing the light image on the film

anatomic crown portion of the tooth that is covered by enamel

anatomic landmark an anatomic structure that is used to identify a location on the face or oral cavity for film or pid placement

anatomy study of the shape and structure of the human body

anesthetic medicine that produces temporary loss of sensation or feeling

anode positive terminal in the X-ray tube head; contains the tungsten target

antiseptic a chemical agent that can be applied to living tissues to destroy or inhibit microorganisms

apex tip of the root of a tooth

apical foramen opening at the apex

appointment book matrix the framework around which appointments are made, such as daily start/ending time, holidays, vacations, lunch hours, staff meetings, and seminars

area monitoring level of radiation monitoring in a specific area

asepsis disease-free

assignment of benefits authorization by the subscriber for the dental carrier to issue benefits directly to the provider, which is the treating dentist

assignment of duties dentist's act of delegating duties to assistants and hygienists

autoclave method of sterilization of instruments using steam under pressure

auto-cure a self-setting material

autonomy independence

back-ordered supply a supply that was ordered but is not in stock that will be shipped when available

barrier a barrier of radiation-absorbing material used for protection (lead, concrete, or plaster)

base an insulating layer placed under a restoration to protect the pulp from hot and cold temperatures

benefit plan summary a description of the subscriber's benefit plan that is required by the employer to give to an employee

bioburden blood, saliva, and other body fluids

biohazard container for disposal of any bioburden

biologic indicators (BI) (spore tests) strips that contain harmless bacterial spores that are used to determine whether sterilization has been reached

biopsy removal of tissue for diagnostic purposes

birthday rule a method of determining which carrier is primary and which carrier is secondary when dual coverage is involved

biteblock styrofoam a plastic film holder that stabilizes the film in the patient's oral cavity

bitewing radiograph a film that shows images of the crowns, coronal thirds of the roots, and crestal bone levels of both maxillary and mandibular teeth in occlusion

blood-borne disease microorganisms that are carried in the blood; for example, Hepatitis B, Hepatitis C and HIV

blood-borne pathogens disease-causing organisms transferred through blood or other body fluids

board of dentistry a collection of dental professionals and lay people that enforce the state's Dental Practice Act

bookkeeping the recording of financial transactions

bramsstrahlung radiation also termed "braking radiation"; describes the deceleration of electrons as they interact with the highly positive-charged nuclei in the X-ray tube head when X-rays are generated

broken appointment an appointment that is scheduled, but the patient does not come and does not call to cancel the appointment

buccal surface of posterior teeth closest to the cheek

buffer period short amount of time set aside per day, usually 20 minutes, to accommodate emergency patients, or used for chairside assistant to catch up from a hectic schedule

calculus hardened plaque that adheres to the enamel

capital supplies large costly supplies that are infrequently replaced

capitation a benefits-delivery system where dentists contract with the program's administrator and services are performed for a fixed monthly payment per patient per capita; this is also called a dental health maintenance organization (DHMO)

carcinoma malignant tumor in epithelial tissue

caries dental decay

carrier the dental insurance company

catalyst a part of the mixture that encourages setting

cathode negative terminal in the X-ray tube head contains the tungsten filament

cavity pitted area in a tooth that was caused by decay

cementoblasts cells that form cementum

cementoclasts cells that absorb cementum

cementum layer of the tooth that covers the root

Centers For Disease Control (CDC) an advisory agency that conducts lengthy research regarding infection-control protocols and makes recommendations based on their research results

central nervous system body system concerned with the brain and spinal cord

chain of infection conditions that must be present for an infection to occur

charting symbols symbol or shorthand for dental conditions and treatment that is entered on tooth symbols on a patient's clinical chart

chemical vapor sterilization (chemiclave) method of sterilization of instruments using hot formaldehyde vapors under pressure

child abuse mistreatment of a child that endangers the child's physical, emotional, and developmental health

cidal agents chemicals that kill microorganisms by an action that is not reversible

cingulum raised, rounded area on cervical third of lingual surfaces of anterior teeth

clinical abbreviations initials or shorter terms used to document clinical treatment performed on the patient's chart; for example, hhr = health history reviewed, 1 carp 2 lido w/1:100,000 = description of local anesthetic

clinical crown portion of the tooth visible in the patient's mouth

clinical record a collection of all of the patient's information related to her or his dental treatment; for example, clinical chart, radiographs, lab requisitions, referral letters, prescriptions, health history, registration form, and consent forms

code of ethics a set of voluntary moral standards a profession establishes

composite a tooth-colored, resin-based restoration material

confidentiality keeping patients' personal, health, and financial information private and secure

consent voluntary acceptance of treatment being presented to patient

consent form a document signed by the patient or parent/guardian of a minor patient that grants permission for administration of dental treatment

cranium the structure made up of eight bones that cover and protect the brain

credit balance total amount owed to the patient by the dental practice

critical instruments any instrument used to penetrate soft tissue or bone

crossbite condition in which a tooth is not properly aligned with its opposing tooth

cross-contamination passage of microorganisms from one person or inanimate object to another

cross-infection passage of microorganisms from one person to another

Current Dental Terminology (CDT) a listing of all current dental procedure codes and descriptions of dental procedures, published by the American Dental Association (ADA)

cusp raised area of enamel on chewing surfaces of cuspids and posterior teeth

custom acrylic provisional a temporary coverage for a tooth preparation custom-made for the patient from acrylic materials

custom tray an impression tray specifically designed to the arch of the patient having his or her final impression taken

debit balance total amount owed to the dental practice

deciduous teeth primary dentition teeth

deductible the amount a patient must pay first before her or his dental benefits begin

defamation of character injury to a professional's reputation by communication of false information to a third party

defendant the person or party being sued

demineralization loss of minerals from a tooth

Dental Practice Act the legal scope of dental practice and the requirements necessary to practice dentistry as defined by each state

dental sealant flowable resin that covers the pits and fissures of teeth

dentin second and largest layer of the tooth; capable of rebuilding itself

dentition a set of teeth

dependent spouse or child of the subscriber that is insured under the subscriber's plan

direct contact touching or contact with a patient's blood or saliva

direct reimbursement plan a plan where the employee is reimbursed directly a certain percent of the cost of the dental treatment

direct supervision level of supervision by the dentist, which gives permission to a dental assistant to perform certain duties only when the dentist is present

disinfectant a chemical agent that is applied onto inanimate surfaces

disinfection destruction of most microorganisms, but not highly resistant forms such as bacterial spores

disposables items that are only used once, then thrown away; single-use items

distal surface of the teeth farthest away from the midline

dosimeter a device used to measure the operator's dose of radiation

dovetailing when a second patient is scheduled at the same time as a first patient; usually a short procedure that the doctor breaks away from the first patient (a longer appointment) to treat the second patient

dry heat sterilizer method of sterilization of instruments using heated air

dual-cure when a material is cured by both self-cure and light-cure

dual insurance when a patient is covered by two separate insurance policies

due care the absence of negligence; proper care

elder abuse treatment of an elderly individual that endangers the person's physical, financial, or emotional health

electron a negatively charged particle

elongation distortion of an image where it appears longer than the actual size caused by improper vertical angulation of the cone/pid

embrasure triangular space in between the teeth next to the gingival border

enamel protective outer layer of the tooth

endodontics dental specialty that diagnoses, treats, and helps prevent diseases of the dental pulp and the periradicular tissues

eruption natural process of a tooth coming into the mouth

etchant a chemical that prepares the tooth surface to receive a restorative material

ethics morals or rules that influence behavioral choices

exfoliation the shedding of the primary (baby) teeth

exothermic release of heat during setting process

expendable supplies supplies that are only used once, then thrown away; single-use items

expert witness a person who is within the same field of practice as the defendant and can offer his or her opinion as to whether the care met acceptable standards

fact witness a person who was present when an act was committed and tells what she or he witnessed

Fair Debt Collection Practices Act act to protect the patient from unethical collection procedures

fee schedule dental insurance plan in which payment is made based on a set fee allowance for each dental procedure

felony a serious crime that may result in jail time

film badge a container of radiographic film worn by an operator that measures the radiation exposure of the operator

filter aluminum filter used to filter out the long-wave low energy waves

financial record documents that pertain to financial transactions; for example, ledger, statement, and payment receipt

fixer a solution used for processing X-rays

fluoride a naturally occurring mineral that strengthens enamel

foreshortening distortion of an image where it appears shorter than the actual size caused by using too little vertical angulation

four-handed dentistry process where the operator and the dental assistant work together to perform clinical tasks in an ergonomically structured environment

framework the metal portion of the removable partial denture

fraud deceit, trickery, sharp practice, or breach of confidence, perpetrated for profit or to gain some unfair or dishonest advantage

full denture a removable prosthesis that replaces all of the missing teeth in one arch

galvanic an electrical reaction that occurs when two different metals come in contact with each other

general supervision level of supervision by the dentist that gives permission to a dental assistant to perform certain duties without the dentist being present

gingiva tissue that covers the bone and acts as a supporting structure in the mouth

gingivitis inflammation of the gingiva; first stage of periodontal disease

glossitis inflammation of the tongue

glutaraldehyde high-level disinfectant usually utilized as "cold sterile" in dental offices (used on instruments that cannot be heat sterilized and not on hard surfaces)

gold a type of dental material that can be used for restorative purposes

gutta percha a rubber-based material that is solid at room temperature and flowable when warmed that is used to fill the canals of endodontically treated roots

Health Insurance Portability and Accountability Act (HIPAA) the 1996 act setting national standards for electronic healthcare transactions to ensure patients' privacy

hematoma swollen area indicating a collection of blood under the skin

high-volume evacuator (HVE) oral evacuation system used by dental assistants to remove water and debris from the treatment area

histology study of body tissues under a microscope

homogeneous the state at which a mixture is all one color, texture, and consistency

hydroxyapatite the first mineral lost during the decay process

immediate denture a temporary denture that is worn by a patient immediately following the extractions of the remaining teeth

implant a titanium screw placed into healthy bone to replace a missing tooth

implied consent when a patient's actions act as a consent to treatment

incipient caries beginning stage of decay

incisal biting surface of anterior teeth

inflammation redness, irritation, and possible swelling due to the presence of an irritant

informed consent permission given to office by a patient to perform treatment after being presented all options of care

integumentary system body system concerned with the skin

interproximal mesial and distal surfaces, "in between" surfaces of the teeth

invasion of privacy publicly exposing someone's personal life without that person's permission

inventory system a list of stock of supplies used in the dental office recording cost of the supply, date supply was ordered, rate of use, and product manufacturer name, address, and phone number

invoice a list of the contents with the price of each item

iodophor intermediate-level disinfectant used to disinfect treatment rooms in dental offices

justice fair treatment

labial/facial surface of anterior teeth closest to the lip/face

labial frenum band of tissue that connects the lip to the mucosa on the maxillary arch

lactobacilli (LB) bacteria produced from a carbohydrate-rich diet

lamina dura thin compact bone that lines the alveolar socket

lesion area of pathology

licensure national- or state-approved permission to practice dentistry after completing written and practical examinations

light-cure an ultraviolet light that hardens dental materials

limitations restrictions stated in the benefit plan summary; restrictions may include age limits for particular procedures, waiting periods, and frequency of certain services

liner a medicament placed when decay is deep and close to the pulp to stimulate secondary dentin

lingual surface of teeth closest to the tongue

lingual frenum band of tissue that connects the tongue to the floor of the mouth

litigation the process of a lawsuit

luting viscous cement

malocclusion occlusion that is deviated from normal

malpractice professional misconduct, illegal or immoral, that is intentional or unintentional

mamelon rounded enamel prominences on incisal edges of incisors noticeable just after eruption

mandated reporters certain professionals that are required by law to report any suspicious or known acts of child abuse

mandibular the lower arch (jaw)

marginal ridge rounded, raised border on chewing surfaces of posterior teeth

masseter strongest muscle of mastication

maxillary the upper arch (jaw)

maximum allowable amount the highest total amount an insurance carrier will pay toward the cost of dental treatment in a given benefit period

mesial surface of the teeth closest to the midline

microleakage an area between the filling/sealant and the tooth structure where bacteria are trapped

midline imaginary line that divides the mouth into right and left sides

misdemeanor a less serious crime that may result in a fine or community service

mixed dentition mixture of permanent and primary teeth together in the mouth at one time (between ages six and 12 years)

mobility to have movement, as in "loose" teeth

morphology study of the form and shape of teeth

mutans streptococci (MS) bacteria primarily responsible for caries

National Practitioner Data Bank a centralized agency that holds information regarding paid malpractice claims and licensure issues

negligence the act of forgetting or choosing not to do something that a reasonable professional would do, or doing something that a reasonable professional would not do

nitrous oxide mixture of nitrous oxide gas and oxygen

noncritical instruments any instrument that comes in contact with only intact skin

non-expendable supplies supplies that are reused after they have been sterilized

nonmaleficence do no harm to the patient

non-participating dentist a dentist who does not have a contract with a dental benefits carrier

nutrients chemicals in food that supply energy

occlusal biting surface of posterior teeth

occlusion natural contact of the maxillary and mandibular teeth in all positions

Occupational Safety and Health Administration (OSHA) regulatory agency that operates on federal and state levels to protect the employee. It creates regulations that must be adhered to in a dental practice

odontoblasts cells that form dentin

odontoclasts cells that absorb dentin

operating zones based on the face of a clock, time zones described for positioning of the dental team (dentist and dental assistant)

orthodontics dental specialty that focuses on prevention, interception, and correction of malocclusions

osseointegration the acceptance of the bone to the newly placed implant

osteoblasts cells that form bone

osteoclasts cells that absorb bone

other potentially infectious materials (OPIM) any body fluid or tissue other than blood that has the potential to cause disease

overbite increased vertical overlap of the maxillary incisors

overlapping a condition in which teeth appear overlapped and the mesial and distal surfaces overlap each other, caused by incorrect horizontal angulation

packing slip document that comes with supplies, which is an enumeration of the enclosed items

parotid salivary gland one of the three major salivary glands

partial denture a removable prosthesis that replaces some missing teeth within the same arch

patient of record a patient who has been examined, diagnosed, and has had treatment planned by the dentist

pedodontics dental specialty that deals with neonatal through adolescent patients, as well as patients with special needs in these age groups

penumbra the blurriness that surrounds the radiographic image

petty cash a small amount of money kept in the office for incidental expenses

percutaneous through the skin, such as needle stick or cut

periodontal disease infections of the structures that support the teeth (gums and bone)

periodontal dressing (perio pak) a dressing placed over a surgical site for protection while the tissue is healing

periodontics dental specialty involved with the diagnosis and treatment of diseases of the supporting structures

periodontitis inflammation of the supporting tissues of the mouth that occurs in stages

periodontium the supporting structures of the mouth (bone, connective tissue, gingival tissue)

peripheral nervous system body system concerned with the spinal and cranial nerves

permanent cement dental cement utilized under permanent restoration, such as a crown or a bridge

permucosal contact with mucous membranes, such as eyes or mouth

personal protective equipment (PPE) scrubs, leather shoes, lab coat, mask, safety glasses/face shield, and gloves

photon a bundle of energy with no mass or weight that travels as a wave at the speed of light

physiology study of the functions of the human body

planes imaginary lines used to divide the body into sections

plaque soft, sticky substance that adheres to enamel

polyvinyl siloxane hydrophilic elastomeric impression material used to take final impressions

polymerization hardening process of light-sensitive materials

predeterminiation submission of a treatment plan on a claim form requesting an estimate from the carrier of what they will pay

pre-natal period of human development from pregnancy to birth

preventive dentistry a patient care program that incorporates fluoride, patient education, proper nutrition, and dental sealants

primary radiation the primary penetrating X-ray beam produced at the target in the anode

prime time appointment times most often requested by patients (usually first appointment in the morning and last appointment in the afternoon)

prism a structure formed by a single ameloblast; prisms make up the enamel

process indicators tapes, strips, or tabs with heat-sensitive chemicals that change color when exposed to certain temperatures

productivity cost of the dental treatment rendered

prophy paste an abrasive pastelike material used to polish stains from the coronal portion of teeth

prosthodontics dental specialty that provides restoration and replacement of natural teeth

provisional temporary crown worn while permanent crown is being fabricated

pulp nerve and blood vessel center of the tooth (heart of the tooth)

purchase order a standardized order for supplies, which is used in large institutions

quadrant one of four sections of the mouth

radiolucent the black or dark areas on an X-ray; soft matter appears radiolucent on a radiograph

radiopaque the light or white areas on an X-ray; hard structures that block the radiation appear radiopaque on a radiograph

rampant caries rapidly forming decay that spreads quickly

recall/continuing care system a system of notifying the patient of routine dental care

reciprocity a process that allows a licensed group of professionals to obtain licensure in another state without retesting

relining a procedure that can be done at the chair or in the lab that restores a more accurate fit to the tissue side of the partial or full denture

remineralization replacement of minerals in the tooth

resorption the body's process of eliminating bone or hard tissue

respondeat superior legal doctrine that holds an employer liable for the acts of the employee

retention the act of holding a restoration in place by mechanical or chemical means

reversible pulpitis form of inflammation of the pulp that may be reversible

route of entry way in which disease can enter the body

saliva ejector less powerful suction system than the HVE for removing excess fluids

sanitization the use of chemicals or processes that keep the microbial flora at a safe public health level

sarcoma malignant tumor in muscle or bone

scatter radiation secondary radiation that results from the primary beam interacting with matter, and the deflecting X-rays are considered scatter

sealant thin resin film applied to the pits and fissures of molars and premolars to prevent tooth decay

secondary dentin the deposition of dentin throughout the lifetime of the tooth

sedative a material that has a calming effect

semi-critical instrument any instrument that comes in contact with oral tissue but does not penetrate

sepsis presence of disease

Sharpey's fibers tissues that anchor the periosteum to the bone

sharps pointed or cutting instruments, including needles, scalpel blades, burs, and orthodontic wires

shelf life the length of time a supply may be used before it expires

six-handed dentistry when a circulating assistant and a chairside assistant both work with the dentist, assisting with manipulation of materials, exchanging instruments, and oral evacuation at the chairside

smear layer an oily residue found on newly prepared teeth that is removed with acid etchant

sodium hypochlorite usually referred to as common household bleach; sometimes used to disinfect surfaces

spatulate to mix together a dental material using a spatula

spores the form some bacteria take to protect themselves from being destroyed

standard of care level at which dental professionals deliver dental care to patients in similar situations

standard precautions standard of care regarding disinfection and sterilization procedures specific to each office

statement document that informs the patient of his or her balance, along with the charges, payments, and adjustments made on the patient's account

static agents chemicals that act by inhibiting the growth of microorganisms without killing them

stent a template, made of acrylic, that is placed over the alveolar ridge to guide the proper placement of a dental implant

sterilization destruction or removal of all forms of life

stomodeum primitive mouth

subgingival under the gingival or gum

sublingual under the tongue, for example, a means of administering a drug

sublingual salivary gland one of the three major salivary glands

submandibular salivary gland one of the three major salivary glands

subscriber employee who owns the dental insurance plan

subsupine lying-down position in which the patient's head is lower than the chest and knees

succedaneous teeth permanent dentition that replaces primary teeth

supine lying-down position in which the patient's head, chest, and knees are at the same level

supragingival above the gingival or gum line

surface wipes a cloth-like wipe impregnated with an iodophor disinfectant used for surface disinfecting

temporary cement dental cement used under provisional to provide temporary coverage while the new restoration is being designed by the lab

temporomandibular joint (TMJ) the articular joint of the temporal bone and the mandible; the only moving joint in the cranium

traumatic intrusion displacement of a tooth into its socket

trituration process of mixing two materials together at a high rate of speed

truth in lending form document used when a treatment plan is extended to four or more monthly payments

ultrasonic cleaner pre-cleaning step prior to sterilization that loosens any debris that might adhere to the instruments by immersion into a cleaning solution in which sound waves travel

ultrasonic scaler device using high-frequency sound waves for rapid removal of calculus from teeth

universal precautions treating all human blood, bodily fluids, and secretions, including saliva, as potentially infectious

usual, customary, and reasonable (UCR) a dental insurance plan where payments are based upon a UCR fee criteria

uvula "punching bag" projection at the end of the soft palate

vacuum former (suck down machine) a machine found in the lab that heats and softens the plastic sheet of material, and then delivers a pull-down rush of air to fabricate custom-made appliances, like bleach trays, for the patient

vasoconstrictor type of drug that constricts the blood vessels used to prolong anesthetic action

veracity being truthful; not lying to the patient

vermilion border darker outer lining of the lips

vestibule space between the teeth and lining of the cheeks

viewbox a lighted box used to view radiographs on

virulence the strength of the microorganism's ability to cause disease

viscosity thickness of a material

vital record a very essential document that cannot be replaced

xerostomia dryness of the mouth

X-radiation high energy ionizing electromagnetic radiation

NOTES

NOTES

NOTES

NOTES

NOTES

NOTES

NOTES

NOTES

Special FREE Offer from LearningExpress

LearningExpress guarantees that you will be better prepared for, and score higher on, the dental assisting exam

Go to the LearningExpress Practice Center at www.LearningExpressFreeOffer.com, an interactive online resource exclusively for LearningExpress customers.

Now that you've purchased LearningExpress's *Dental Assisting Exam*, you have **FREE** access to:

- **A full-length dental assisting practice exam** that mirrors official dental assisting exams
- **Multiple-choice questions covering** chairside assisting, radiation health and safety, and infection control
- **Immediate scoring** and **detailed answer explanations**
- Benchmark your skills and focus your study with our **customized diagnostic report**

Follow the simple instructions on the scratch card in your copy of *Dental Assisting Exam*. Use your individualized access code found on the scratch card and go to www.LearningExpressFreeOffer.com to sign in. Start practicing online for the dental assisting exam right away!

Once you've logged on, use the spaces below to write in your access code and newly created password for easy reference:

Access Code: _____   Password: _____